MAXIMIZING STUDY ABROAD

A Students' Guide to Strategies for Language and Culture Learning and Use

Second Edition

MAXIMIZING STUDY ABROAD

A Students' Guide to Strategies for Language and Culture Learning and Use

Second Edition

R. Michael Paige

Andrew D. Cohen

Barbara Kappler

Julie C. Chi

James P. Lassegard

Center for Advanced Research
on Language Acquisition

UNIVERSITY OF MINNESOTA

MAXIMIZING STUDY ABROAD:
A Students' Guide to Strategies for Language and Culture Learning and Use—Second edition

Produced by
Center for Advanced Research on Language Acquisition
University of Minnesota
140 University International Center
331 - 17th Avenue Southeast
Minneapolis, MN 55414

ISBN: 0-9722545-5-2

Second Edition, Sixth Printing
Printed in the United States of America

Background

As with all successful collaborative efforts, the development of the *Maximizing Study Abroad* series has a long history and has involved the participation of many people. In 1999 the Center for Advanced Research on Language Acquisition (CARLA) at the University of Minnesota received funding from the U.S. Department of Education's Title VI Language Resource Center program to create a set of user-friendly materials on language- and culture-learning strategies designed to maximize students' study abroad experiences. This project was a logical extension of previous work conducted at CARLA on culture and language learning and strategies-based instruction that began in 1993.

During the period 1999-2003 the project leaders created, field-tested, and revised the following set of three guides as part of the *Maximizing Study Abroad* series:

> ***Maximizing Study Abroad: A Students' Guide to Strategies for Language and Culture Learning and Use***
>
> ***Maximizing Study Abroad: A Program Professionals' Guide to Strategies for Language and Culture Learning and Use***
>
> ***Maximizing Study Abroad: A Language Instructors' Guide to Strategies for Language and Culture Learning and Use***

Phases of the project

The initial writing phase (1999-2000)

The initial writing phase of this project took place during the 1999-2000 academic year. The writing team was led by Professor Andrew D. Cohen on the language-learning strategies sections and Professor R. Michael Paige on the culture-learning strategies sections. Two graduate research assistants, Julie C. Chi and James P. Lassegard, worked in collaboration with Professors Cohen and Paige throughout the initial development of the guides.

The field-testing and revision phase – part 1 (2000-2001)

The field-testing and revision phase of the project was coordinated by Dr. Barbara Kappler (University of Minnesota International Student and Scholar Services) during the 2000-2001 academic year. The three guides were piloted with volunteer groups of language instructors, students engaged in study abroad programs, and study abroad program professionals and advisers at the University of Minnesota and selected sites throughout the country. Based on the rich feedback received, the guides were extensively reformatted and revised to be more appealing and accessible to end-users.

The field-testing and implementation phase – part 2 (2001-2002)

During the third and final phase of field-testing and development of the guides, prototypes were used to fully explore the range of options in which the materials could be used effectively. The core leadership group (Cohen, Kappler, and Paige) worked with faculty and staff from the Department of Spanish and Portuguese and the Learning Abroad Center at the University of Minnesota to demonstrate how the guides could be used in a wide range of teaching and study abroad contexts. As part of this demonstration phase, Margaret Meagher, a seasoned instructor of Spanish, taught a special study abroad section of beginning third-year Spanish using materials from the instructor and student guides. Each student in this special course section received a copy of the *Students' Guide*. Their response was very positive.

In addition to using the materials in a language course, special workshops were held in fall 2001 and spring 2002 for students planning to study abroad. Dr. Kappler facilitated another round of focus groups with language instructors from various language departments and program professionals from the Learning Abroad Center. In May 2002, CARLA sponsored an intensive workshop on how to use the guides, which attracted the participation of more than 40 language instructors and study abroad program professionals. Half of the participants were staff and faculty at the University of Minnesota, while the other half came from study abroad programs in Minnesota, Wisconsin, Missouri, Maryland, and Colorado.

By fall 2002, the first editions of the *Students' Guide* and the *Program Professionals' Guide* were published as part of the CARLA working paper series. Both guides were widely circulated to a national audience of leaders in the field of study abroad, and the response from students and professionals indicated these publications met a national need.

Final development phase for the *Instructors' Guide* (2002–2003)
The third guide in the *Maximizing Study Abroad* series was targeted at the needs of language instructors, and while the materials and philosophy behind the guide were complementary to the first two guides, the needs and focus of the classroom language teacher in using the materials were quite different because not all students in language classrooms are directly preparing for study abroad. Given this difference, the authors and the development team at CARLA thought that it was critical to take additional time to make sure the materials were further tested and revised by practicing language teachers.

In fall 2002 Margaret Meagher joined the team of authors to help create and revise activities for teachers to use in the classroom and to provide input on writing throughout the guide based on her experience in regularly using the materials in her Spanish classes at the University and with a group of Spanish instructors at a study abroad site in Spain. After another round of major revisions to the guide, a draft was circulated to a group of colleagues at the University of Minnesota, Brigham Young University, and St. Cloud State University who provided in-depth feedback and ideas to make the final guide appropriate for the language-teaching context. The first version of the *Instructors' Guide* was published in 2003.

Research on the guides and another round of revisions (2002–2006)
A U.S. Department of Education research project, "Maximizing study abroad through language and culture strategies," began in September 2002 under the direction of Professors Cohen and Paige with active support from research assistants Holly Emert, Joseph Hoff, and Rachel Shively. The research included three related studies that investigated the use and impact of the *Maximizing Study Abroad* guidebook series for

students, program professionals, and language instructors. The research questions for each of the three studies were:

- ***Students:*** Do study abroad students use the strategies in the *Students' Guide* in order to deal with the target language and culture? How, and in which contexts, do they utilize these strategies? How frequently do they use the language and culture strategies?
- ***Program Professionals:*** What are ways that program professionals use the *Program Professionals' Guide* in student orientation? How do they actually use the guide? How do they perceive the role of this guide in the student orientation process?
- ***Language Instructors:*** In what ways do language instructors utilize the *Instructors' Guide* in their language teaching and advising?

Based on the extensive feedback gleaned by the researchers from study participants, a core team of *Maximizing Study Abroad* authors decided to take on the task of crafting another revision to make the *Maximizing Study Abroad* series the best that it could be. Cohen also brought insights he gained from using the *Students' Guide* annually in his undergraduate course, "Practical Language Learning for International Communication," whose students tended to be either those returning from study abroad experiences or preparing to embark on them (or both).

Also as a result of the feedback from study abroad program professionals and language instructors, the three lead authors worked on merging, revising, and expanding the *Program Professionals'* and *Language Instructors'* guides into one comprehensive volume for use in a variety of study abroad and language instruction settings. This effort was led by Dr. Kappler Mikk with the active input of Professors Cohen and Paige and the tireless editing and desktop publishing support of Jennifer Schulz from the Office of International Programs. *Maximizing Study Abroad: An Instructional Guide to Strategies for Language and Culture Learning and Use* brings together the materials from both guides and adds facilitation support for the new activities found in the *Students' Guide*.

We are pleased to be able to share the thoroughly revised and field-tested *Maximizing Study Abroad* guides nationally with a broad audience of people involved in study abroad. As we all know, enhancing students' language and culture learning during their study abroad experiences is a holistic endeavor that ultimately requires the efforts of the students themselves, study abroad professionals, and language teachers. It is our greatest hope that these guides can provide support for the important goal of preparing students to make the most of their study abroad experiences.

Acknowledgments

CARLA wishes to thank the many students, teachers, and study abroad professionals who have contributed to the development of the *Maximizing Study Abroad* series. Those listed below are from the University of Minnesota unless otherwise noted.

Maximizing Study Abroad project leaders

The initial vision and the background research for this project came from Professor Andrew Cohen and Professor R. Michael Paige, both leaders in their fields and active members of CARLA since its inception. Cohen's research on styles- and strategies-based language instruction and Paige's work on integrating concepts of intercultural communication into the second language classroom made this project possible. The collaborative scholarship provided both a solid research-based foundation and a framework to synthesize information from both fields into a new body of materials to support study abroad. We are deeply grateful to both for their vision for this project and their continued leadership within the center.

Professors Cohen and Paige were aided greatly in the first year of the project by two graduate students, Julie Chi and James Lassegard. Former graduate assistant Susan J. Weaver also contributed to materials for the first draft of the guide for language instructors. Chi continued to contribute time and energy to this project beyond the time of her initial work as a graduate student, and Lassegard helped with some final details after he graduated and left the University. After the first drafts of all three guides had been completed, the materials needed to be piloted and revised, and Dr. Barbara Kappler, an assistant director of International Student and Scholar Services, was invited to lead the effort. She gathered and incorporated feedback from students, study abroad program professionals, and language instructors into the final publications. It was a tremendous task to synthesize the volumes of feedback and create more user-friendly texts from an academic framework, especially for the *Students' Guide*. Kappler's in-depth background in intercultural communication, her insights into study abroad experiences, and her skills as both a writer and editor helped transform the guides into a set of lively and informative materials that are engaging for students, program professionals, and language instructors alike.

Students

Many students gave feedback on the development of the *Students' Guide* during workshops, focus groups, and classes held at the University of Minnesota and other local institutions. Special recognition goes to students who, as part of the Undergraduate Research Opportunities Program at the University of Minnesota, used the *Students' Guide* during their own study abroad experience or gave feedback based on previous study abroad experience, including Jacob Dick, Kelly Lavin, Tammy Yach, and Molly Zahn. For the second edition, we are grateful to the students participating in Cohen's undergraduate course, "Practical Language Learning for International Communication," for their input on what students really need and for their course papers, which provided the writing team with a rich source of quotes about language use in study abroad.

Study abroad program professionals and program staff

Throughout the process of creating materials, gathering feedback, and revising, many of the staff members in the Learning Abroad Center and other departments at the University of Minnesota assisted in the task of distilling a vast quantity of information into a work that would be read by students. We are grateful to study abroad program professionals Sheila Collins, Sophie Gladding, Holly Zimmerman LeVoir, Heidi Soneson, and Susan Wiese for their willingness to let us "try out" the draft materials on their student audiences and for giving us feedback from their perspectives as program leaders. In addition we are grateful to other staff and students who helped review the guides, including Bill Baldus, Joan Brzezinski, Michelle Cumming, Amy Greeley, Joe Hoff, April Knutson, Jodi Malmgren, Gayla Marty, Rachel Sullivan-Nightengale, Barbara Pilling, Gayle Woodruff, and Yelena Yershova. Thanks also to Hanae Tsukada for collecting quotes from international students and for helping to rewrite the section on learning characters. We appreciate the contributions of Christine Anderson, who helped to revise the social relations chapter and wrote the section on dating and sexual harassment based on her master's degree work. Alexandra Booij's feedback on the debriefing section and assistance in collecting international perspectives was much appreciated. Special recognition goes to Chip Peterson, a veteran in the field of study abroad, for his ongoing support, expertise, and uncanny ability to see both the big picture and the small details at the same time. For their overall support of this project, we express our warmest thanks to Al Balkcum, director of the Learning Abroad Center, and Kay Thomas, director of International Student and Scholar Services, and to their staff members who gave their valuable practitioner feedback.

Language instructors

Specific feedback on all of the guides came from a wide network of language instructors at and around the University of Minnesota. Blair Bateman (Brigham Young University), Eleanora Bertranou, Lucy Carlone, Elaine Fuller Carter (St. Cloud State University), Isabelle Clavel, Kelly Conroy, Francine Klein, Muisi Krosi, Magara Maeda, Patricia Mougel, Allison Spenader, Susan Villar, and Ellen Wormwood gave enormously helpful feedback on the *Language Instructors' Guide* as part of an initial series of focus groups with language instructors. Bateman, Carter, Klein, Villar, Wormwood, María Emilce López, and Kathleen Ganley read the final draft of the *Language Instructors' Guide* during an especially busy time of the year and provided the detailed feedback needed to make the final publication a success. Based on teacher feedback, a new section was added that focused on the intersection between language and culture in foreign language instruction. Klein, who wrote her dissertation on the topic, was the lead author of this new chapter, along with Professor Cohen. Both Bateman and Klein were very helpful in providing important information for the reference section.

Special thanks goes to Charlotte Melin, Patricia Mougel, and Susan Villar for their ongoing help in supporting this work through their language departments and by providing a set of quotes that helped make connections to the language classroom. We greatly appreciate the enthusiasm and support of faculty and staff of the

Department of Spanish and Portuguese for this project, including Department Chair Carol Klee, Margaret Meagher, Kathleen Ganley, and Susan Villar. Special thanks goes to Meagher, who brought many years of experience in language teaching and study abroad program coordination to the challenge of incorporating materials from the guides into her third-year Spanish language course. Her skills, insight, and zeal helped us to do a "real life" test of the materials and gave us a wealth of feedback that was incorporated into each of the guides. We were especially grateful that she chose to join the team of authors in the final phase of writing and revising the guide for language instructors, given her experience with the project and her perspective as a language instructor who was in the classroom when she was writing the materials.

Feedback from far and wide

The writing team at CARLA also solicited feedback from experts outside the University of Minnesota. We appreciate the helpful comments received from Anna Uhl Chamot (The George Washington University), Rebecca Oxford and Gloria Park (University of Maryland-College Park), Jonathon Rees (University of Birmingham), and Joan Rubin during various stages of the development of the material. For the latest round of revisions, we are grateful for the insights provided by Julie Chi, who was an original author, but had been away from the text long enough that she could look at the revisions with fresh eyes.

Researching the impact of the guides

Professors Cohen and Paige proved that they are researchers at heart by obtaining a grant from the U.S. Department of Education through the Title VI International Research and Studies Program. Their aim was to take a close look at the impact that these materials have on students and how materials are used by program professionals and language instructors. They were fortunate to be assisted for three years of the grant by research assistants Holly Emert, Joseph Hoff, and Rachel Shively, who brought their own rich experience in study abroad and language instruction to the research and who contributed greatly to getting the word out about these materials to the study abroad and language teaching community. The research was strengthened through the professional insights of the project advisory committee members: Dr. Barbara Freed, Carnegie Mellon University (language); Dr. Mitch Hammer, School of International Service, American University (culture); and Dr. Bruce LaBrack, School of International Studies, University of the Pacific (study abroad).

Behind the scenes

Given the level of truth in the adage "the devil is in the details," we wish to thank those working in the CARLA office and in the Office of International Programs whose efforts have proved critical to the success of this project. For the first round of publications we wish to give special recognition to Dan Supalla, a student worker with an incredible eye for proofreading; student Jesse Houchins for his fantastic cover design; and Suzanne Hay, the secretary of CARLA, who brought tremendous skill, background knowledge of study abroad, and good humor to the job of word processing, formatting, and editing through a series of drafts that became too numerous to count. Not enough can be said about the contributions of Jennifer

Schulz, the communications coordinator in the Office of International Programs, who developed the original template for the guides and did the layout, as well as all of the copyediting and proofreading and much of the editing for each edition of the guides. We cannot thank her enough.

A heartfelt note of thanks goes to our partners in the Office of International Programs, especially C. Eugene Allen, who served as the associate vice president when the project began, for his championing of *Maximizing Study Abroad* during critical points along the way, and Fiscal Officer Elaine Randolph, for her help with all of the financing involved in this project.

Revising the Instructional Guide—*a final word of thanks*

It is no wonder *Maximizing Study Abroad* guides have received national acclaim from those who are most active in the field of study abroad, given the amount of collaboration and real-life testing that has gone into these publications. Merging the best materials from two independent guides (*Program Professionals'* and *Language Instructors'* guides) and adding all the wonderful new materials that were created for the *Students' Guide* was a Herculean undertaking that went well beyond the typical process of revision. Dr. Barbara Kappler Mikk agreed to lead this effort, which entailed combing through the guides for the best of the materials from both publications, reorganizing the guide for a better "flow," and ensuring that the guide had a consistent "voice" throughout. She created new activities to parallel additions made to the *Students' Guide* and wrote the facilitation guidelines for those activities—all of which were strengthened by further input from Professors Cohen and Paige. Jennifer Schulz, our wonderful publication coordinator who has been part of this effort from the beginning, was a leading partner in the effort to mold these materials into a new shape. Her willingness and ability to take an active role in editing and conceptualizing many parts of this latest installment of the *Maximizing Study Abroad* project are greatly appreciated. Without her support, skill, and insight, this project could not have been completed.

Elaine Tarone	*Karin Larson*
Director	*Coordinator*
CARLA	*CARLA*

Revised March 2009

Table of Contents

Post-Study Abroad Unit

Section II: Language-Learning Strategies

Welcome to Study Abroad!

As a study abroad student, you are not going to be just a tourist—you are embarking on something much richer, doing the kinds of things that most tourists can only dream about. You will be with the locals, immersing yourself in the culture and perhaps coming to understand the culture as an insider. Being a tourist is easy—studying abroad takes work to learn another language and the culture of your hosts. And it's rewarding work!

> *My entire trip was the most meaningful, exciting, life-changing four months I have ever had. Every day I learned something new, and I know that sounds a little clichéd, but it's absolutely true. Studying abroad was the best thing I could have done. ~ Seth Lengkeek, England*

> *Study abroad let me finally get a grip on the Spanish language...the only way to learn a language is to speak and hear it. ~ Dan Jakab, Spain*

What does this guide offer?

This guide provides specific strategies for improving your language and culture learning so that your time spent abroad will be as meaningful and productive as you hope. These tools have been developed based on the experiences of students and the authors and solid research in the fields of language acquisition, international education, and intercultural communication. This revision incorporates findings from a major research study on the first edition of the guide conducted over a three-year period.

Why do I need a guide?

While you have probably studied the language and culture of your destination, chances are that you have not been taught strategies you can use to make the most of study abroad. Quite simply, if language and culture were easy to learn, everyone would be fluent in another language and competent in another culture. Clearly, this is not the case. It's hard to do all of this learning on your own, so this guide is prepared to lead you through the process.

Why this guide?

This guide is unique in linking language- and culture-learning strategies into one workbook. The two are inseparable—you cannot be competent in another culture without skills in both language and culture.

How do I use this guide?

This guide was not written for you to read cover to cover. Begin by taking surveys of your learning styles and language- and culture-learning strategies (starting on p. 10). The strategies surveys will introduce you to culture- and language-learning approaches, provide you with a self-assessment, and direct you to the different sections of the book where you can learn more about specific strategies. Then, you can practice using them during your study abroad program. The idea is that you will read some of the guide before you go, consult the guide while abroad, and check out the suggestions for strategies to maintain or improve your language skills upon returning home.

But a whole guide?

> *The guide is long only because it's comprehensive—and if used correctly, it is not time consuming. ~ Jacob Dick, Italy*

Some of you may be so ready to study abroad that you want to jump in right now and get going. We agree that getting involved and participating is essential. Yet we also know that there are numerous examples of "ugly travelers" (and not just Americans) whose lack of cultural sensitivity makes them instantly recognizable in an unpleasant sort of way and, moreover, reflects a lack of respect for their hosts. Why not try to break that mold, taking time to think about how you are going to interact and spending a little time learning from those who have traveled before? With a few extra minutes of preparation, you can assure yourself that you are doing all you can to make this the most amazing and meaningful journey of your life!

> *I find the guide to be quite thorough with lots of helpful information. I wish I would have had this guide before I went abroad. ~ Laura Seifert, England*

> *This guide gave me the opportunity to be much more self-reflective while I was studying in Germany. Of course everyone who studies abroad realizes at some level that they are operating in a different environment, facing different challenges and different sources of stress. But the guide works through all these new things in a systematic way, which allowed me to get a better sense of what was really going on. It provides a context larger than simply my own experience for my interactions with a different culture. It also contains a lot of valuable insights about language learning—how to overcome typical frustrations (or: 'Why can't I speak this language yet?'); strategies for improving reading, writing, listening, and speaking skills; and suggestions for ways to practice your skills with the help of native speakers. Not every part of the guide will speak to every student, but it contains much that will be of use to anyone who studies abroad. ~ Molly Zahn, Germany*

Personal Goals for Study Abroad

One of the most important things you can do to help yourself be successful in study abroad is to be aware of what you hope to gain from the experience. Take a few moments to write down your own personal goals for this study abroad trip. Make sure to consider language- and culture-learning goals, as well as personal aspirations.

What if this isn't your first study abroad? You've done it before. You may think you know it all, right? Each time there are things to learn, things to be mindful of. You have experience to fall back on, which gives you some comfort. But still…what will be different? What may be the same? What will your goals look like? It is possible that your goals will be more finely tuned than in your first study abroad. You are likely to be more savvy about which language and culture strategies to use and how to use them to benefit from your time abroad. At times you will just be using the same strategies in a slightly different way. For example, you will continue to use the same strategies for speaking with people, but now you will have a better sense of how to use them and what to expect when you do so. At other times you will be using different strategies consistent with your new needs. For example, you may have entirely new ways of approaching reading in the host community, such as reading the daily newspaper—something you didn't do in your previous stint abroad.

Use the space below to list the personal goals you have for your study abroad experience.

-
-
-
-
-
-

General Departure Tips

The next few pages give you quick, essential ideas to help you begin preparing for your study abroad experience. Whether this is your first time out of the country or you are a seasoned traveler, we encourage you to take a moment and see what advice others have for you.

Six easy things to do before you go

1. Buy a dictionary and train yourself how to use it effectively. Consider your skill level and determine if you should have a monolingual dictionary (e.g., Spanish-Spanish) or a bilingual dictionary (Spanish-English).
2. Start a journal. (Journaling is discussed starting on p. 119.)
3. Set language goals. Identify your current level of language proficiency. Write down your goals for where you want your language skills to be by the end of your time abroad. Put these goals on the front page of your journal or on the flap of your dictionary. If you are new to the language, you probably have dreams of carrying on a conversation at a basic level and making friends. If you are an experienced language learner, you undoubtedly want to increase your comprehension and speak more "like a native."

   I knew I had achieved successful competence in German when natives in both Germany and Austria started telling me: 'Mensch Leo, du kannst reden!' ('Gee, Leo, you can converse!'). This distinction between 'speaking' a language and 'conversing' in that language is very important. ~ Leo Papademetre, Germany

4. Make a list of things you would like to learn while abroad. Write these in your journal or notebook.
5. Collect photos and/or postcards of your school, friends, family, home, favorite vacation spot, etc., to share with new friends and hosts while studying abroad.
6. Define for yourself what "survival" skills you personally will need:
   - Do you have special dietary needs (kosher, halal, vegetarian, dairy- or wheat-free)? Do you know how to ask for these things in ways that are culturally appropriate?
   - Do you have any critical health issues or medication needs? Do you know how to explain them?
   - Will you be engaging in any hobbies for which you will need to get equipment or supplies while you are abroad (e.g., photography equipment, paints, batteries, etc.)?

Stress factors to consider about the study abroad experience

In order to prepare for your upcoming study abroad experience, we think it is useful to review what Paige (1993) considers to be the 10 most important cross-cultural stress factors of intercultural experiences. Each trip abroad will have some combination of these elements; taken together, they represent both challenges and opportunities for you. The challenges have to do with the stresses of cultural adjustment. The opportunity they present is for you to gain new intercultural skills and become more effective in your host setting. If all of these are present to a high degree, you can expect that your study abroad experience will be more emotionally intense. Reviewing these is a way to do an initial assessment of your readiness, the challenges awaiting you, and your opportunities for learning. Being informed ahead of time, you can also begin to plan your coping strategies for handling these challenges (see p. 98 for more on coping strategies).

1. Cultural Differences

The first thing to consider is the amount of difference between your own and the host culture in terms of the elements of culture mentioned on p. 40. The greater the differences, the more challenging the experience will be. Many things will be unfamiliar to you, and the ways you are normally accustomed to doing things might not work very well. Initially and when under stress, people tend to negatively evaluate the host culture values and behaviors.

2. Ethnocentrism

Ethnocentrism refers to the tendency to see the world through your own cultural lens and to view your cultural reality as central to the human experience. It can often mean that we extol the virtues of our culture in contrast to other cultures and negatively evaluate various aspects of the other culture. There are two aspects of ethnocentrism that influence study abroad. The first is the degree of ethnocentrism of the visitor. The second is the degree to which the host cultural community is itself accepting of outsiders. Travelers who are more ethnocentric and those in more ethnocentric communities will find the experience to be more stressful.

3. Cultural Immersion

Cultural immersion refers to the amount of contact you will be having with host culture persons, such as being in a homestay environment or being directly enrolled in university courses. Immersion can also mean that you are using a second language frequently. In general, the more immersed you are in another culture, the more stressful it can be. With more immersion, "culture fatigue" is a common problem.

4. Cultural Isolation

With respect to intercultural experiences, cultural isolation describes the degree to which you do or do not have access to persons from your own culture while abroad. The most stressful experiences are when you are immersed and isolated. As a coping strategy, it is helpful to spend time periodically with persons from your own culture. This allows you to affirm your culture and share your experience with others who are having similar experiences.

5. Language

Persons unable to speak the language of the host culture will find the experience more stressful. The more essential language ability is to be successful in the target culture, the greater will be the stress if you don't have the necessary language skills. The ability to speak the target language is not always essential, nor does it assure effective communication or intercultural adjustment. But lack of language skills can lead to social isolation and frustration.

6. Prior Intercultural Experience

Stress is affected by the amount and nature of one's prior intercultural experience. In general, people with a limited intercultural background will experience more stress in a cross-cultural situation. Those with a great deal of previous intercultural experience will generally adapt more effectively because they have already developed effective learning and coping strategies, have realistic expectations, and possess strong intercultural communication skills. Based on your level of experience, you need to be realistic about what you need to learn, the skills you need to develop, and the time it will take to become more proficient in the culture.

7. Expectations

There are two major issues related to expectations in intercultural situations. First, people who have very positive but unrealistic expectations about the new culture often feel let down after a time. The culture just doesn't measure up. Second, people who have high expectations of themselves in terms of their ability to work effectively in new situations may experience frustration when it takes longer to figure out the culture.

8. Visibility and Invisibility

This is a very interesting but not commonly mentioned intercultural problem. Persons who are physically different from members of the host (or dominant) culture are highly visible and thus may become the object of curiosity, unwanted attention, or even discrimination. Alternatively, stress can also occur when an important aspect of one's identity is invisible to members of the host culture (e.g., one's religion or political philosophy) or is concealed because it is not accepted in the host culture (e.g., sexual orientation or being divorced). Concealing something about oneself for fear it could harm one's standing in the community or reduce one's effectiveness may be culturally appropriate to do in those circumstances, but it can cause considerable stress.

9. Status

Persons who feel they are not getting the respect they deserve or, conversely, feel they are receiving unearned recognition will find the experience more stressful. Some cultures, for example, are very hierarchical and ascribe status to individuals on the basis of age, family ties, social class, gender, and other characteristics. Someone from a more egalitarian society might find this very difficult to handle. Alternatively, being granted status on the basis of inherited characteristics (e.g., age, ethnicity, religion, nationality, family background, occupation) rather than personal achievement or other qualities that are important in your culture can also result in discomfort.

10. Power and Control

One of the most consistent research findings is that persons in cultures other than their own feel a loss of power and control over events and people compared to what they possessed at home. And the more power you are used to exercising, the more disturbing the sense of loss. You will feel that your personal efficacy is diminished and that things are out of your control. The less power and control the person has in the intercultural situation, the more stressful the experience will be.

We encourage you to keep these 10 intensity factors in mind as you prepare for your journey and revisit this list throughout your time abroad as you go through the stages of cultural adjustment.

Plan ahead: re-entry tips—before you go!

> *For me, mentally preparing for the time abroad is really important as it helps me set the stage for a positive experience. Part of preparing is making sure my expectations are malleable. Some expectations turn out to be true, and many get turned upside down (in a good way). Of course, part of the fun is discovering which will be which! ~ Kara Galvin, Spain and Japan*

1. Invite your family and friends to save your emails, letters, and postcards so that you can read them again when you return home.
2. Prepare to come back a few days before returning to school and work. It's overwhelming to move, get things from storage, register for classes, go back to work, see friends and family, and catch up on jet lag in a few hours.
3. Look for courses related to your study abroad. For example, one author found that by using her study abroad credits toward electives in communication, she was able to double-major in economics and communications—a combination that was much more rewarding to her than economics alone.
4. Watch out for deadlines that will occur while you are gone. Your university will have special procedures on how you can legally give rights to someone on campus to have them register you for courses, sign up for housing, etc.

> *The world is a great book, of which they who never stir from home read only a page. ~ St. Augustine*

Next steps

We encourage you to complete the language and culture surveys to determine where it's most appropriate for you to focus your time and energy.

Learning Style Survey, p. 10
Language Strategy Use Inventory, p. 21
Culture-Learning Strategies Inventory, p. 29

Terms Used in this Guide

Host culture: the culture(s) of the country in which you are studying

Target or new language: the language of your host culture

Second language: While you may speak many languages, we may occasionally refer to the target or new language as the "second language."

Second language learner strategies: These encompass both second language learning and second language use strategies. "Taken together, they constitute the steps or actions consciously selected by learners either to improve the learning of a second language, the use of it, or both" (Cohen, 1998).

Note:

1. For the purposes of this guide, "tips," "techniques," and "tactics" are all being used synonymously with "strategies." No distinction is being made.
2. While we wrote the guide assuming that most readers are native speakers of U.S. English, it can be used by students of any language.

> *Worried that this guide will spoil the experience? Nothing is going to take away the richness of the experience of your study abroad. ~ R. Michael Paige, co-author*

Discovering Your Styles:
Strategies to Language and Culture Learning

Now is your chance to take three surveys, all intended to give you a better sense of how you learn and how you use specific strategies for culture and language learning. The first survey, the Learning Style Survey, gives you a general overview of your preferences for learning. Understanding your preferences can help you determine your strengths and weaknesses for new learning environments. The second and third surveys give you the chance to consider if you know how to use certain strategies for language and culture learning.

The Learning Style Survey

We all have preferences for how we like to learn. Your classmates may enjoy how a certain professor lectures, while you crave more visuals. You may feel very uncomfortable with role-playing activities but really enjoy independent research projects. While you may have a general sense of your preferences already, this survey can help you deepen your understanding by comparing and contrasting 11 different learning styles. You will then be better prepared to make the most of your upcoming change—from being in a familiar U.S. classroom where you have spent more than a decade to studying abroad.

Learning-style preferences allow us to understand and organize our learning. Since some aspects of learning are usually out of your control (you may have to take a class where the professor lectures nearly 100 percent of the time), you can improve your learning by understanding your strengths and weaknesses. For example, knowing that you prefer a visual style does not give you free license to demand that professors teach to your style. In fact, it may be absolutely culturally inappropriate to make such a request and might reflect your own hesitancy and reluctance to adapt. Instead, knowing that you are a visual learner helps you to understand that you may need to create your own visuals, team with auditory learners, and tap into your own auditory skills that exist but are not fully developed. In short, our goal is to help you "style-stretch" by incorporating approaches that you may have resisted or been unaware of in the past.

Learning Style Survey:
Assessing Your Own Learning Styles

Andrew D. Cohen, Rebecca L. Oxford, and Julie C. Chi

The Learning Style Survey is designed to assess your general approach to learning. It does not predict your behavior in every instance, but it is a clear indication of your overall style preferences. For each item, circle the response that represents your approach. Complete all items. There are 11 major activities representing 12 different aspects of your learning style. When you read the statements, try to think about what you usually do when learning. It typically takes about 30 minutes to complete the survey. Do not spend too much time on any item—indicate your immediate feeling and move on to the next item.

For each item, circle your response:

0 = Never
1 = Rarely
2 = Sometimes
3 = Often
4 = Always

Part 1: HOW I USE MY PHYSICAL SENSES

1. I remember something better if I write it down.	0 1 2 3 4
2. I take detailed notes during lectures.	0 1 2 3 4
3. When I listen, I visualize pictures, numbers, or words in my head.	0 1 2 3 4
4. I prefer to learn with TV or video rather than other media.	0 1 2 3 4
5. I use color-coding to help me as I learn or work.	0 1 2 3 4
6. I need written directions for tasks.	0 1 2 3 4
7. I have to look at people to understand what they say.	0 1 2 3 4
8. I understand lectures better when professors write on the board.	0 1 2 3 4
9. Charts, diagrams, and maps help me understand what someone says.	0 1 2 3 4
10. I remember peoples' faces but not their names.	0 1 2 3 4

A - Total ________

Authors' note: The format of the Learning Style Survey and a number of the dimensions and items are drawn from Oxford, 1995. Other key dimensions and some of the wording of items comes from Ehrman and Leaver, 2003.

11. I remember things better if I discuss them with someone. 0 1 2 3 4
12. I prefer to learn by listening to a lecture rather than reading. 0 1 2 3 4
13. I need oral directions for a task. 0 1 2 3 4
14. Background sound helps me think. 0 1 2 3 4
15. I like to listen to music when I study or work. 0 1 2 3 4
16. I can understand what people say even when I cannot see them. 0 1 2 3 4
17. I remember peoples' names but not their faces. 0 1 2 3 4
18. I easily remember jokes that I hear. 0 1 2 3 4
19. I can identify people by their voices (e.g., on the phone). 0 1 2 3 4
20. When I turn on the TV, I listen to the sound more than I watch the screen. 0 1 2 3 4

B - Total ____________

21. I prefer to start doing things rather than checking the directions first. 0 1 2 3 4
22. I need frequent breaks when I work or study. 0 1 2 3 4
23. I need to eat something when I read or study. 0 1 2 3 4
24. If I have a choice between sitting and standing, I'd rather stand. 0 1 2 3 4
25. I get nervous when I sit still too long. 0 1 2 3 4
26. I think better when I move around (e.g., pacing or tapping my feet). 0 1 2 3 4
27. I play with or bite on my pens during lectures. 0 1 2 3 4
28. Manipulating objects helps me to remember what someone says. 0 1 2 3 4
29. I move my hands when I speak. 0 1 2 3 4
30. I draw lots of pictures (doodles) in my notebook during lectures. 0 1 2 3 4

C - Total ____________

Part 2: HOW I EXPOSE MYSELF TO LEARNING SITUATIONS

1. I learn better when I work or study with others than by myself. 0 1 2 3 4
2. I meet new people easily by jumping into the conversation. 0 1 2 3 4
3. I learn better in the classroom than with a private tutor. 0 1 2 3 4
4. It is easy for me to approach strangers. 0 1 2 3 4
5. Interacting with lots of people gives me energy. 0 1 2 3 4
6. I experience things first and then try to understand them. 0 1 2 3 4

A - Total ____________

7. I am energized by the inner world (what I'm thinking inside). 0 1 2 3 4
8. I prefer individual or one-on-one games and activities. 0 1 2 3 4
9. I have a few interests, and I concentrate deeply on them. 0 1 2 3 4
10. After working in a large group, I am exhausted. 0 1 2 3 4
11. When I am in a large group, I tend to keep silent and listen. 0 1 2 3 4
12. I want to understand something well before I try it. 0 1 2 3 4

B - Total ____________

Part 3: HOW I HANDLE POSSIBILITIES

1. I have a creative imagination.	0 1 2 3 4
2. I try to find many options and possibilities for why something happens.	0 1 2 3 4
3. I plan carefully for future events.	0 1 2 3 4
4. I like to discover things myself rather than have everything explained to me.	0 1 2 3 4
5. I add many original ideas during class discussions.	0 1 2 3 4
6. I am open-minded to new suggestions from my peers.	0 1 2 3 4

A - Total ________

7. I focus on a situation as it is rather than thinking about how it could be.	0 1 2 3 4
8. I read instruction manuals (e.g., for computers or VCRs) before using the device.	0 1 2 3 4
9. I trust concrete facts instead of new, untested ideas.	0 1 2 3 4
10. I prefer things presented in a step-by-step way.	0 1 2 3 4
11. I dislike it if my classmate changes the plan for our project.	0 1 2 3 4
12. I follow directions carefully.	0 1 2 3 4

B - Total ________

Part 4: HOW I DEAL WITH AMBIGUITY AND WITH DEADLINES

1. I like to plan language study sessions carefully and do lessons on time or early.	0 1 2 3 4
2. My notes, handouts, and other school materials are carefully organized.	0 1 2 3 4
3. I like to be certain about what things mean in a target language.	0 1 2 3 4
4. I like to know how rules are applied and why.	0 1 2 3 4

A - Total ________

5. I let deadlines slide if I'm involved in other things.	0 1 2 3 4
6. I let things pile up on my desk to be organized eventually.	0 1 2 3 4
7. I don't worry about comprehending everything.	0 1 2 3 4
8. I don't feel the need to come to rapid conclusions about a topic.	0 1 2 3 4

B - Total ________

Part 5: HOW I RECEIVE INFORMATION

1. I prefer short and simple answers rather than long explanations. 0 1 2 3 4
2. I ignore details that do not seem relevant. 0 1 2 3 4
3. It is easy for me to see the overall plan or big picture. 0 1 2 3 4
4. I get the main idea, and that's enough for me. 0 1 2 3 4
5. When I tell an old story, I tend to forget lots of specific details. 0 1 2 3 4

A - Total ________

6. I need very specific examples in order to understand fully. 0 1 2 3 4
7. I pay attention to specific facts or information. 0 1 2 3 4
8. I'm good at catching new phrases or words when I hear them. 0 1 2 3 4
9. I enjoy activities where I fill in the blank with missing words I hear. 0 1 2 3 4
10. When I try to tell a joke, I remember details but forget the punch line. 0 1 2 3 4

B - Total ________

Part 6: HOW I FURTHER PROCESS INFORMATION

1. I can summarize information easily. 0 1 2 3 4
2. I can quickly paraphrase what other people say. 0 1 2 3 4
3. When I create an outline, I consider the key points first. 0 1 2 3 4
4. I enjoy activities where I have to pull ideas together. 0 1 2 3 4
5. By looking at the whole situation, I can easily understand someone. 0 1 2 3 4

A - Total ________

6. I have a hard time understanding when I don't know every word. 0 1 2 3 4
7. When I tell a story or explain something, it takes a long time. 0 1 2 3 4
8. I like to focus on grammar rules. 0 1 2 3 4
9. I'm good at solving complicated mysteries and puzzles. 0 1 2 3 4
10. I am good at noticing even the smallest details involved in a task. 0 1 2 3 4

B - Total ________

Part 7: HOW I COMMIT MATERIAL TO MEMORY

1. I try to pay attention to all the features of new material as I learn. 0 1 2 3 4
2. When I memorize different bits of language material, I can retrieve these bits easily – as if I had stored them in separate slots in my brain. 0 1 2 3 4
3. As I learn new material in the target language, I make fine distinctions among speech sounds, grammatical forms, and words and phrases. 0 1 2 3 4

A - Total ________

4. When learning new information, I may clump together data by eliminating or reducing differences and focusing on similarities. 0 1 2 3 4
5. I ignore distinctions that would make what I say more accurate in the given context. 0 1 2 3 4
6. Similar memories become blurred in my mind; I merge new learning experiences with previous ones. 0 1 2 3 4

B - Total __________

Part 8: HOW I DEAL WITH LANGUAGE RULES

1. I like to go from general patterns to the specific examples in learning a target language. 0 1 2 3 4
2. I like to start with rules and theories rather than specific examples. 0 1 2 3 4
3. I like to begin with generalizations and then find experiences that relate to those generalizations. 0 1 2 3 4

A - Total __________

4. I like to learn rules of language indirectly by being exposed to examples of grammatical structures and other language features. 0 1 2 3 4
5. I don't really care if I hear a rule stated since I don't remember rules very well anyway. 0 1 2 3 4
6. I figure out rules based on the way I see language forms behaving over time. 0 1 2 3 4

B - Total __________

Part 9: HOW I DEAL WITH MULTIPLE INPUTS

1. I can separate out the relevant and important information in a given context even when distracting information is present. 0 1 2 3 4
2. When I produce an oral or written message in the target language, I make sure that all the grammatical structures are in agreement with each other. 0 1 2 3 4
3. I not only attend to grammar but check for appropriate levels of formality and politeness. 0 1 2 3 4

A - Total __________

4. When speaking or writing, I feel that focusing on grammar is less important than paying attention to the content of the message. 0 1 2 3 4
5. It is a challenge for me to both focus on communication in speech or writing while at the same time paying attention to grammatical agreement (e.g., person, number, tense, or gender). 0 1 2 3 4
6. When I am using lengthy sentences in a target language, I get distracted and neglect aspects of grammar and style. 0 1 2 3 4

B - Total __________

Part 10: HOW I DEAL WITH RESPONSE TIME

1.	I react quickly in language situations.	0 1 2 3 4
2.	I go with my instincts in the target language.	0 1 2 3 4
3.	I jump in, see what happens, and make corrections if needed.	0 1 2 3 4

A - Total ________

4.	I need to think things through before speaking or writing.	0 1 2 3 4
5.	I like to look before I leap when determining what to say or write in a target language.	0 1 2 3 4
6.	I attempt to find supporting material in my mind before I set about producing language.	0 1 2 3 4

B - Total ________

Part 11: HOW LITERALLY I TAKE REALITY

1.	I find that building metaphors in my mind helps me deal with language (e.g., viewing the language like a machine with component parts that can be disassembled).	0 1 2 3 4
2.	I learn things through metaphors and associations with other things. I find that stories and examples help me learn.	0 1 2 3 4

A - Total ________

3.	I take learning language literally and don't deal in metaphors.	0 1 2 3 4
4.	I take things at face value, so I like language material that says what it means directly.	0 1 2 3 4

B - Total ________

Understanding your totals

Once you have totaled your points, write the results in the blanks below. Circle the higher number in each part (if they are close, circle both). Read about your learning styles on the next page.

Part 1:
A ____ Visual
B ____ Auditory
C ____ Tactile/Kinesthetic

Part 2:
A ____ Extroverted
B ____ Introverted

Part 3:
A ____ Random-Intuitive
B ____ Concrete-Sequential

Part 4:
A ____ Closure-Oriented
B ____ Open

Part 5:
A ____ Global
B ____ Particular

Part 6:
A ____ Synthesizing
B ____ Analytic

Part 7:
A ____ Sharpener
B ____ Leveler

Part 8:
A ____ Deductive
B ____ Inductive

Part 9:
A ____ Field-Independent
B ____ Field-Dependent

Part 10:
A ____ Impulsive
B ____ Reflective

Part 11:
A ____ Metaphoric
B ____ Literal

Note: Before reading the next section, understand that this is only a general description of your learning-style preferences. It does not describe you *all of the time*, but gives you an idea of your tendencies when you learn. Note that in some learning situations, you may have one set of style preferences and in a different situation, another set of preferences. Also, there are both advantages and disadvantages to every style preference.

If on the sensory style preferences (visual, auditory, tactile/kinesthetic) you prefer two or all three of these senses (i.e., your totals for the categories are within 5 points or so), you are likely to be flexible enough to enjoy a wide variety of activities in the language classroom. On the other dimensions, although they appear to be in opposition, it is possible for you to have high scores on both, meaning that you do not have a preference one way or the other. Here are three examples: on the extroversion-introversion distinction, you are able to work effectively with others as well as by yourself; on the closure-open distinction, you enjoy the freedom of limited structure yet can still get the task done before the deadline without stress; on the global-particular distinction, you can handle both the gist and the details easily.

Furthermore, learning-style preferences change throughout your life, and you can also stretch them, so don't feel that you are constrained to one style.

Part 1: HOW I USE MY PHYSICAL SENSES

If you came out as more visual than auditory, you rely more on the sense of sight, and you learn best through visual means (books, video, charts, pictures). If you are more auditory, you prefer listening and speaking activities (discussions, lectures, audiotapes, role-plays). If you have a tactile/kinesthetic style preference, you benefit from doing projects, working with objects, and moving around (playing games, building models, conducting experiments).

Part 2: HOW I EXPOSE MYSELF TO LEARNING SITUATIONS

If you came out more extroverted on this survey, you probably enjoy a wide range of social, interactive learning tasks (games, conversations, discussions, debates, role-plays, simulations). If you came out more introverted, you probably like to do more independent work (studying or reading by yourself or learning with a computer) or enjoy working with one other person you know well.

Part 3: HOW I HANDLE POSSIBILITIES

If you scored more random-intuitive, you are most likely more future-oriented, prefer what can be over what is, like to speculate about possibilities, enjoy abstract thinking, and tend to disfavor step-by-step instruction. If your style preference was more concrete-sequential, you are likely to be more present-oriented, prefer one-step-at-a-time activities, and want to know where you are going in your learning at every moment.

Part 4: HOW I DEAL WITH AMBIGUITY AND WITH DEADLINES

If you are more closure-oriented, you probably focus carefully on most or all learning tasks, strive to meet deadlines, plan ahead for assignments, and want explicit directions. If you are more open in your orientation, you enjoy discovery learning (in which you pick up information naturally) and prefer to relax and enjoy your learning without concern for deadlines or rules.

Part 5: HOW I RECEIVE INFORMATION

If you have a more global style preference, you enjoy getting the gist or main idea and are comfortable communicating even if you don't know all the words or concepts. If you are more particular in preference, you focus more on details and remember specific information about a topic well.

Part 6: HOW I FURTHER PROCESS INFORMATION

If you are a synthesizing person, you can summarize material well, enjoy guessing meanings and predicting outcomes, and notice similarities quickly. If you are analytic, you can pull ideas apart and do well on logical analysis and contrast tasks, and you tend to focus on grammar rules.

Part 7: HOW I COMMIT MATERIAL TO MEMORY

If you are a sharpener, you tend to notice differences and seek distinctions among items as you commit material to memory. You like to distinguish small differences and to separate memories of prior experiences from memories of current ones. You can easily retrieve the different items because you store them separately. You like to make fine distinctions among speech sounds, grammatical forms, and meaningful elements of language (words and phrases). If you are a leveler, you are likely to clump material together in order to remember it by eliminating or reducing differences, and by focusing almost exclusively on similarities. You are likely to blur similar memories and to merge new experiences readily with previous ones. If you are concerned about accuracy and getting it all right, then the sharpener approach is perhaps preferable. If you are concerned about expediency, then being a leveler may be the key to communication.

Part 8: HOW I DEAL WITH LANGUAGE RULES

If you are a more deductive learner, you like to go from the general to the specific, to apply generalizations to experience, and to start with rules and theories rather than with specific examples. If you are a more inductive learner, you like to go from specific to general and prefer to begin with examples rather than rules or theories.

Part 9: HOW I DEAL WITH MULTIPLE INPUTS

If you are more field-independent in style preference, you like to separate or abstract material from within a given context, even in the presence of distractions. You may, however, have less facility dealing with information holistically. If you are more field-dependent in preference, you tend to deal with information in a more holistic or gestalt way. Consequently you may have greater difficulty in separating or abstracting material from its context. You work best without distractions.

Part 10: HOW I DEAL WITH RESPONSE TIME

If you are a more impulsive learner, you react quickly in acting or speaking, without thinking the situation through. For you, thought often follows action. If you are a more reflective learner, you think things through before taking action and often do not trust your gut reactions. In your case, action usually follows thought.

Part 11: HOW LITERALLY I TAKE REALITY

If you are a metaphoric learner, you learn material more effectively if you conceptualize aspects of it, such as the grammar system, in metaphorical terms. You make the material more comprehensible by developing and applying an extended metaphor to it (e.g., visualizing the grammar system of a given language as an engine that can be assembled and disassembled). If you are a literal learner, you prefer a relatively literal representation of concepts and like to work with language material more or less as it is on the surface.

Tips for the learner

Each style preference offers significant strengths in learning and working. Recognize your strengths to take advantage of ways you learn best. Also, enhance your learning and working power by being aware of and developing the style areas that you do *not* normally use. Tasks that do not seem quite as suited to your style preferences will help you stretch beyond your ordinary comfort zone, expanding your learning and working potential.

For example, if you are a highly global person, you might need to learn to pay more attention to detail in order to learn more effectively. If you are an extremely detail-oriented person, you might be missing out on some useful global characteristics, like getting the main idea quickly. You can develop such qualities in yourself through practice. You won't lose your basic strengths by trying something new; you will simply develop another side of yourself that is likely to be very helpful to your language learning.

If you aren't sure how to attempt new behaviors that go *beyond* your favored style, then ask your colleagues, friends, or teachers to give you a hand. Talk with someone who has a different style from yours and see how that person does it. Improve your learning or working situation by stretching your style!

Language Strategy Use Inventory

Andrew D. Cohen, Rebecca L. Oxford, and Julie C. Chi

The purpose of this inventory is to find out more about yourself as a language learner and to help you discover strategies that can help you master a new language. Check the box that describes your use of each listed strategy. The categories are: ***I use this strategy and like it***; ***I have tried this strategy and would use it again***; ***I've never used this strategy but am interested in it***; and ***This strategy doesn't fit for me***. By referring to the page numbers at the end of each section, you can use this inventory as an index to find out more about the strategies that interest you. Please note that "target" language refers to the new language you are learning.

Listening Strategy Use

	I use this strategy and like it	I have tried this strategy and would use it again	I've never used this strategy but am interested in it	This strategy doesn't fit for me
Strategies to increase my exposure to the target language:				
1. Attend out-of-class events where the new language is spoken.	☐	☐	☐	☐
2. Listen to talk shows on the radio, watch TV shows, or see movies in the target language.	☐	☐	☐	☐
3. Listen to the language in a restaurant or store where the staff speak the target language.	☐	☐	☐	☐
4. Listen in on people who are having conversations in the target language to try to catch the gist of what they are saying.	☐	☐	☐	☐
Strategies to become more familiar with the sounds in the target language:				
5. Practice sounds in the target language that are very different from sounds in my own language to become comfortable with them.	☐	☐	☐	☐
6. Look for associations between the sound of a word or phrase in the new language with the sound of a familiar word.	☐	☐	☐	☐
7. Imitate the way native speakers talk.	☐	☐	☐	☐
8. Ask a native speaker about unfamiliar sounds that I hear.	☐	☐	☐	☐
Strategies to prepare to listen to conversation in the target language:				
9. Pay special attention to specific aspects of the language; for example, the way the speaker pronounces certain sounds.	☐	☐	☐	☐
10. Try to predict what the other person is going to say based on what has been said so far.	☐	☐	☐	☐
11. Prepare for talks and performances I will hear in the target language by reading some background materials beforehand.	☐	☐	☐	☐

Authors' note: This inventory includes revised items from Oxford's Strategy Inventory for Language Learning (in Oxford, 1990) as well as strategies identified and described in Cohen (1990).

Strategies to listen to conversation in the target language:	I use this strategy and like it	I have tried this strategy and would use it again	I've never used this strategy but am interested in it	This strategy doesn't fit for me
12. Listen for key words that seem to carry the bulk of the meaning.	☐	☐	☐	☐
13. Listen for word and sentence stress to see what native speakers emphasize when they speak.	☐	☐	☐	☐
14. Pay attention to when and how long people tend to pause.	☐	☐	☐	☐
15. Pay attention to the rise and fall of speech by native speakers—the "music" of it.	☐	☐	☐	☐
16. Practice "skim listening" by paying attention to some parts and ignoring others.	☐	☐	☐	☐
17. Try to understand what I hear without translating it word for word.	☐	☐	☐	☐
18. Focus on the context of what people are saying.	☐	☐	☐	☐
19. Listen for specific details to see whether I can understand them.	☐	☐	☐	☐
Strategies for when I do not understand some or most of what someone says in the target language:				
20. Ask speakers to repeat what they said if it wasn't clear to me.	☐	☐	☐	☐
21. Ask speakers to slow down if they are speaking too fast.	☐	☐	☐	☐
22. Ask for clarification if I don't understand it the first time around.	☐	☐	☐	☐
23. Use the speakers' tone of voice as a clue to the meaning of what they are saying.	☐	☐	☐	☐
24. Make educated guesses about the topic based on what has already been said.	☐	☐	☐	☐
25. Draw on my general background knowledge to get the main idea.	☐	☐	☐	☐
26. Watch speakers' gestures and general body language to help me figure out the meaning of what they are saying.	☐	☐	☐	☐

For more information on listening strategies, see pp. 173-186.

Vocabulary Strategy Use

Strategies to learn new words:	I use this strategy and like it	I have tried this strategy and would use it again	I've never used this strategy but am interested in it	This strategy doesn't fit for me
27. Pay attention to the structure of the new word.	☐	☐	☐	☐
28. Break the word into parts that I can identify.	☐	☐	☐	☐
29. Group words according to parts of speech (e.g., nouns, verbs).	☐	☐	☐	☐
30. Associate the sound of the new word with the sound of a word that is familiar to me.	☐	☐	☐	☐
31. Use rhyming to remember new words.	☐	☐	☐	☐
32. Make a mental image of new words.	☐	☐	☐	☐
33. List new words with other words that are related to it.	☐	☐	☐	☐
34. Write out new words in meaningful sentences.	☐	☐	☐	☐
35. Practice new action verbs by acting them out.	☐	☐	☐	☐
36. Use flash cards in a systematic way to learn new words.	☐	☐	☐	☐
Strategies to review vocabulary:				
37. Go over new words often when I first learn them to help me remember them.	☐	☐	☐	☐
38. Review words periodically so I don't forget them.	☐	☐	☐	☐
Strategies to recall vocabulary:				
39. Look at meaningful parts of the word (e.g., the prefix or the suffix) to remind me of the meaning of the word.	☐	☐	☐	☐
40. Make an effort to remember the situation where I first heard or saw the word or remember the page or sign where I saw it written.	☐	☐	☐	☐
41. Visualize the spelling of new words in my mind.	☐	☐	☐	☐
Strategies to make use of new vocabulary:				
42. Try using new words in a variety of ways.	☐	☐	☐	☐
43. Practice using familiar words in different ways.	☐	☐	☐	☐
44. Make an effort to use idiomatic expressions in the new language.	☐	☐	☐	☐

For more information on vocabulary strategies, see pp. 187-201.

Speaking Strategy Use

Strategies to practice speaking:	I use this strategy and like it	I have tried this strategy and would use it again	I've never used this strategy but am interested in it	This strategy doesn't fit for me
45. Practice saying new expressions to myself.	☐	☐	☐	☐
46. Practice new grammatical structures in different situations to build my confidence level in using them.	☐	☐	☐	☐
47. Think about how a native speaker might say something and practice saying it that way.	☐	☐	☐	☐
Strategies to engage in conversation:				
48. Regularly seek out opportunities to talk with native speakers.	☐	☐	☐	☐
49. Initiate conversations in the target language as often as possible.	☐	☐	☐	☐
50. Direct the conversation to familiar topics.	☐	☐	☐	☐
51. Plan out in advance what I want to say.	☐	☐	☐	☐
52. Ask questions as a way to be involved in the conversation.	☐	☐	☐	☐
53. Anticipate what will be said based on what has been said so far.	☐	☐	☐	☐
54. Try topics even when they aren't familiar to me.	☐	☐	☐	☐
55. Encourage others to correct errors in my speaking.	☐	☐	☐	☐
56. Try to figure out and model native speakers' language patterns when requesting, apologizing, or complaining.	☐	☐	☐	☐
Strategies for when I can't think of a word or expression:				
57. Ask for help from my conversation partner.	☐	☐	☐	☐
58. Look for a different way to express the idea, like using a synonym.	☐	☐	☐	☐
59. Use words from my own language, but say them in a way that sounds like words in the target language.	☐	☐	☐	☐
60. Make up new words or guess if I don't know the right ones to use.	☐	☐	☐	☐
61. Use gestures as a way to try to get my meaning across.	☐	☐	☐	☐
62. Switch back to my own language momentarily if I know that the person I'm talking to can understand what is being said.	☐	☐	☐	☐

For more information on speaking strategies, see pp. 203-224.

Reading Strategy Use

	I use this strategy and like it	I have tried this strategy and would use it again	I've never used this strategy but am interested in it	This strategy doesn't fit for me
Strategies to improve my reading ability:				
63. Read as much as possible in the target language.	☐	☐	☐	☐
64. Try to find things to read for pleasure in the target language.	☐	☐	☐	☐
65. Find reading material that is at or near my level.	☐	☐	☐	☐
66. Plan out in advance how I'm going to read the text, monitor to see how I'm doing, and then check to see how much I understand.	☐	☐	☐	☐
67. Skim an academic text first to get the main idea and then go back and read it more carefully.	☐	☐	☐	☐
68. Read a story or dialogue several times until I understand it.	☐	☐	☐	☐
69. Pay attention to the organization of the text, especially headings and subheadings.	☐	☐	☐	☐
70. Make ongoing summaries of the reading either in my mind or in the margins of the text.	☐	☐	☐	☐
71. Make predictions as to what will happen next.	☐	☐	☐	☐
Strategies for when words and grammatical structures are not understood:				
72. Guess the approximate meaning by using clues from the context of the reading material.	☐	☐	☐	☐
73. Use a bilingual dictionary to get a sense of what the equivalent word in my native language would be.	☐	☐	☐	☐
74. Use a target language dictionary to see how words are defined by means of other target language words.	☐	☐	☐	☐

For more information on reading strategies, see pp. 225-236.

Writing Strategy Use

	I use this strategy and like it	I have tried this strategy and would use it again	I've never used this strategy but am interested in it	This strategy doesn't fit for me
Strategies for basic writing:				
75. Practice writing the alphabet and/or new words in the target language.	☐	☐	☐	☐
76. Plan out in advance how to write academic papers, monitor how my writing is going, and check to see how well my writing reflects what I want to say.	☐	☐	☐	☐
77. Try writing different kinds of texts in the target language (e.g., personal notes, messages, letters, and course papers).	☐	☐	☐	☐
78. Take class notes in the target language as much as I can.	☐	☐	☐	☐
Strategies for writing an essay or academic paper:				
79. Find a different way to express the idea when I don't know the correct expression (e.g., use a synonym or describe the idea).	☐	☐	☐	☐
80. Review what I have already written before continuing to write more.	☐	☐	☐	☐
81. Use reference materials such as a glossary, a dictionary, or a thesaurus to help find or verify words in the target language.	☐	☐	☐	☐
82. Wait to edit my writing until all my ideas are down on paper.	☐	☐	☐	☐
Strategies to use after writing a draft of an essay or paper:				
83. Revise my writing once or twice to improve the language and content.	☐	☐	☐	☐
84. Try to get feedback from others, especially native speakers of the language.	☐	☐	☐	☐

For more information on writing strategies, see pp. 237-245.

Translation Strategy Use

	I use this strategy and like it	I have tried this strategy and would use it again	I've never used this strategy but am interested in it	This strategy doesn't fit for me
Strategies for translation:				
85. Plan out what to say or write in my own language and then translate it into the target language.	☐	☐	☐	☐
86. Translate in my head while I am reading to help me understand the text.	☐	☐	☐	☐
87. Translate parts of a conversation into my own language to help me remember the conversation.	☐	☐	☐	☐
Strategies for working directly in the target language as much as possible:				
88. Put my own language out of mind and think only in the target language as much as possible.	☐	☐	☐	☐
89. Try to understand what has been heard or read without translating it word for word into my own language.	☐	☐	☐	☐
90. Use caution when directly transferring words and ideas from my own language into the target language.	☐	☐	☐	☐

For more information on translation strategies, see pp. 247-251.

Comments regarding the Language Strategy Use Inventory and Index

- The purpose for completing the survey is to become more aware of the strategies that you use and could use to enhance your language learning and use. You should then use this guide to learn more about those strategies and how to make them work for you. Being an effective strategy user starts with paying greater attention to the strategies you do use, as well as to how you use them and to the results you are getting from using them.
- Just because you use certain strategies frequently doesn't mean you are using them effectively. One goal of this survey is to help you reduce your reliance on a single strategy and increase your ability to use others more. Taking stock with regard to your strategy use can involve cleaning house a bit; it can lead to using strategies that simply don't work less often and using others that have more potential.
- You may also find that you have been too hasty in rejecting a strategy just because it didn't work on a given task. Perhaps it would pay to give that strategy a second chance on another or the same task, but this time taking more care to make sure that it produces the results you want. Strategies aren't good or bad—their impact depends on our preferences and sometimes our ability to make the most of the strategy.
- This inventory doesn't provide you a score on your language strategy use for a given skill or for the language overall. You will notice that the instrument purposely avoids having you rate the strategies by frequency of use. We believe that this approach isn't very helpful for those exploring the options for strategy use to enhance language development. In fact, "frequency" is deceptive because the reason you use a strategy a lot is because you need to use it a lot to make it work!
- Not all strategies listed in this inventory will be useful for the language-learning tasks you may encounter, but many of them are thought to have some value, depending on your style preferences and the learning contexts in which you find yourself.
- The listing of strategies in this inventory should in no way be viewed as all-inclusive of strategies within the skill area. Rather, it is seen as a place to start. We encourage you to cultivate your own personal repertoire of strategies, picking and choosing from strategies to suit your needs. Research has shown that the broader the repertoire of strategies a learner has, the greater the likelihood of success.

Culture-Learning Strategies Inventory

R. M. Paige, J. Rong, W. Zheng, and B. Kappler

The purpose of this inventory is to find out more about yourself as a culture learner and to help you discover strategies that can help you understand and adapt to cultures that are different from your own. Culture-learning strategies can be difficult to pinpoint because when we function well in an environment, we are often no longer conscious of the strategies we use. And perhaps more important, we may not always be conscious that we are *not* functioning well in a new environment! This inventory asks you to consider what you do and what you might do to be effective in a new culture. The specific strategies listed here, while not exhaustive, are comprehensive in terms of what research, theory, and experience suggest are important to consider for how you acquire the knowledge and skills to function well in a new environment.

When taking this inventory, check the box that describes your use of each listed strategy. The categories are: ***I use this strategy and like it***; ***I have tried this strategy and would use it again***; ***I've never used this strategy but am interested in it***; and ***This strategy doesn't fit for me***. By referring to the page numbers at the end of each section, you can use this inventory as an index to find out more about the strategies that interest you.

Pre-Departure Strategies

Strategies for when I am in surroundings that are culturally different from what I am used to:	I use this strategy and like it	I have tried this strategy and would use it again	I've never used this strategy but am interested in it	This strategy doesn't fit for me
1. Consider ways in which different cultures might view things in different ways (e.g., how different cultures value "alone time" or independence).	☐	☐	☐	☐
2. Figure out what cultural values might be involved when I encounter a conflict or when something goes wrong.	☐	☐	☐	☐
3. Think about different cross-cultural perspectives to examine situations in which I seem to offend someone or do something wrong.	☐	☐	☐	☐
4. Use generalizations instead of stereotypes when I make statements about people who are different from me.	☐	☐	☐	☐
5. Counter stereotypes others use about people from my country by using generalizations and cultural values instead.	☐	☐	☐	☐
6. Make distinctions between behavior that is personal (unique to the person), cultural (representative of the person's culture), and universal (shared by humans).	☐	☐	☐	☐
7. Look at similarities as well as differences among people of different backgrounds.	☐	☐	☐	☐

For more information on pre-departure strategies, see pp. 43-75.

The next portion of the Culture-Learning Strategies Inventory looks at the culture-learning strategies you think you will use once you are in the country of your study abroad experience, referred to in this inventory as your "host country." If you have studied abroad before, you may want to complete this inventory according to what you did last time. Or you can fill it out by indicating which strategies you think you *will likely* use in a variety of situations.

In-Country Strategies

Strategies I (will likely) use to adjust to a new culture and cope with culture shock:	I use this strategy and like it	I have tried this strategy and would use it again	I've never used this strategy but am interested in it	This strategy doesn't fit for me
8. Explain my cross-cultural experiences (the good *and* the difficult) to my family and friends at home.	☐	☐	☐	☐
9. Consider what my friends living in the host country say about people from my own culture, using what I know about cultural bias.	☐	☐	☐	☐
10. Strive to keep myself physically healthy.	☐	☐	☐	☐
11. Assume that some moments of culture shock are normal culture-learning experiences and not worry about them too much.	☐	☐	☐	☐
12. Use a variety of coping strategies when I feel I have "culture shock overload."	☐	☐	☐	☐
13. Keep reasonable expectations of my ability to adjust to the new culture, given the length of my stay and my particular study abroad program.	☐	☐	☐	☐

For more information on strategies for cross-cultural adjustment and culture shock, see pp. 91-106.

Strategies for dealing with difficult times in the new culture:	I use this strategy and like it	I have tried this strategy and would use it again	I've never used this strategy but am interested in it	This strategy doesn't fit for me
14. Keep in touch with friends and family back home by writing letters and emails.	☐	☐	☐	☐
15. Keep a journal or a diary about my experiences.	☐	☐	☐	☐
16. Participate in sports and other activities while abroad.	☐	☐	☐	☐
17. Find someone from my own culture to talk to about my cultural experiences.	☐	☐	☐	☐
18. Relax when I'm stressed out in my host country by doing what I normally do back home to make myself comfortable.	☐	☐	☐	☐

For more information on strategies for dealing with difficult times in the new culture, see pp. 91-106.

Strategies for making judgments about another culture:	I use this strategy and like it	I have tried this strategy and would use it again	I've never used this strategy but am interested in it	This strategy doesn't fit for me
19. Observe the behavior of people from my host country very carefully.	☐	☐	☐	☐
20. Analyze things that happen in my host country that seem strange to me from as many perspectives as I can.	☐	☐	☐	☐
21. Consider my own cultural biases when trying to understand another culture.	☐	☐	☐	☐
22. Refrain from making quick judgments about another culture.	☐	☐	☐	☐

For more information on strategies for making cultural judgments, see pp. 52-61, 63-74, and 107-117.

Strategies for communicating with people from another culture:

23. Don't assume that everyone from the same culture is the same.	☐	☐	☐	☐
24. Investigate common areas of miscommunication between people from my host culture and my own culture by reading books and by talking to people who know the two cultures well.	☐	☐	☐	☐
25. Read local newspapers to better understand the current political and social issues in my host country.	☐	☐	☐	☐
26. Build relations with local people by finding opportunities to spend time with them.	☐	☐	☐	☐
27. Help people in my host country understand me by explaining my behaviors and attitudes in terms of my personality and culture.	☐	☐	☐	☐

For more information on strategies for communicating with people from other cultures, see pp. 125-132.

Strategies to deal with different communication styles:	I use this strategy and like it	I have tried this strategy and would use it again	I've never used this strategy but am interested in it	This strategy doesn't fit for me
28. Consider using different types of communication styles when talking with someone from a different culture.	☐	☐	☐	☐
29. Try a different approach when my communication style doesn't seem to be working well.	☐	☐	☐	☐
30. Listen to whether my conversation partners are indirect or direct in their communication styles.	☐	☐	☐	☐
31. Mirror the communication style of my conversation partners (i.e., if they are always indirect, I try to be indirect too).	☐	☐	☐	☐
32. Respect the way people from other cultures express their emotions.	☐	☐	☐	☐
33. Refrain from disagreeing right away so that I have a chance to listen to what others are trying to communicate.	☐	☐	☐	☐

For more information on strategies to deal with different communication styles, see pp. 125-132.

Strategies to understand nonverbal communication in another culture:				
34. Learn about the ways in which people in my host country use nonverbal communication.	☐	☐	☐	☐
35. Examine how my own nonverbal communication is influenced by my culture.	☐	☐	☐	☐
36. Observe which nonverbal communication differences are most difficult for me to adjust to in my host country.	☐	☐	☐	☐
37. Practice using a variety of different nonverbal communication patterns.	☐	☐	☐	☐
38. Figure out how far people stand from each other in my host country and try to keep the "right" distance from others.	☐	☐	☐	☐
39. Observe the gestures that people use in my host country.	☐	☐	☐	☐
40. Ask friends in my host country to explain the meaning of different gestures to me.	☐	☐	☐	☐
41. Try to use eye contact in a way that is appropriate in my host country.	☐	☐	☐	☐

For more information on strategies for nonverbal communication, see pp. 133-142.

Strategies to interact with people in the host culture:	I use this strategy and like it	I have tried this strategy and would use it again	I've never used this strategy but am interested in it	This strategy doesn't fit for me
42. Join clubs or organizations to meet people who have interests like mine.	☐	☐	☐	☐
43. Ask people in my host country about their perceptions of my country and culture.	☐	☐	☐	☐
44. Go to the market in my host country and interact with people in the shops.	☐	☐	☐	☐
45. Hold back on making judgments about other people based on my first impressions.	☐	☐	☐	☐

For more information on strategies for interacting with hosts, see pp. 77-89.

Strategies to use with my homestay family:				
46. Find out from my homestay family what I can do to help around the house.	☐	☐	☐	☐
47. Ask my homestay family about smoking rules in the house and observe those rules if I smoke or invite over friends who smoke.	☐	☐	☐	☐
48. Get permission before bringing someone to my homestay family's house.	☐	☐	☐	☐
49. Share pictures of my own family with my homestay family.	☐	☐	☐	☐
50. Teach games common in my own country to my homestay family.	☐	☐	☐	☐
51. Enlist the help of a friend in my host country when I have a conflict with my homestay family to help me understand the situation.	☐	☐	☐	☐
52. Figure out the household rules for eating, smoking, using the bathroom, dressing around the house, and helping out by observing and asking questions.	☐	☐	☐	☐
53. Ask my host family about their views on privacy and being alone rather than assume that we share the same views.	☐	☐	☐	☐

For more information on strategies for interacting with homestay families, see pp. 85-89.

Post-Study Abroad

Strategies to use when I return home:	I use this strategy and like it	I have tried this strategy and would use it again	I've never used this strategy but am interested in it	This strategy doesn't fit for me
54. Find a group of people who have had similar study abroad experiences to talk to and share experiences.	☐	☐	☐	☐
55. Participate in activities sponsored by study abroad and international groups back home.	☐	☐	☐	☐
56. Take a language class that will help me keep up with the language of the country I studied in (if applicable) and/or take classes on subjects I became interested in during my study abroad adventure.	☐	☐	☐	☐
57. Volunteer for an international organization or work with international students.	☐	☐	☐	☐
58. Share my feelings and experiences with friends and family, without expecting that they will relate to all that I say.	☐	☐	☐	☐
59. Try to stay connected with friends I made while studying abroad.	☐	☐	☐	☐
60. Give myself time to readjust to my own country.	☐	☐	☐	☐

For more information on strategies for returning home, see pp. 143-162.

Comments regarding the Culture-Learning Strategies Inventory

- The purpose for completing this survey is to become more aware of the strategies you use and could use to enhance your culture learning. You should then use this guide to learn more about those strategies and how to make them work for you. Being an effective strategy user starts with paying greater attention to the strategies you do use, as well as to how you use them and to the results you are getting from using them.
- Just because you use certain strategies frequently doesn't mean you are using them effectively. One goal of this survey is to help you reduce the use of a single strategy and use others more. Taking stock with regard to your strategy use can involve cleaning house a bit; it can lead to using strategies that simply don't work less often and using others that have more potential.
- You may also find that you have been too hasty in rejecting a strategy just because it didn't work on a given task. Perhaps it would pay to give that strategy a second chance on another or the same task, but this time taking more care to make sure that it produces the results you want. Strategies aren't good or bad—their impact depends on our preferences and sometimes our ability to make the most of the strategy.
- This inventory doesn't provide you a score on your culture learning for a given strategy or for your culture learning overall. You will notice that the instrument purposely avoids having you rate the strategies by frequency of use. We felt that this approach isn't very helpful for those exploring the options for strategy use to enhance cultural proficiency. In fact, "frequency" is deceptive because the reason you use a strategy a lot is because you need to use it a lot to make it work!
- Not all strategies listed in this inventory will be useful for the culture-learning tasks you may encounter, but many of them are thought to have some value, depending on your style preferences and the learning contexts in which you find yourself.
- The listing of strategies in this inventory is in no way viewed as all-inclusive of strategies within the skill area. Rather, it is seen as a place to start. We encourage you to cultivate your own personal repertoire of strategies, picking and choosing from strategies to suit your needs. Research has shown that the broader the repertoire of strategies a learner has, the greater the likelihood of success.

Section I
Culture-Learning Strategies

INTRODUCTION: CULTURE-LEARNING STRATEGIES

Living abroad has certainly expanded my perspective of the world. By trying to get comfortable in other cultures, trying to learn other ways of doing everything, I have learned much more about myself. Also, by being exposed to new beliefs, ideas, and values, and by analyzing many aspects of my own culture under a new and richer light, I have broadened my viewpoint on many issues. Furthermore, I have acquired the recognition that in international affairs, language is not enough—that for the synergy of business and cultural relations to take place, deep intercultural understanding is required. My international experience is a source of richness that sets me apart from many people and has been a continuous benefit to my career.
~ Antonella Corsi-Bunker; Switzerland, Italy, and France

For some, the ability to learn how to get along in a host culture comes naturally and fairly easily. For most of us, though, it does not. The following sections have been designed to provide you with a wide variety of culture-learning strategies (i.e., ways to help you effectively learn about the host culture).

In learning about cultures, there seem to be two main pieces of advice that are polar opposites:

- Jump in and just go with the flow.
- Wait until you understand what's going on around you.

We suggest a balanced approach. If you go solely for immersion, you run the risk of repeatedly being an "ugly traveler" and, perhaps worse, you run the risk of not really understanding the culture because others are simply constantly adapting to you. On the other hand, waiting until you have gathered everything you need to know will lead you to feel too anxious, and your time may run out before you feel ready. In order to learn about the host culture, you need to be immersed in it and you need to take time to reflect upon your experiences. This section of the guide helps you find this balance.

There are a number of culture-related activities throughout this section to help you prepare for your study abroad experience, with suggested answers provided for each activity. These answers are not meant to be definitive. For many of the activities, there are no right or wrong answers. It may very well be that you disagree with some of the suggested answers, which may spur you to examine how issues of culture can vary from person to person. The answers, like the exercises themselves, are intended to stimulate reflection and further discussion.

The Dimensions of Culture Learning

In this guide, we define culture learning in terms of process and content. The many strategies you will be reading about pertain to the process of learning a new culture in its own context. We organize the content of culture learning into five main categories, as presented by Paige (2005).

1. ***Learning about the Self as a Cultural Being:*** This refers to becoming aware of how the culture(s) we are raised in contribute to our individual identities. We aren't all identical clones of our culture, and yet our individual patterns often reflect influences of the larger cultural groups that surround us. Cultural self-awareness is the foundation for intercultural competence because it enables us first of all to understand that culture influences all of our interactions and that culture isn't something found just in others. Second, it enables us to compare and contrast our own culture(s) with others, as well as to predict those areas where culture clashes may be the most likely to occur and which clashes may be the most challenging.
2. ***Learning about the Elements of Culture:*** To be effective culture learners, we need to know what culture is. In this guide, we use Paige's definition: "Culture refers to values, beliefs, attitudes, preferences, customs, learning styles, communication styles, history/historical interpretations, achievements/accomplishments, technology, the arts, literature, etc.—the sum total of what a particular group of people has created together, share, and transmit."
3. ***Culture-Specific Learning:*** One of the most common ways to think about culture is to consider the cultural elements of the host culture you will be visiting. Culture-specific learning thus refers to becoming knowledgeable about the elements of culture in your specific cultural setting. Those who have lived in another culture frequently comment on how satisfying it was to learn the culture and become more proficient in it. The study abroad experience can also be the launch for a lifetime of study of a country and its cultures.
4. ***Culture-General Learning:*** Culture-general learning refers more broadly to the intercultural experiences that are common to all who visit another culture, as well as the common ways cultures can differ. The key concepts here are values and communication styles, as well as phenomena like intercultural adjustment, adaptation, culture shock, acculturation, and assimilation. These are phenomena that occur whenever individuals move across cultural boundaries and interact with people from other cultures. These experiences can be psychologically and emotionally intense; therefore, we have included many suggestions in this guide for handling cultural adjustment. Understanding the concepts of values and communication styles in general terms is a strategy that can help you develop strengths in culture-specific learning. For example, knowing that individualism is a value can help you to be aware of it and develop an understanding of how individualism is manifested in a particular culture.
5. ***Learning about Learning:*** The premise of this book is that strategic learners are self-empowered and more effective language and culture learners. The main purpose of this guide is to identify strategies you can use in the field, including learning from the media, observing the culture, interacting with host culture persons, and practicing the culture. This kind of learning is grounded on two

principal approaches. The first is to test and refine your understanding of the culture (the hypothesis-testing approach proposed by Crawford-Lange and Lange, 1984). The second is to participate in the culture, reflect upon your experiences, and build your competence (the experiential learning cycle put forward by Kolb, 1984).

These five dimensions of culture learning are the guiding theoretical framework underlying this book. Mastery of all five dimensions can truly be a lifetime endeavor. During your study abroad experience, we encourage you to focus on all five, taking more time to delve into the dimension you feel you need the most. If this is your first time studying abroad, our experience and research indicate that more time will typically be spent in the first and third dimensions. For those who are abroad for the second time and beyond, focusing on all five is our challenge to you.

Coming home story: Beginning at the end

April 28th was the day I chose. I don't even know why. I knew I had to return to Minnesota sometime, so I picked an unimportant date. I had lived in Mexico for four months and, although I didn't consider it home, it just felt more like my home than Minnesota. In the week before I left, I continued my life in Mexico as normal except for packing a little and buying some gifts. I spent my last Saturday, my last Sunday, my last Monday, Tuesday, Wednesday, and Thursday in Cuernavaca. And then Friday, April 28th, arrived. I wasn't excited. I wasn't scared. I wasn't sad. I was just numb, in total disbelief.

I decided not to tell anyone when I was coming home. My mother would ask and I would say, 'Oh, sometime at the end of April or early May.' I finished classes at the beginning of April and since then, my friends were wondering when I was coming home so they could meet me at the airport. I pictured the scene: my mom almost crying with happiness when she sees me, a stern hug from my dad, a quick 'welcome home roughing up' from my brothers, friends giving hugs and asking how the trip was, etc.

The whole idea scared me to death. I haven't seen these people in four months, and they want to come together in one place and bombard me the moment I get off the plane? No way! So I decided to tell only two friends when my flight came in—Matt and Carlos are the two people who I knew would not stress me out.

The morning of the 28th I took a taxi to the bus station and a bus to the airport in Mexico City with my friend Alberto. We got to the airport with about 15 minutes before I had to board the plane and nervously talked. He and I had become really good friends, and I think we were nervous about saying goodbye. About seven minutes before I boarded the plane it hit me. I was leaving. I didn't want to leave Mexico. I didn't want to leave this wonderful culture and beautiful language. I didn't want to leave my friends. And I didn't want to leave the new 'me' that I had discovered. I started to cry. Alberto gave me a hug, we said goodbye, and I walked to the gate. I knew that if I looked back at him I would just walk back to him and say, 'Let's go back to Cuernavaca. I can't leave!' Instead I walked to my gate and boarded the plane.

I had a layover in Houston, and it was terrible. I walked off the plane and was surrounded by white people. Everyone was speaking English. I hadn't seen so many people like me in so long. It seems like I should have been fine with it, but I was very uncomfortable. I kept thinking about Alberto and my other Mexican friends, and I kept thinking about all the places I had seen every day that I may never see again. My 40-minute layover seemed to last forever.

My plane ride to Minneapolis was uneventful except for my thoughts of how I didn't want to be going there. I stepped off the plane and saw Matt and Carlos and almost started to cry. I wanted to cry because no matter how great it was to see them, I didn't want to see them. I wanted to be in Mexico.
~ Susie Peltzman, Mexico

We all come home at some point. And that is often when we begin to realize just how much we have learned about ourselves, about living in another culture and speaking a second language, about profound cultural differences and wonderful human commonalities, and about the pain of leaving our new home and the mixed emotions about returning to our old one. It is quite a journey, as Susie's story suggests.

The purpose of this guide is to be a companion and a help along the way. The learning is always going to be uniquely yours. Our hope is that the strategies and ideas presented here will enhance your experience.

The Culture-Learning Strategies portion of this guide is divided into three major sections: Pre-Departure, In-Country, and Post-Study Abroad (also referred to as re-entry).

PRE-DEPARTURE CULTURE STRATEGIES PART I:
WHAT IS CULTURE, ANYWAY?

We live it. We are surrounded by it. What is it?

> *Culture refers to values, beliefs, attitudes, preferences, customs, learning styles, communication styles, history/historical interpretations, achievements/accomplishments, technology, the arts, literature, etc.—the sum total of what a particular group of people has created together, share, and transmit. ~ R. Michael Paige, co-author*

We all belong to several cultures, each infusing us with ideas and patterns that make us unique and connected with others in our cultural groups. When you think about study abroad, it's natural to focus on learning about the "other"—the other's language, traditions, values, and all the things you want to delve into during your time abroad. We certainly encourage this exploration and yet ask you to consider that the foundation for being successful lies first in understanding yourself. What cultures do you operate in on a daily basis? How does being a particular gender, for example, influence your own values and beliefs? How did your family influence you? How does your ethnicity influence you? In what ways have religious organizations been a part of your life? Answering these questions is where we encourage you to begin your intercultural journey.

You as a Culturally Diverse Person

> *Most of us are not aware we have a culture until we step outside of it. ~ Jacob Dick, Italy*

You are embarking on study abroad to meet real people from other countries. You'll want to learn as much as you can about them—their cultural backgrounds, their personalities, their likes and dislikes. In exchange, they'll want to know about you. This next activity helps you reflect upon the cultural groups and categories to which you belong. All of our experiences growing up have contributed to who we are today, particularly in terms of what we value, what we believe, what we know, and how we behave.

ACTIVITY: Discovering your cultural diversity

Take a few minutes to complete this diagram. In as many circles as you can, write a word you feel describes you or is a significant part of who you are or how you choose to identify yourself to others.

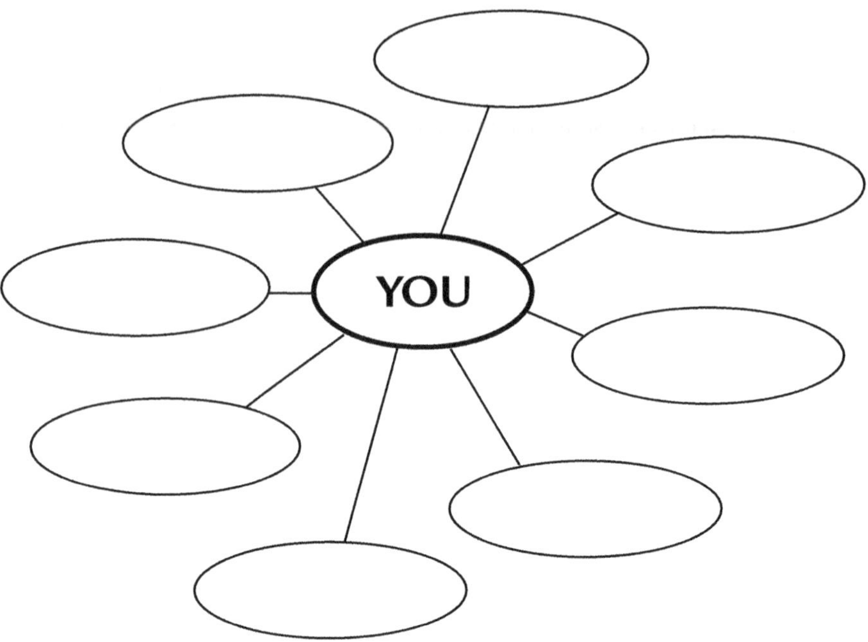

Reflection questions

- If you had to pick just one circle, which would it be? Two circles? Why are these the most important parts of your cultural identity?
- Did you have difficulty filling in eight circles? Did you find eight was not enough? What insights have you gained about yourself from this exercise? Is there an identity that others don't readily recognize in you? Is this OK? Or is it frustrating?
- Go back to the diagram and add some of the values you attribute to the circles. For example, if one circle says "student," values from being a student might be "independence," "respect for knowledge," or "question authority." After adding in the values, consider if there are places where the values conflict. How have you managed to cope with these conflicts?
- How might these circles change when you are abroad? For example, did you list your nationality in one of the circles? Your social class? Did you list the languages you speak? How might it feel to be seen as just one or another circle—such as U.S. American?
- How might the roles you play in the U.S. be similar and different in your host country?

(Adapted from Gardenswartz and Rowe, 1994.)

The various roles that we play in life have an impact on our identity, shaping our sense of who and what we are. Below are some of the identities given by three study abroad students who filled out a personal culture diagram, followed by the reactions they had to this activity.

Student #1
- Hispanic
- woman
- writer
- activist
- lover of books
- cat owner
- photographer

Student #2
- black
- male
- math major
- student
- brother
- waiter
- biker

Student #3
- parent/mom
- sister
- Irish heritage
- Catholic
- pre-law student
- friend

Student #1

My number one identity is Chicana. It shapes everything I do, and I'm very proud of this. However, my identity is also very tied up with being a woman, specifically a woman of color. Culture and gender are huge issues for me because they've had to be. It's impossible to be a minority woman in this country and not confront these identifiers as a part of life because that's how everyone else sees me.

Student #2

People always ask me if I play sports. Sports are not part of my identity, but their asking shows that they're stereotyping me. I had a hard time selecting one circle. All of these circles really affect me. Being black is important, but I socialize with people from all different backgrounds. It's important to get along with everyone.

Student #3

I've never spent much time thinking about my identity. I say I'm Irish, but if I picked one or two circles, it would never be that. I'm really an American, and I didn't even put that as one of my circles. Now that I am a mom, I realize how much this shapes me and brings out my values. I suppose I'm also middle class, but because I'm a student paying my own tuition, I always feel so poor!

It is difficult to address all the complexities about study abroad and identity in a book. We strongly encourage you to seek the support of your study abroad coordinators and advisers for questions that naturally may arise out of this identity exercise. For example, are certain circles going to be less visible in another country? You may be a student that is returning to a country of heritage, a place from where you were adopted, or a place from where your relatives were enslaved. How will you be seen by people from the host country? Do they see you as a member of their culture? Do they see you solely as a U.S. American?

For many students who are connected by heritage to the study abroad location, the experience is powerful:

> *My parents are from Laos and spent some years in the refugee camps in Thailand. I was born and raised in the United States and sometimes feel disconnected from my heritage. I felt a yearning to experience Southeast*

Asia for myself. I wanted to see, hear, and feel the same atmosphere my parents grew up in. When I saw the opportunity open up to study in Thailand, I jumped at it.

I had little knowledge of the Thai language except a few words that had been integrated into the Hmong language, so it was a challenge to communicate with people. But I discovered that gestures and facial expressions could carry a conversation all on their own. Then, when we visited a Hmong village it was refreshing to be able to communicate with everyone there. At first I was nervous about what they would think of us. But we sat in on a celebration ceremony for a group of local Hmong boys and had lunch (also refreshing to have authentic Hmong food again), and it felt like having lunch at one of my aunts' houses.

Our excursions also brought us into rural life. We spent a weekend at a Buddhist community where we learned how to plant rice. I've often heard stories from my parents and grandparents about working in the fields and here I was actually taking part in it. Now I knew what they meant when they said it was hard work! The experience really connected me with my roots. I got to experience a life that was very much a part of my history and blood. It is something that I will treasure and look back on as one of the proudest moments of my life. ~ Bee Lee, Thailand

Although you know the many cultures that you belong to, others you meet will not automatically appreciate your complex cultural identity. One challenge about studying abroad is that you may feel as if you are seen only as a U.S. American, rich, female, etc. Similarly, it is important to realize that all people are complex and have multiple layers of identity so that you don't fall into the trap of limiting them to one identity, just as you don't think of yourself as being only U.S. American. One strategy is to try to learn at least eight aspects of your host's identity.

Becoming Familiar with Culture: The Iceberg Analogy

Culture shock in Sydney didn't hit me when the meat tasted slimy or even when every other sentence was 'No worries, mate.' It hit when I went to register for classes and spent an entire day trying not to rip out all of my hair due to the process that was so slow it was painful. I took registration on the Internet for granted. No longer will I do that. ~ Elizabeth Hook, Australia

My first bit of advice would be patience. You are no longer in the land of instant gratification. France, for the foreigner, is an acquired taste. ~ Joy Wildermuth, France

You know there will be differences and similarities. But how do you recognize and understand these when you are face-to-face with these similarities and differences? Understanding culture does not simply mean knowing a list of values that a culture has. Culture is a system, meaning you cannot say, "U.S. Americans value time and don't value relationships." We value both. There are times when relationships are going to be the most important thing to a U.S. American. And there are times when being on time to work, being independent, and being practical are going to come first. The key to understanding another culture is understanding the system of decision making—what value or rule comes out on top in specific situations.

One strategy for learning this system it to understand the iceberg concept of culture. This concept helps greatly in developing your skills in the second and third dimensions of culture learning (culture-specific and culture-general) and is a tool for the fifth dimension (learning about learning), see p. 40. The following story helps us understand the role of using the iceberg in everyday intercultural situations.

Joshua's story

> *During the third week of my 15-week stay in Venezuela, it became time to iron some of my clothes. Upon doing so, the iron fell off the ironing board and onto the tile floor. The piece designed to make the iron stand up had broken off, so I decided I had better tell my host mother what had happened. It wasn't easy, but with body language, showing her the iron, and my beginning-level Spanish, she understood what I had done. I could not help but notice she looked somewhat agitated and concerned. She fidgeted around with the iron for awhile and left the room and went about her business. I, thinking it was not a big deal, went to class and forgot about the incident.*
>
> *However, the next day I woke up to an empty house and a note addressed to me lying on the kitchen table. After an hour of using my Spanish-English dictionary, I figured out what it said. My host mother, using many kind and genial words, was asking me to go into town to buy the super glue that would repair the broken iron. This involved a great deal of uncertainty for me. In the beginning, I hated going anywhere in the city alone, so I called every person I knew and either nobody was home or they could not go with me. Not wanting to disappoint my host mom, I set out alone to find the glue.*
>
> *On the note were the directions to get to the carpenter's shop, so basically I knew where I was going. I needed to take the bus because it was too far to walk, and besides, I had been avoiding the bus as much as possible; therefore, I felt it necessary to overcome my fear. However, as soon as I stepped onto the bus I knew I was going to have a problem because I got pushed to the back of the bus, which meant I was going to have to shout 'Por la parada, por favor' at the top of my lungs to get off the bus. It is one thing to speak in Spanish, but it is an entirely different thing to shout in Spanish.*
> *~ Joshua Bleskan, Venezuela*

ACTIVITY: *Joshua and the iceberg*

Joshua faces a number of challenges in this situation. To help sort through these, the analogy of an iceberg is helpful. The tip of the iceberg represents the pieces of culture that we can see. The area below the water line represents deeper cultural meaning.

1. What do you see happening in Joshua's example? Place these items on the iceberg above the line.
2. What might be some deeper cultural differences that lie below the surface? Place these items on the iceberg as well.

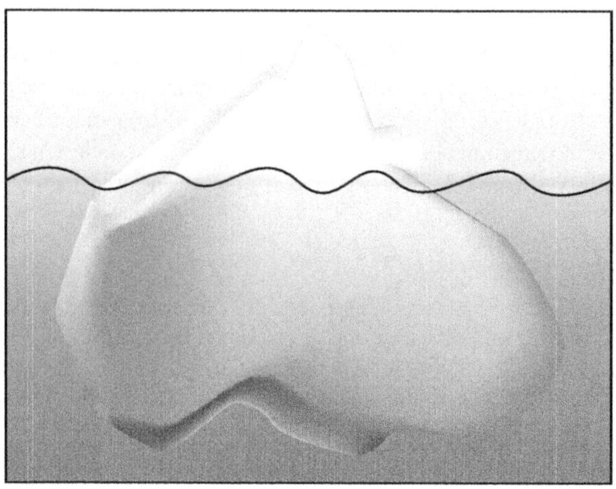

Other students who have looked at this incident have placed the following items above the line on the iceberg as the observable elements of culture:

- *Language* – Joshua's host is using Spanish; his Spanish is limited
- *Indirect communication* – his host did not directly discuss the incident with him
- *Formal and polite communication* – his host's note
- *Yelling on the bus* – people in the back yell to get off the bus

The tricky part is, of course, what lies beneath the surface. Notice that the portion of the iceberg beneath the water is much larger. The portion that is invisible includes peoples' values, norms, and belief systems. Here's a look at what other students have said were some of the deeper cultural differences Joshua encountered:

- His own culture's emphasis on independence and individualism
- His assumption that nothing being said on the day of the accident meant that nothing was wrong; the absence of words can mean no conflict or no problem
- His host country's rules of behavior in public places

Here's a bit of an explanation of these differences:

- Joshua's culture emphasizes independence. His language inadequacy and unfamiliarity with public transportation made him feel uneasy and dependent on others. He experienced frustration that he felt dependent on his friends, but finding none available, he was determined to go out on his own and find the glue. Joshua experienced a desire to be independent, a strong U.S. American value. In this sense, Joshua's clash with cultures was not directly with Venezuela, but with himself. In the end, it is also the value that helped him through the situation.

- When the host mother did not immediately tell Joshua that he needed to fix the iron, he assumed it was not a big deal. But as Joshua himself later realized, the iron needed to be fixed. The note was not just a way to communicate but potentially a sign of a preferred way to communicate because it's a way to save face.
- To Joshua, yelling in public places may be considered very inappropriate. But in Venezuela it was apparently OK in one public place—a crowded bus—so he experienced a different norm for behavior in a public place.
- Joshua's willingness to step outside of his comfort zone and understand the elements below the surface helped him in this situation. In addition, he and his host mom had something in common. They both held the belief that people are responsible for their own actions.

Consider what lies beneath the surface in this situation. Why do you think Joshua's host mother wrote the note? Write your response below.

Here is what people with experience in Venezuela had to say about the note:

- *Perhaps she is being sensitive to his limited language skills, and so she wrote a note to help him.*
- *This may not have much to do with culture, but more to do with social class—this may be an issue of money and income. This family may not have the money to fix or replace the item, so it is important that Joshua take care of it.*
- *There may be a value difference here. The perception of Venezuelans may be that U.S. Americans are wasteful. Perhaps she has had U.S. American students in the past, and when incidents like this have occurred they have bought new things instead of having them fixed. She may be trying to teach him that it's OK to fix the iron instead of replacing it.*
- *For Venezuelans and his host mom it may be more appropriate to give messages indirectly, especially when you are at the beginning of a relationship. It is a way to save face and not embarrass Joshua.*
- *As a Venezuelan, I can see that the note is written not necessarily to avoid conflict, but to emphasize that in taking care of things you are taking care of your relationships with other people, and that is the most important thing. He needs to fix the iron not because it's an iron, but because it will show that he cares for her.*

Here's what Joshua had to say about this:

> *Because of the success I had with the iron incident, my host mother gained a lot of confidence in me and we became the best of friends. So when I shattered the sink during my 10th week, there was no longer a need to write me a note to fix it. She told me that she would pay for half if I paid for the other half. Now, had I not done what at the time seemed like a rather insignificant thing—go to the store and buy some glue—breaking the sink*

could have been a very uncomfortable situation. Fortunately, I did what I was politely asked, and it benefited me greatly in the future. For this reason, I believe there is nothing more detrimental in cultural adaptation than avoiding the uncomfortable. What is the worst that can happen? More times than not, the worst that can happen comes from the avoidance.

The iceberg analogy has some key points for learning about a culture:

- The things we observe almost always have deeper meaning, that is, they represent a more fundamental cultural value. Although the iceberg separates culture into visible and invisible elements, these are almost always interrelated (such as the written note being a sign of a deeper communication pattern in the culture).
- What we think we see is not always what is going on. Even trickier is how a visible aspect of culture, something so seemingly obvious as laughing, can have very different meanings in different cultures. For example, laughing can mean "That's funny" or "I'm embarrassed."
- We interpret what we see in the host culture as we would in our own, but the actual meaning may be quite different.

I like this iceberg strategy. It's an easy-to-use mental image. ~ Jacob Dick, Italy

ACTIVITY: Identifying aspects of culture

What kinds of things typically lie above or below the surface? Take a look at these sample items and place them on the iceberg—the more visible elements going above the water line and the less visible below.

____ Clothing	____ Methods of worship	____ Rules of politeness
____ Views on equality	____ Time management	____ Relationship with nature
____ Religious beliefs	____ Tipping customs	____ Attitudes toward sexuality
____ Personal distance	____ Gestures	____ Degree of eye contact
____ Works of art	____ Concept of beauty	____ Food

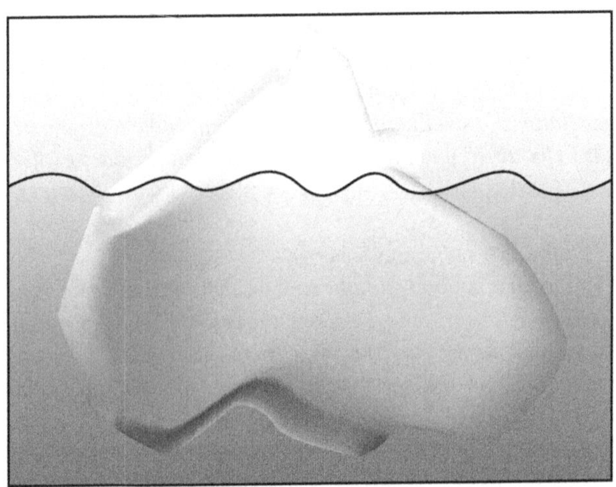

Reflection questions

- Did you place some items both above and below? If so, why?

- Were some items difficult to place?

- Where did you place methods of worship? If you don't have any visible signs of worship (like going to a public place of worship), what does that mean? How would someone come to learn about your own religious beliefs?

- Most would place "views on equality" in the deep aspects of culture. What might be visible signs that you are a feminist or support gender equality among men and women? Are there signs in the way you dress? Speak? What visible signs are there about equality among social classes?

Suggested answers

- Clothing
- Personal distance
- Works of art
- Methods of worship
- Tipping customs
- Gestures
- Degree of eye contact
- Food

- Views on equality
- Religious beliefs
- Time management
- Rules of politeness
- Relationship with nature
- Attitudes toward sexuality
- Concept of beauty

Examining the connections between surface and deep aspects of culture is a critical strategy for being effective in crossing cultures. For example, certain gestures may be signs of religious beliefs, such as some Muslim women not shaking hands with men when they greet each other. And, in the case with Joshua, understanding the note as a way to maintain the relationship and a preference for indirect communication was critical to Joshua's success with his host. Of course, some visible signs may not be connected to a deeper meaning—it may just be the way things are!

Differentiating Cultural from Personal and Universal

It was really hard to tell in the beginning if something was cultural or just personal. I remember one time asking my host parents out to dinner at what for me was kind of an expensive restaurant. When we were getting ready to go, I was a little frustrated when I saw my host father's brother and his family had arrived to join us. I didn't say anything because I know family is important in Mexico, and what would I say, anyway?

When the bill came, I figured that my host father would help out—after all, he was the one who invited his brother and his brother's family. As it turns out, I got stuck with the bill and felt really taken advantage of. I had found Mexicans to be so generous and then this really made me think my host father was a jerk. ~ Kelly Lavin, Mexico

Kelly's experience brings up an issue that can be challenging: How do you sort out what's normal cultural behavior and what's not? In this case, is the host father really a "jerk," or is he following some cultural rule or norm? How can you figure this out?

Let's start with some definitions from *Culture Matters: The Peace Corps Cross-Cultural Workbook*:

- ***Cultural***: refers to what a group of people have in common with each other and how they are different from other groups
- ***Personal***: refers to ways in which each person is different from everyone else, including those in the same group
- ***Universal***: refers to ways in which all people in all groups are basically the same

(Storti and Bennhold-Samaan, 1997.)

Some important points to remember

- Personal preferences exist everywhere. Often a preference may very well have cultural and historical roots. The longer you are in the country, the better you can distinguish between what is cultural and what is more personal.
- When something is cultural, this means there is a recognizable pattern of behavior. When you have learned the patterns, then you know when something is out of the norm. You'll be better able to know, for example, when someone is being unusually friendly.
- Awareness of cultural patterns also helps you figure out your own perceptions of events and your adaptation strategies.

Kelly found out several weeks later that an invitation to one family member is, in fact, an invitation to other family members who know about the upcoming event. This became clear when she saw her host father in a similar situation when people who she knew hadn't been directly invited showed up to the restaurant, and he paid the bill for everyone.

She also learned something important about distinguishing between universal (in this case, hosting a social event) and culturally specific patterns—the details that differ between cultures during such events.

ACTIVITY: Cultural, personal, or universal?

Read the list of behaviors below. Indicate if you think the behavior is universal, cultural, or personal. If you feel that there is more than one answer, think of some examples to show how this may be true.

U = Universal
C = Cultural
P = Personal

1. _____ Eating with chopsticks
2. _____ Women walking five steps behind men
3. _____ Walking rather than riding the bus
4. _____ Feeling sorry after accidentally stepping on someone's foot
5. _____ Respecting your elders
6. _____ Making a slurping sound when eating soup or noodles
7. _____ Wearing warmer clothing when it is cold
8. _____ Being depressed after the death of a loved one
9. _____ Sleeping with a light on
10. _____ Shaking hands with someone you first meet

(Adapted from Storti and Bennhold-Samaan, 1997.)

Suggested answers

Cultural

1. Eating with chopsticks
2. Women walking five steps behind men
5. Respecting your elders
6. Making a slurping sound when eating soup or noodles
10. Shaking hands with someone you first meet

These statements are considered to be cultural because there are places in the world where a majority of the people would engage in the behavior. While it can also be true that these are personal behaviors, there are often rules regarding the behaviors—suggesting personal variation is the exception, not the rule. For example, in the U.S. Midwest, some may make a slurping sound when eating soup or noodles; however, by general Midwest standards, it is considered to be improper etiquette.

Universal

4. Feeling sorry after accidentally stepping on someone's foot
5. Respecting your elders
7. Wearing warmer clothing when it is cold
8. Being depressed after the death of a loved one

The above represent behaviors and beliefs found in all cultures. Of course, this does not mean that you respond exactly the same way in each culture—you may apologize profusely in one culture for stepping on someone's foot and in another you simply say "excuse me" or nothing at all. Notice that "Respecting your elders" is on both the cultural and universal list because, while this belief is common throughout cultures, the extent to which respect is shown varies so greatly that it can seem to differ across cultures.

Personal
3. Walking rather than riding the bus
9. Sleeping with a light on

These reflect individual preferences, rather than cultural norms. Of course, there are some cultures where riding the bus is the only realistic option given distances between sites. Whether one walks or rides the bus may still be a matter of choice.

When encountering new or puzzling behaviors, ask yourself these questions:

- Is this behavior likely to be personal, cultural, or universal?
- If it's universal, such as grieving for a loss of a loved one, how do I find out the culturally appropriate ways to respond in this particular culture?
- If I think the behavior is personal, how can I really know it isn't cultural?

The answer is complex, of course, as humans are complex. One strategy is to try out behaviors in different situations and watch for reactions and look for how it is perceived—do others react as if the behavior was natural or not? If you think the behavior is cultural, what additional information do you need to ensure that you am correct? (For example, in Estonia it is not necessary to say "nice to meet you" when you meet someone for the first time.) How many times do you need to observe something to understand that it is more than simply personal differences? How many times do you need to observe something to know if age, gender, and time constraints are also factors involved?

The biggest challenge is perhaps distinguishing the personal from the cultural and usually requires collecting information over a period of time. Being able to make these distinctions allows you to be more comfortable with the cultural nuances and to be more effective in your communication with others.

Some Strategies for Culture-Specific Learning

> *Learn about and try to understand the culture that you'll be going to. Learn about the history and politics of the country and how they have affected the present-day culture. Also, try to understand your own culture as this will help you to better understand another. ~ Jessica Novotny, Spain*

How to learn about your host culture

Don't wait until you are overseas to learn about the host culture(s) of your study abroad country. Why not? A little bit of knowledge can go a long way to establish good relations. Should you bring a gift? If so, what's appropriate? How formal should you be with your hosts? What should you expect in terms of how to register for your classes? What are some major political issues facing the country? Knowing the answers to these questions will help you get off to a good start and will build your confidence. Also, many find themselves intimidated by the knowledge people from other countries have not only about their own politics, history, and culture, but also about U.S. American politics and culture. Feeling insecure, it's easy to shut yourself off from these conversations, further preventing you from gaining the knowledge you seek! We're not suggesting you "know everything," but, rather, prepare yourself with a few key pieces of information.

Here are a few suggestions for getting prepared. Of course, you can't do all these before you go. Select the areas that are most interesting or most challenging to you.

People from the country and culture you are visiting:

- Check out the international organizations or university groups at your home college or university
- Find out if there are professional organizations in your area with an international exchange focus (e.g., Rotary International or AFS/Youth for Understanding)
- Visit with other students who have studied abroad in your host country; ask your campus study abroad office about how you can meet returnees
- Meet with returned volunteers from the Peace Corps or other agencies

Literature:

- Check out novels, short stories, poetry, etc; learn about the major literary figures and their works
- Discover the Intercultural Press—a wonderful resource for intercultural and culture-specific books, both fiction and nonfiction
- Explore books written for second language learners and textbooks for cultural information
- Read nonfiction books on history, geography, politics, etc.
- Seek out travel writing
- Look for Culturgrams—publications outlining key cultural information on more than 180 countries and cultures of the world; available on the Internet and through public libraries

Film:

- Rent videos from the international section of the video store or the library
- Watch film festival listings for movies made about or in your host country

Newspapers and magazines:

- Check out your school library's special collections for newspapers and magazines from your host country
- Pay attention to cultural trends and hot topics, such as:
  - What societal issues are considered important to the people?
  - What sports teams does the country have? What are their records?
  - What artists or musicians are currently popular?

Internet:

- Read online newspapers
- Listen to online radio
- Search the Internet for country-specific information about topics of interest (If you enjoy cooking, Rollerblading, or pottery, find organizations related to these interests. You could even start up dialogues with people before you leave.)
- Look up maps of the country; have an understanding of where the major cities and other important geographical areas are located

Much of the above could be considered required knowledge before you leave for your study abroad. You can think of it as a great way to expand upon your cultural literacy of the target country without a huge expenditure of time.

ACTIVITY: Basic things you should know before you go

It's strategic to have some basic facts about your host country at your fingertips. This helps you to get into conversations and shows your respect for the culture. Take some time to investigate the following topics—use the Internet, foreign newspapers, and magazines, or ask a person from your host country.

- Names of famous artists
- Famous movies and popular movie stars, TV shows, newspapers, etc.
- Names of popular singers
- Popular sports or sports teams
- Ethnic groups and cultural heritages that make up the country
- Cultural diversity (e.g., immigration and refugee populations)
- Major religion(s)/spiritual beliefs and their effect on the host country
- National holidays and traditional customs
- Traditional foods, most popular foods
- Types of gifts, if any, that are appropriate to bring to host families, new friends, etc.
- Names of political leaders
- Names of political parties
- Type of government
- Year of independence and circumstances
- Hot topics of the day (e.g., government scandals)
- Recent conflicts and the role of the U.S. in those conflicts
- U.S. role in local economy, politics, culture, etc.
- Economic conditions
- Class structure (e.g., What will your status as a student be in this country? What percentage of students in your host country go to college?)
- Weather conditions

Working with Stereotypes and Testing Hypotheses

You've probably heard the saying, "When in Rome, do as the Romans do." But what's a Roman? We probably assume that all Romans are not alike, just as we know that all persons from our country or region are not the same. At the same time, we might have a lot of images in our mind about Romans from books, the news, television, and movies. So, we are in a quandary. What does it mean to behave like a Roman? How can we speak about Roman culture without just stereotyping it? How can we make any sense of how Romans do things? If the images are incorrect, how can we correct them? In other words, what does understanding a culture really mean?

There are several ways to answer these questions, and we will suggest some strategies to use. First, it is useful to acknowledge that we do have stereotypical cultural images in our mind. They may be simplistic and crude, but they are there.

Did you ever hear anyone say:

- The French are rude.
- Spaniards love their siestas.
- Brits have a wonderful, dry sense of humor.
- U.S. Americans are self-centered.
- U.S. Americans are friendly.
- Asian students are good in science and math.

Are these statements true? Of course not; they are ***stereotypes****—the automatic application of information we have about a country or culture group, both positive and negative, to every individual in it.* This information is often based on limited experience with the culture, so it is incomplete at best and downright wrong at worst. If you consider only stereotypes when learning about a culture, you limit your understanding of the host culture and can make serious mistakes.

What's the alternative? A ***generalization***. This means *using initial ideas about a group to form hypotheses*. For example, you've been watching British television and note the dry sense of humor that forms the basis for several sitcoms. Then you meet several Brits who also have a dry sense of humor. You begin to form a general idea about British humor.

Generalizing recognizes that there may be a tendency for people within a culture group to share certain values, beliefs, and behaviors. Generalizations can also be based on incomplete or false information, but you are less likely to get into trouble with a generalization because you are using that information with caution, you are constantly testing and revising your ideas, and while you are searching for general patterns in the culture, you never assume that every person will act in the same way.

The way to test a generalization is to form one or more ***hypotheses***. The hypothesis is recognized as a guess; it leaves open the possibility that you could be wrong and that you need to collect more information. The best hypotheses are stated as questions and are in neutral or descriptive language so that they can be used to gather more information rather than reveal your personal judgment (positive or negative) about the situation. Your desire to learn more about the culture will sound much more authentic if you resist the temptation to exaggerate and stereotype. For example, instead of saying, "Women are second-class citizens in Japan," you might change this to a hypothesis and collect more information: "Are women treated equally to men in employment? For example, I have only seen women making tea, never men, even when I thought they had the same positions." Note that the statement includes the observable behavior that led you to the generalization. The extra detail in the revised statement makes it preferable to the original stereotyped statement. You haven't concluded anything, and yet you see a pattern emerging from the information you are learning about the country. This allows the listener to see what your hypothesis is based on and can lead to further discussion about whether your assumption is accurate and what additional information you might need (for example, that the roles are based on age, that this used to be more common and is changing, or that other definitions of "equality" exist).

ACTIVITY: Changing stereotypes into generalizations and hypotheses

This exercise gives you some practice in changing stereotypes into generalizations. By being able to transition from stereotypes to generalizations, you can help yourself and can also help fellow travelers and host nationals to develop stronger skills in understanding cultures.

Example:

Stereotype: Americans are very friendly.
Changing it to a generalization: Many Americans are friendly in the way they act toward people from other countries.
Changing it to hypotheses (questions with an observable component): What do Americans do to appear very friendly? Do they talk more readily to strangers than people from other cultures? Do they smile more? Do they smile more often at people they don't know?

Practice Statements:

1. Americans are superficial.
Changing it to a generalization:
Changing it to hypotheses (questions with an observable component):

2. The French are rude.
Changing it to a generalization:
Changing it to hypotheses (questions with an observable component):

3. Spaniards are laid-back.
Changing it to a generalization:
Changing it to hypotheses (questions with an observable component):

Suggested answers:

1. Americans are superficial.
Changing it to a generalization: Many Americans seem superficial to people from other countries. Many Americans come across as superficial in the way they talk to others.
Changing it to hypotheses (questions with an observable component): What do Americans do that seems superficial? Do they have more small talk in their conversations than others? Do they seem hesitant to get into deeper political conversations? Do they have brief conversations about topics that do not lead into longer discussions?

2. The French are rude.
Changing it to a generalization: Many French seem to respond rudely to U.S. Americans.
Changing it to hypotheses (questions with an observable component): What is it that the French are doing (and to whom) that seems rude? What do I think is rude in the situation? Is it that they are speaking loudly? Is it that I speak to them in French and they respond in English? Are some French particular about the way French is spoken? Is there something specific between France and the U.S. in the political world that would bring about animosity?

3. Spaniards are laid-back.
Changing it to a generalization: Some Spaniards seem more laid-back when compared to northern Europeans.
Changing it to hypotheses (questions with an observable component): What are the observable differences between Spaniards and northern Europeans? Do the Spaniards take a siesta and the British typically do not? Do Spaniards seem to be more relaxed about what time a meeting begins than you are used to?

Using Generalizations to Respond to Stereotypes about You

While you are abroad you are likely to encounter many occasions when the host nationals or other international students will make stereotypical comments about the U.S. and its citizens.

How can you respond? One of the things you can do is explain your culture in terms of its general patterns. This assumes that you know what they are, which interestingly is something most of us don't think about very often. The following section will introduce you to the numerous values that underlie the actions and thoughts of some people living in the United States. For example, imagine that your Thai host father has commented on how individualistic U.S. Americans are. He claims, "They always want to express their own ideas, and they look after their own welfare rather than their family's." Using generalizations, you can give a cultural overview, saying something like James Lassegard did:

> *Yes, Americans like to be independent and to see themselves as in control of their lives. These values are reflected in the popular song 'My Way' or in the emphasis on 'self-expression' or 'self-empowerment' in today's society. Of course, this does not mean that all people living in the U.S. value individualism in the same way or to the same extent. It simply means that many, if not most, Americans appear to have this value, and that the culture views this as a positive attribute. ~ James Lassegard, Japan*

The wealthy American?

One challenging stereotype people may have of you is that you are rich. The reality may be that you are going into personal debt to be on this trip or that you have saved for months for the opportunity to study abroad. In either case, you may feel far removed from wealth and very much like a poor student!

Yet by world standards, you may very well be wealthy. Consider the following:

- Did you have access to a job to save money for study abroad?
- Will you be able to find a job when you return?
- Although attending college in the U.S. may not feel like elitism, *USA Today* reported in 2005 that fewer than 30 percent of U.S. Americans between the ages of 25 and 29 have a college degree, with members of certain ethnic groups less likely to have a college degree than members of other ethnic groups. Do you know what the ratio is in your host country and how it may vary by ethnic group? If the numbers are not readily available, what might this suggest?

While access to jobs and education may not put money directly into your bank account, it does make you wealthy in comparison to those you might meet in your host country.

In many countries, there exists an image of the United States as a land of limitless wealth and opportunity. For over a century now an idealized image—"where the streets are paved with gold"—has drawn people from around the world to the U.S. and, with mass media, what is now "known" abroad about the United States often comes via movies, pop music, and television shows. The lives depicted on U.S. soap operas and in most Hollywood movies probably bear little resemblance to your own, and it may seem laughable that those depictions would be accepted as reality anywhere. However, there are often few alternative images to counterbalance the impact of shows like *Baywatch* or *As the World Turns*. (Try to imagine the scenes from a movie about your life, if you are an average college student: purchasing a month's supply of ramen noodles in the grocery store or moving your aunt's avocado-and-rust colored plaid couch, circa 1973, up four flights of narrow stairs into your apartment. Not exactly a lifestyle that translates easily into international blockbuster material!) With the imbalance of superstars, pop singers, and multimillionaire athletes versus ordinary U.S. citizens represented in the media, it is not surprising that there is the stereotype of U.S. Americans as rich and materialistic, and by extension, greedy, shallow, and wasteful. Depending on your host country, you may find a strange mix of curiosity and antipathy directed toward you because of these stereotypes about the U.S.

As an American, you may hold strong views about the United States. Some of you may feel that your home country is the land of opportunity, a special place in the world where those who work hard can achieve unlimited personal success. Others may feel that this is a country riddled with social problems and gross inequalities. Still others of you may not have given these issues much consideration up to this point, and you accept the United States as it is. Regardless of your opinions, it will be worthwhile to pay attention to the differences in wealth and personal opportunities that you notice between your host country and your home country. Some differences may be overt and some may be subtle, so look closely. Write down what you see, hear, and observe, and talk with your friends and host family if you can. In the end, the point is not to come away with a definitive answer or opinion, or to define which value system is right and which is wrong. The goal is to discover what you feel is valuable in both cultures and ultimately have a greater understanding of what you have in the U.S., both in terms of physical possessions as well as opportunities.

And here is some final advice from another traveler about being a U.S. American abroad:

> *I remember feeling as though people judged me unfairly because of my nationality while traveling in eastern Europe. I was with a group of kids about my age while in Slovakia, and I felt that they were overly critical of me as an individual because of my government's military actions in Belgrade. The anger I felt toward them for judging me actually helped me. It is very important to remember the golden rule of intercultural interaction: Don't judge a person completely because of cultural stereotypes if you don't want them to be equally critical of you. I now realize that no one is responsible for their government. We are all individuals and deserve to be evaluated on our own merits, not those of our elected officials. ~ Dan Jakab, Spain*

PRE-DEPARTURE CULTURE STRATEGIES PART II:

UNDERSTANDING THE WAYS CULTURES CAN DIFFER IN VALUES

Before studying in England, I had not traveled much. I really did not know if I was a 'typical' American or not. I was just me. And I expected to find my British family to be a British family—whatever that would be. I was not expecting to find major differences and, in many ways, I did not. What I did find was that they saw me as very different from them. I was an American. Through their eyes and reactions to me, I learned much more about myself than I was able to learn about them. ~ Barbara Kappler, England

You've heard this before: going to a foreign country leads people to "discover themselves." Of course, you don't need to travel thousands of miles to encounter differences and make such discoveries. But this experience will undoubtedly be different because, as a foreign student traveling to another country, you are immersed in the host culture. Often, you become essentially a minority. Your next-door neighbors, fellow students, and hosts will probably share some, but certainly not all or even very many, of your values and beliefs. Confronting and experiencing these value differences is what leads to the exciting—and sometimes challenging—opportunity to get to know your cultural self.

Making sense of value differences is not easy. Before you can fully understand another culture, it is important to become familiar with the basic ways that cultures can differ, and with your own values and beliefs. In this section, you will have the opportunity to learn about cultural values as a way of understanding culture and then to look specifically at U.S. American cultural values as a way of understanding yourself as a cultural person.

Core Cultural Values: The Key to Understanding Culture

Every human community lives by a set of values that guide how people communicate and relate to one another, interpret behavior, and evaluate each other. How do we know if someone is behaving "normally"? That concept only makes sense if we have a shared standard that frames what is normal or appropriate. Cultural values are those standards. A value system does not tell people exactly how they should behave, but it does set the standard by which they are judged. Most of the time, these standards are not written down; they are simply understood by most people in the culture.

Core Cultural Values

Now let's look at a set of nine core cultural values. These are presented in terms of value contrasts to illustrate how cultures can vary and to show the range of cultural expression on a particular matter. For example, a culture that places its primary emphasis on the individual stands in clear contrast to a culture that places greater importance on the collective group. This should not be interpreted to mean that a person from a more individualistic culture is not a part of groups or that community life is unimportant. It means that the organizing principle for behavior is the person, not the group. A given culture group will have a dominant cultural pattern that resides somewhere on a continuum. One of the most important aspects of intercultural communication is how your own cultural values align with the values of your study abroad site. Extremely contrasting values can be a challenge because our tendency, at least initially, may be to evaluate negatively those cultural values that are at odds with our own. Later we will suggest a culture mapping activity to use for the purpose of exploring these value differences.

Here is a description of some core cultural values, presented as contrasting value orientations. Since little about humans can be thought of as either/or choices, we placed these values on continua. Using the contrasting values described, think about where your own personal values fit and mark the appropriate box. While chances are that you are relatively high in one value and low in another, you may be high in both, even if they are frequently viewed as opposites.

1A. Individualism (primary importance of the self)	**1B. Collectivism (primary importance of the group)**
While you may seek input from others, you are ultimately responsible for your own decisions regarding where you live, what your major is, or where you decide to study abroad. You have a sense of pride in being responsible for yourself and know that others expect you to be independent. If you do something wrong, you feel guilty and are concerned about how this reflects upon you.	You make important life decisions based on the needs of the group and put the well-being of the group ahead of your own. You make major life decisions in consultation with your family, friends, and co-workers. You believe that looking out for others protects one's self and that group harmony is the greatest good. As a child, you're taught to depend and rely upon others, who in turn could rely upon you. Identity is a function of one's membership or role in a primary group. If you do something wrong, you feel ashamed and are concerned about how this reflects on your group.

	LOW ←								→ HIGH
Individualism	☐	☐	☐	☐	☐	☐	☐	☐	☐
Collectivism	☐	☐	☐	☐	☐	☐	☐	☐	☐

2A. Equality	**2B. Hierarchy**
You believe that people should interact with each other on a level playing field. While differences such as age and economic standing obviously exist, you don't feel these should be used as the basis for interacting with others. For example, you prefer to be on a first-name basis with your instructors, boss, and co-workers.	You believe strongly in status differences and that people should be treated according to their standing. Teachers, for example, are experts and should be referred to by their titles. At school or at work, you would defer to the views of your seniors and use forms of address congruent with their standing. Hierarchy is the fact of life and gives everyone a sense of their place in the world.

	LOW ←								→ HIGH
Equality	☐	☐	☐	☐	☐	☐	☐	☐	☐
Hierarchy	☐	☐	☐	☐	☐	☐	☐	☐	☐

3A. Polychronic Time (time as an unlimited good)	3B. Monochronic Time (time as a precious commodity)
You feel that time is an unlimited good and available as needed. People should take the amount of time necessary to do what they need to do. Life does not follow a clock; things happen when they are supposed to happen. Promising to meet someone at a certain time is not a commitment set in stone. Rather, appointments and social gatherings happen when the time is right. For example, a wedding won't start until all the people are there who were invited; when they have arrived is when the wedding is supposed to begin.	You feel that time is a precious good. It should not be wasted. Human activities must be organized with careful recognition of this fact. You take great care to plan your day to make sure you arrive to class, work, and meetings with friends and family on time. It is unthinkable to waste someone else's time. A wedding must start at the designated time out of respect for everyone's time commitments and other obligations.

	LOW ⟵								⟶ HIGH
Polychronic	☐	☐	☐	☐	☐	☐	☐	☐	☐
Monochronic	☐	☐	☐	☐	☐	☐	☐	☐	☐

4A. Meritocracy (achievement based on what you do)	4B. Ascription (achievement based on who you are)
You believe that people should be judged on merit and that they should earn their position and status in life. What is fair for one is fair for all. You know that when you graduate, the jobs you get will be because you have earned them. They won't be given to you because of who you are, but because of what you have accomplished. You wouldn't select people to do a job, for example, simply on the basis of their age; being older in your culture does not automatically mean being wiser.	You believe that a person's family background, age, gender, ethnicity, and other characteristics are very important in determining a person's status or standing in the community. This also establishes how you should interact with the person. For example, you would likely assume that older persons are going to be much more knowledgeable than younger ones and that their knowledge should be respected. That is how things work in the world.

	LOW ⟵								⟶ HIGH
Meritocracy	☐	☐	☐	☐	☐	☐	☐	☐	☐
Ascription	☐	☐	☐	☐	☐	☐	☐	☐	☐

5A. Activity	5B. People
Your day is scheduled with a number of activities including work, studying, and social time with friends. You are strongly motivated to be doing something constantly. In your culture, for example, you ask people upon first meeting them what their job is ("What do you do?") or what activities they have been engaged in ("What have you been doing"?) Even when getting together with family and friends, you may plan an activity, like playing a sport or going to a movie. You are likely to be very task-oriented. Fundamentally, a high and positive value is placed on activity.	Who you are with is more important than what you are doing. Rather than schedule specific activities, you are most likely just to spend time with your friends and family. Being with others is particularly important in your culture. The quality of your interpersonal relations is very important; you would not let a task get in the way of a relationship.

	LOW ⟵								⟶ HIGH
Activity	☐	☐	☐	☐	☐	☐	☐	☐	☐
People	☐	☐	☐	☐	☐	☐	☐	☐	☐

6A. Change, Progress, Risk Taking	6B. Stability, Tradition, Risk Aversion
You know that almost everything around you will change—even the friends you have throughout your lifetime. You look forward to change and feel that it brings many positives to your life. Change in your culture is a good thing; it means progress. Lack of change leads to stagnation. This emphasis on change translates into people being willing to take risks and try new things.	You feel it's important to keep traditions in the world around you because these bring a positive and expected rhythm to your life. The friends that you have had since you were very small will be the most important friends you have throughout your life. Stability gives meaning to life. Change for its own sake doesn't make any sense because it disrupts the rhythms, pace, and meaning of life. It can also disrupt longstanding relationships. This value orientation means that people are uncomfortable about taking risks, preferring to do things as they have been done in the past.

	LOW ←								→ HIGH
Change	☐	☐	☐	☐	☐	☐	☐	☐	☐
Stability	☐	☐	☐	☐	☐	☐	☐	☐	☐

7A. Formality	7B. Informality
You feel that people should communicate and relate to each other in a manner that strictly conforms to what is considered to be appropriate. For example, a younger person would be obligated to address and interact with an older person in a particular way that shows deference to that person's age and status; depending on the culture, using one's first name in such an encounter might be unacceptable.	Formality does not need to be adhered to rigidly; in fact, being overly formal is thought to stifle good communication and interaction. The communication and interaction rules in your culture are relaxed and flexible.

	LOW ←								→ HIGH
Formality	☐	☐	☐	☐	☐	☐	☐	☐	☐
Informality	☐	☐	☐	☐	☐	☐	☐	☐	☐

8A. Fate and Destiny	8B. Personal Efficacy
You believe that human destiny is a matter of fate, something beyond one's ability to control. You are likely to see your fate being in the hands of others, such as your family, your government, or a higher being. To behave as if you can control destiny seems supremely arrogant to you, and you distrust people who hold that belief.	You believe that what you do in life matters, that you have control of your destiny, and that you must in fact exercise that control to make things happen. You are impatient with people who have a fatalistic attitude and value people who do everything they can to take control of their lives. To do anything less means to be irresponsible.

	LOW ←								→ HIGH
Fate and Destiny	☐	☐	☐	☐	☐	☐	☐	☐	☐
Personal Efficacy	☐	☐	☐	☐	☐	☐	☐	☐	☐

9A. Directness	9B. Indirectness
In your culture, being direct is the way to communicate and interact. If there are problems, it is important to have face-to-face conversations to resolve them. If you are not direct, you feel you are doing the other person a disservice. You are also concerned that you might be seen as dishonest if you are not forthright. Trust in your culture is based on direct, open, person-to-person communication.	You believe that indirect communication is the best way to respect the integrity of others and to allow them to save face. If you are facing a problem with another person, you might ask a third party to intervene, or you might leave subtle clues that there is a problem. A direct, face-to-face confrontation with the other person would be seen as rude and offensive. In your culture, you assume that people will extract meaning from the context of the situation and don't need to be told to their face about an issue. The indirect approach gives people more latitude to respond, helps them save face, and maintains the harmony of the community.

	LOW ⟵								⟶ HIGH
Directness	☐	☐	☐	☐	☐	☐	☐	☐	☐
Indirectness	☐	☐	☐	☐	☐	☐	☐	☐	☐

ACTIVITY: Culture mapping

Culture mapping is an exercise in discovering oneself, one's home culture, and one's host culture. Start by reviewing where you placed your own personal values on the above continua. The second step is to think about and identify the dominant cultural values in your society. (Discussing this step with others from your home culture will provide broader insights.) The final step will be to hypothesize what the dominant cultural values will be in your host culture environment. (Initially, this third step might be difficult to do until you have more experience and information.)

Step One: Assessing My Personal Values

As you review where you placed your personal values on the continua, we would like you to reflect on the following questions:

- Do you have any marks on the far ends (either the highest or lowest circle) of the value continua? If so, that means you have a strong value orientation in those particular areas. Think about how this might be a source of strength for you, but also consider how your values could be a challenge in the host culture.
- Were there certain values where you felt strongly about both sides of the continuum? Sometimes, the situations we are in require us to behave in different ways, for example, being very focused on activities at times but focused on people at others. How might this be a source of strength for you in the host culture?

Step Two: Assessing My Culture Group's Values

Now we suggest you work with a group from your own culture and discuss U.S. American values. Go back to the previous charts and place a mark where you think many U.S. Americans would be on these value continua. In the next section, we include some comments from intercultural experts about where they think many U.S. Americans fall on these continua. We encourage you to wait to look at that section until you have had a chance to complete this step for yourself.

Step Three: Assessing Host Culture Values for Further Comparison

Find someone who is from your host country or has spent a lot of time there. Discuss the value dimensions together and plot on the previous charts what you think the core values might be for your host country. Keep in mind that these are generalizations based on what you know at this point and are likely to change as you learn more. Consider the following questions: What are the main similarities and differences between your host country and home country? What are the main similarities and differences between you, in particular, and the host country? How might these common values vary for different groups within the host country? What might be some of the reasons for the differences?

ACTIVITY: Core U.S. American cultural values: What the experts say

Now let's take a look at what intercultural experts such as Althen (1988), Hofstede (2003), and Stewart and Bennett (1991) identify as core U.S. cultural values. Keep in mind that these are generalizations, not absolutes—that is, these are the dominant cultural patterns that can be readily found in the U.S., but not the only values that are present. While these authors might discuss the values in slightly different terms, they agree that the following values are reflective of mainstream U.S. American culture, as evidenced by the sayings and comments listed below. The charts present general cultural patterns for the U.S. and provide room for you to add phrases that you feel reflect your host country's values, both now and after you have spent time there.

Individualism

U.S. American Views	Host Country Views (before arriving)	Host Country Views (after arriving)
• If you don't take care of it yourself, nobody else will. • It's important to know who you are and what you want out of life. No one else can do that for you. • Be true to yourself.		

Equality

U.S. American Views	Host Country Views (before arriving)	Host Country Views (after arriving)
• We are all equal under the law. • People should all have the same opportunities for success.		

Monochronic Time

U.S. American Views	Host Country Views (before arriving)	Host Country Views (after arriving)
• Time is of the essence. Every second counts. • It is important to make the most of your time. Don't waste it. • There are only 24 hours in a day. Make every minute count.		

Meritocracy

U.S. American Views	Host Country Views (before arriving)	Host Country Views (after arriving)
• It's not who you are, it's what you do. • Actions speak louder than words.		

Activity

U.S. American Views	Host Country Views (before arriving)	Host Country Views (after arriving)
• Taking action is more important than just talking about it. • You feel like you should be doing something on a weekday afternoon rather than relaxing at home.		

Change, Progress, Risk Taking

U.S. American Views	Host Country Views (before arriving)	Host Country Views (after arriving)
• You can always pick up, move, and start over somewhere else. • It's important to reinvent yourself.		

Informality

U.S. American Views	Host Country Views (before arriving)	Host Country Views (after arriving)
• Make yourself at home; you're family here. • "Come as you are."		

Personal Efficacy

U.S. American Views	Host Country Views (before arriving)	Host Country Views (after arriving)
• Success is due to hard work and talent, more than luck. • You are responsible for your successes or failures. • If at first you don't succeed, try, try again.		

Directness

U.S. American Views	Host Country Views (before arriving)	Host Country Views (after arriving)
• "I can't guess what you are thinking if you don't tell me." • Being direct is equated with telling the truth.		

Reflection questions

- How did your answers compare in terms of how you perceived U.S. cultural values?
- What were the similarities and what were the differences?
- Can you pinpoint aspects of your background and personal history that may have influenced your system of values and beliefs?
- Were there some U.S. values you disagreed with? If in reading some of the statements about U.S. Americans you found yourself saying, "That's not me!" or "That's not true!" you may have discovered a value where you differ from the mainstream. Think about why this might be. Are there certain groups (political, ethnic, class) that you feel a part of that may help explain this difference?
- If you were thinking, "This isn't how it is anymore," you are right to a degree. Cultures change, of course, but the rate of change is often slower than we think. And, perhaps just as important, your hosts may expect you to behave as a "typical" U.S. American. Hence, the image they form of you may or may not be a true reflection because they are seeing you through their own value lens.
- Were you able to write down anything for the host culture? If you are unsure of the host culture's view, it would be easy to make the mistake of assuming that its values are probably similar. Keep this list handy and record what you find as time goes on in your study abroad experience.

(Adapted from Storti and Bennhold-Samaan, 1997.)

International perspectives on U.S. Americans

Another way to get a glimpse of U.S. values and cultures is to see what people from other countries have to say about their experiences in the U.S. or about meeting U.S. Americans in their home countries. We asked international students and hosts of U.S. students to comment on their first impressions of life in the U.S. and of U.S. Americans. This will give you a sense of what "outsiders" notice about life in the U.S. and how they may view you, knowing you are a U.S. American. Take a look at the following statements and jot down the cultural values that are being described by these international students. The perceptions may be incorrect. They may be accurate. They may be held as stereotypes. They are not, however, uncommon. What insights can you gain about the U.S. culture in reading these comments? About yourself?

Australia

My perceptions of Americans with regards to travelling is that they are very insular. Yes, they are endeavouring to travel abroad and see the world, which is to their credit; however, you will more often than not find a busload of American tourists doing an organized tour than you would, say, a group of Brits or Germans, who will just pick up their day pack and stride off into the wilderness. They expect high levels of service everywhere and are willing to pay for it. It very much feels like a money-orientated society. Also, they are definitely more reserved than other European cultures.

Students always seem to try and get away with whatever they can. From getting their grades raised to free drinks, they seem a little bit sneakier than most when it comes to getting their own way.

In saying that, though, it is definitely a more positive culture in terms of attaining success. Americans will build you up and compliment you on your work ethic and efforts, praising your successes, whereas Australians will try and pull you down and resent you for it. Also, American students study much more than Australian students, and definitely put in the work required to excel.

Germany

Americans are very patriotic, almost nationalistic. Americans are convinced that theirs is the best country and that other nations need to learn and absorb the American belief system. There is little if any introspection and reflection of what can be learned from others. Even though the U.S. stands for freedom of speech, liberty, and the pursuit of happiness, its core values continue to reflect the white, male, Christian thinking of the Founding Fathers.

Hong Kong

I have noticed the following differences in friendship:

- *Americans talk about politics and sports with their friends whereas we talk with our friends about deeper subject matters such as ideas, beliefs, and our goals in life.*
- *There is a deeper commitment among friends in my culture. I can expect my friends to be there for me even when we are far apart or vice versa.*

Iceland

Of all the things I thought of Americans before I came, two issues have remained as still true. They are incredibly loud and take up a lot of space in public places. The sound level at an American restaurant is as high as a cliff full of birds in my country of Iceland. It is hard to pass Americans on the sidewalk because they usually take up half the space themselves just by the way they walk and swing their arms. Every time I go home to Iceland, I'm stopped by someone who tells me I'm taking up too much space on the sidewalk!

Italy

Americans are extremely ethnocentric and superficial in their approach to a different culture. They act friendly and have a positive attitude toward people, but they rarely relax in a genuine way. They have a very efficient approach to work, they're good planners, but they're technology-addicted and individualist.

Americans are friendly and enthusiastic towards new people, new cultures, and new places; however, I find that they lack critical sense and thus they tend to stereotype too much. They are very self-proud, but at the same time ready to recognize other people's skills.

Japan

Americans have high self-esteem and respect others' individuality.

One of the things that I found interesting or odd about U.S. Americans after I came to the United States is that they seem to be busy all the time and proud to tell people how busy they are. I sometimes felt as if they were implying that they were too busy with other things to be bothered with me. They seem to be very friendly and easy-going, but you have to make an appointment for whatever you do with them, even going out for coffee with friends sometimes. Otherwise, people would leave you saying, 'I gotta go.' It took awhile for me to get used to it.

Korea

Americans are individual-oriented. Each individual's opinion, perspective, and way of living are considered to be unique in the society. Americans are polite to strangers in general; however, that politeness is often superficial. In other words, they act politely for the sake of politeness (meaning that they act politely not necessarily because they respect others but because they know that they ought to be polite). Americans love food...lots of food. They love eating out. Restaurants are serving more than enough food to the customers and wasting more than what is needed to feed the starved people in extremely poor countries.

Kyrgyzstan

Many people from former Soviet Union countries would say, 'People in the USA are very friendly, but they hardly be real friends' or 'Americans are very busy people and hardly have time for socialization with each other.'

Mongolia

I have very positive thoughts about U.S. Americans. First of all, they are very friendly. Even if they are in a bad mood, they do their best to be friendly. Second, I think U.S. Americans are very good communicators. Talking with others and sharing information all the time seems to be important for them; however, they are forgetful. They ask you a question and you give them the answer, but when you see them again, they ask you the same question again. Third, Americans are very good at timing and planning things ahead of time. I have always been so amazed at how they plan events and activities of all types including their work and vacations. Once they plan to do something they do it no matter what. Moreover, they are good at meeting deadlines and doing things on time.

Spain

I felt that in the United States so much had to do with money—how much you made, the car you drove, the brand on your clothes. It was amazing how materialistic people were. I also felt that the family values were not very strong. I always include cousins, uncles, grandparents, etc., when I talk about my family. The family to many Americans just includes their nuclear family. Work is a huge priority in people's lives—it's all about making a lot of money fast and then hopefully being able to retire young. That is if they are healthy enough once they get to retirement. I also felt that the number one social activity, pastime, you name it—was eating out! For birthdays they would take you out for breakfast, lunch, and dinner for an entire week. If someone hadn't seen you for awhile they would take you out to eat. In Spain you meet up for coffee or go to the park to have a drink in a terraza. Spaniards do enjoy their food but in a different way. I felt like in the U.S. the number one distraction was eating out and shopping!

Uzbekistan

My fellow Uzbek friends say that Americans are 'freedom-lovers,' 'free to express themselves,' and 'open-minded.' To that I can add that Americans adore their country and are real patriots of their native land. They do not know limits. For example, a 46-year-old can decide to go to college to get a bachelor's degree. They also love money and spend most of their time earning and saving. At the same time, they like recreational activities a lot, such as sports, travel, etc. Also, they are into the 'political correctness' thing a lot. Americans are very 'environmentally conscious,' meaning they care about the environment and ecology a lot and enforce environmentally friendly practices such as reuse/recycle.

Reflection questions

- What insights can you gain about U.S. culture in reading these comments? About yourself?
- How might you respond to these comments if they were made to you directly?
- How might you explain the behaviors of U.S. Americans differently?
- How might you explain how you are similar or different from the images of U.S. Americans given above?
- What questions might you have for these international students to gain a better understanding of how they reached their conclusions?

Experiencing value differences

Now, take a look at the following quotes and see what they suggest about value differences between some study abroad students and their hosts.

- *I was so surprised to find out that my host mom would come into my room every day and clean things up. While I knew she was being helpful, it just really bugged me that she was in my space.*
- *Eating out was a very social activity—you almost never saw anyone dining alone or even drinking a cup of coffee alone at a café. Also, when you went out to a restaurant, the expectation was that you would sit and enjoy the meal and then linger, possibly for several hours, with your companions. At first this seemed slow and inefficient to me, but gradually I came to really enjoy not feeling rushed.*
- *I went overseas pretty open-minded. I knew there were differences in how men and women were treated. But no matter how hard I tried, I could not get used to men calling out to me and whistling. I know it wasn't just me—they did it to the women from the country as well.*
- *I knew I'd have to make a difficult decision to be open about being gay. I was prepared for that—and expected people to be pretty homophobic. What I was not prepared for was that nobody talked about gays at all. It was like they wanted to pretend we did not even exist. The silence was unbearable.*
- *I wanted to travel every weekend. Paris, the sea—everything was just a few hours away. I also wanted to get to know my host family better. I tried to spend time with them during the week so that I would not feel bad about leaving them on the weekend. It seemed to work OK.*

What do these quotes reflect about the following set of value differences? Think about the contrast of values and where your values fit compared with the host country. How might these impact your stay?

- High privacy norm versus low privacy norm (including an expectation of privacy in public places—e.g., no one will whistle when you walk by)
- High personal independence versus low personal independence
- Strict gender roles versus open gender roles
- Liberal tolerance of sexual orientation versus conservative tolerance
- Strong family commitment versus weak family commitment

A few key points to wrap up the chapter:

- The ability to recognize values and beliefs that are culturally based improves with practice, familiarity with the culture, and increased contact with members of that culture.
- Understanding the predominant values and beliefs of your own culture and those of others provides the foundation for much of intercultural learning.
- Again, the point here is not to overly emphasize differences that exist between cultural groups, but to recognize them as they are and be aware of the impact they have on a given individual's behaviors and actions.
- Recognizing, accepting, and even appreciating the cultural differences in others are steps on the path toward becoming interculturally competent and will provide opportunities for further culture learning.

Conclusion to the Pre-Departure Section

Congratulations! You have completed a critical part of your study abroad journey. Getting to know a bit more about yourself and your hosts will surely make your experience an even greater one.

> *Many people think that the study abroad experience begins the day you step off of the plane, but it really begins before you go, during the time that you are preparing to go. There are many questions running through your head that are important. Only if you are aware of these can you help yourself.*
> *~ A. J. Fleming, Spain*

IN-COUNTRY CULTURE STRATEGIES PART I:

STRATEGIES FOR SOCIAL RELATIONS

Khoo Ah Au liked Americans. Above all he found their personal relationships easy to read. His own people were always very careful not to give themselves away, to expose crude feelings about one another. Americans seemed not to care how much was understood by strangers. It was almost as if they enjoyed being transparent. ~ "Passage of Arms," Eric Ambler

In the book, Khoo Ah Au was able to learn what he liked about U.S. Americans because he spent time with them. In studying abroad, there can be real obstacles to spending time with locals, and then when you do have the opportunity, there can be challenges in friendships, dating, and host family stays. In this chapter, we share students' tips about overcoming obstacles for making connections, as well as comments on friendships, dating, sexual harassment, host family preparation, and host family conflicts.

Overcoming Obstacles for Making Connections

One obstacle is the tendency for students to form tight groups consisting entirely of fellow international students or home country students. Having the opportunity to get together and talk gives you a way to provide fellowship and support for each other. Of course, it isn't recommended that you use these groups exclusively for support and friendship to the extent that you neglect opportunities to interact with the host culture. Finding ways to immerse yourself in the culture—while periodically taking time out to be with your home country friends—will provide you with a more enriching study abroad experience.

A second obstacle is anxiety about meeting and talking with people. The ironic thing is that the best cure for anxiety is meeting and talking with people! As the tips in the language section will describe, if anxiety is something that you encounter, try planning out your conversations in advance, developing a list of topics you want to talk about, or coming up with a set of questions you like to ask others. Being prepared can help ease you into these anxious situations.

A third obstacle is that there may be a limited number of options for you to meet host nationals in your program. You often need to be the one to initiate the opportunities. The following are some tips from fellow travelers. Some options may not be available where you are studying, but if there is a need for a program that doesn't exist, you might want to make efforts toward its creation.

- *At the beginning of my stay, I never wore a watch, so I was forced to ask people on the bus or on the street what time it was. This built my confidence and helped me meet people. ~ A. J. Fleming, Spain*
- *Try to develop a routine that integrates you into the culture. With repetition, that is, frequenting a certain restaurant or café, locals will become comfortable seeing you and you might make new acquaintances. ~ Julie Radmar, France*

- *Adjust your expectations about what you can get done. In the U.S., I am constantly on the go, and I can get a lot done in a day. However, I remember taking a two-hour train trip to Halkis from Athens, conducting a 45-minute interview in Greek (which I was not fluent in), and then returning home on the train. It was only 2 p.m., but that was it for the day. The language, the traveling, the heat of summer—I was wiped out, physically and mentally. ~ Suzanne Hay, Greece*
- What are you interested in? Soccer? Classical music? Juggling? Find a local group, club, or society with locals who have similar interests. Or find out what might be common local pastimes and see how you might be involved in a new hobby or interest. You could join a rowing team on the Thames or a table tennis team in Calcutta, or make model airplanes in Johannesburg.
- Start or join a study group to study the language or to learn about each other's culture.
- Make a meal for some fellow students or your hosts. One author of this text made tacos in Malaysia. It was tricky finding the ingredients but well worth the effort. Another made chocolate chip cookies with a friend in Taiwan and sold them at a local market.
- Join a school club. There usually is an international student organization on campus. This can be a great way to meet local students who are interested in you.
- Give presentations to local schools, community organizations, and businesses. Often the university or school where you are studying will have opportunities, whether volunteer or paid, for foreign students to give short presentations about their home countries or about a topic of interest to you. Here's your chance to deepen your audience's cultural knowledge of the U.S. and to debunk stereotypes in the process!
- Join in political activities. However, be careful: some countries discourage or even prohibit foreign students from engaging in such activities. Check with your study abroad program administrators before participating.
- Attend religious/spiritual activities. Just because you are in a foreign country doesn't mean you have to stop being spiritual. You may or may not find a place to worship of the same denomination to which you belong, but you can be adventurous and explore the spiritual and religious beliefs of the local community.

Making Friends

Making new friends can be rewarding but can also be a challenge. Some of you may be entering educational systems where fellow students have known each other and have been the closest of friends since kindergarten. Sometimes these groups can be hard to break into, as friendship can be viewed as a deep commitment that takes years to develop. Others among you may find your time in the host country is simply too short to develop true friendships. And yet, there are times when these barriers are overcome and connections are made. The rewards of such close ties are related best by the following study abroad returnees, as well as tips on how they developed their friendships in the first place:

I was a Peace Corps volunteer in Kiribati. One way that I made friends was by learning traditional songs and dances. My teachers took pride in helping me develop these skills, and I felt more a part of the community. These activities allowed me to befriend people with whom I would not otherwise have interacted.

The husband of the head teacher at our school did not speak English. When I found out that he played chess, we played on a regular basis and developed a friendship. Although we could not communicate verbally because I had just started learning the I-Kiribati language, we both enjoyed our chess games. I learned that just being present with someone is sometimes more important than any words that are said. ~ Eric Kroetsch, Kiribati

During my time in Japan as an English instructor, I was able to become good friends with some of my students and co-workers. As a result, it helped me to get out more. I saw many new places and participated in popular activities, like going to the hot springs. I probably would not have experienced as much as I did if it were not for the relationships I developed. These relationships helped me to get out of my safety zone and to try new things. My entire stay was enriched by these relationships and experiences. I am still in touch with one of my friends, several years later. We talk about raising children in our respective countries. ~ Stacey Buachart, Japan

And, of course, your fellow travel companions from around the world as well as from your home country may open new doors of friendship:

I made many good friends during my time studying abroad, but one friend especially has had an influence on me in many ways. I was in Puerto Rico working on my Spanish before going on my year-long study abroad and got connected with a Puerto Rican, Paul, who was studying at the time at my undergrad university and was actually going on my same study abroad program to Ecuador and Chile. Paul and I traveled together, memorized Pablo Neruda poetry together, and followed Che Guevara's route through Latin America on buses, carts, cars, bicycles, etc. We went to the water festivals in Bolivia, we hiked the Inca Trail in Peru, we rode Jeeps in Argentina, and we are still close friends today. When back in the U.S., we decided to go to Spain for spring break to visit a friend we had met during our time studying in South America. When we were in Madrid, Paul met his current wife at a rock concert. I subsequently went to their wedding in Spain. Later on, Paul and I walked across the Spanish Pyrenees together for 36 days, camping and sleeping outside. I learned many things from my friendship with Paul, but more importantly I learned a tremendous amount about literature and the value of reading. I took mostly economics classes during my study abroad. Paul convinced me to take an art history course. I also ended up falling in love with Shakespeare during this time, as Paul was an English Lit major and had the books around. In addition, Paul's love of life (having the Puerto Rican blood) highly influenced me later in life. And he also taught me how to cook during our semester living together in Chile.

So, overall, he had quite a significant influence on who I am today. He is not a local I met while studying abroad, but he was a friend from that period who also went through study abroad with me. ~ Daniel Cohen, Ecuador and Chile

In addition to strategizing about how to make friends, take a moment to think about the meaning of friendship. How do you answer the question, "What is a friend?" Is it someone who you enjoy being with, can talk with about everyday events, seek advice from, and turn to when you need help? While the broad definition might be similar in many locations around the world, it may differ in some specific ways:

- How friendships develop (Can you befriend someone from a different social class, for example?)
- Extent to which one changes friends (For example, do you make new friends over a lifetime and, if so, what happens to your friends from childhood?)
- Ways in which one may rely on friends (Money? A place to stay? Help in the middle of the night? Do you worry about bothering your friends for help, or is it understood that you would not be bothering them with such requests?)

Spending time with host nationals will help you develop a sense of the rhythm of friendship within the particular cultures you interact with, as well as find places of difference and commonality.

Dating

Dating someone from a different culture is truly a unique experience. Not only did it help improve my language skills, but it also exposed me to a new perspective on romance. While living and studying in Madrid, I was astonished by the differences between the U.S. and Spanish dating styles. For example, public displays of affection, which are often frowned upon in the U.S., were much more noticeable in the Spanish dating scene. Couples were often seen kissing in parks, metro trains, and other community areas. At first I was a little uneasy about being intimate in public areas, but eventually I came to accept the cultural difference. ~ Matt, Spain

Aside from the obvious benefits of romance and companionship, dating someone from your host country may provide you with a built-in cultural informant, an incentive to learn the language, and perhaps a friendship that lasts beyond your stay in the country. Dating someone from your host culture can be very exciting. You may enjoy the new language and a different way of being treated, coupled with interesting surroundings. Another aspect of this relationship could be different expectations of you and your actions. As you are entering into a dating situation with your own set of U.S. American dating customs, the other person is bringing his or her society's dating beliefs and values. These two different sets of expectations could lead to some embarrassing moments, laughter, or a potentially dangerous situation if cultural cues are not properly understood. In addition, perhaps for the first time, you are being seen as a *U.S. American* potential partner rather than just a potential partner.

The following are some questions to consider before beginning to date. First, think about your own cultural norms surrounding dating. This will give you a base upon which you can begin to look at another society's dating assumptions.

- What is considered a "date" and what is considered "just hanging out"?
- What types of activities are customary for a first date?
- Who initiates a date?
- When going out for coffee, a meal, or a drink, who pays?
- Do you date in groups or is it OK to be alone?
- Is it acceptable for a date to be in a private setting, such as your home, or should it be more public?
- Is physical contact OK? If so, what types and when?

Some additional questions to consider tie in politics, history, and values, and are relevant to dating across cultures:

- What significance does your being a U.S. American have to a person from your host country?
- How might media stereotypes about U.S. Americans affect how a potential partner views you?
- Are you viewed as having a lot of money?
- Are you seen as having a more liberal attitude toward sexual intimacy?

The following comments from study abroad students in Mexico highlight how these cultural differences can come to life:

> *In relationships with their Mexican girlfriends, the guys were very respectful as far as holding on to those traditions. They would date with a group of friends because once they did stuff alone they were seen as being more serious, as planning to get married. With American women they can go off and be alone because that's the way we are use to dating. (And they will take advantage of that.)*

> *Men were a lot more willing to get closer to you, whereas if they were dancing with a Mexican woman, they were a lot more in tune or aware of how much space was between their bodies and how they were dancing.*

ACTIVITY: Dating scenarios

One way to approach unraveling the dating cues and assumptions of both your host culture and your own culture is to consider different styles of communication. (We discuss the topic of communication styles later in this guide on p. 126. You may want to jump ahead and read this information now.)

Scenario: You have been dancing with someone most of the evening, sometimes closely, sometimes not, when he invites you back to his house for a small party.

- What is the sense of personal space in your host country? What body language cues may you have unknowingly sent?

- What type of communication style predominates in your host country? Does "small party" actually mean a small party or, depending on the situation, could it mean something else?

Scenario: You meet a woman through a study group. A couple of times you have suggested that just the two of you should meet sometime. She never says no or makes an excuse for why she can't go; she just lowers her eyes, smiles, and looks away.

- What are the norms regarding the use of eye contact in your host country? Do they vary depending upon gender?

- Consider your host country's communication styles. Are you living in a country that rarely replies with a no?

- Are there any differences in the way privacy between the genders is viewed? Would it be respectable for a woman to be in a private setting with a man?

Scenario: Your host brother hugs you when you run into him outside of the home. You have never had another male hug you this way. You wonder if his use of a physical hello means more than just a greeting.

- What is the customary public greeting for males? Is it common to see a man touching another man? Or a woman with whom he may not be in a romantic relationship?

Reflection questions

- Consider how you would respond to these scenarios in your home environment. What would you do if you needed to seek advice? What would you do if you felt a situation was not safe?
- The scenarios are not set up to include only heterosexual or same-sex individuals. How did you interpret the scenarios? How might your responses differ if the scenarios referred to heterosexuals or to those of the same sex (for example, the openness of the family or host culture environment to gay culture or how the host culture views opposite-sex friendships or relationships before marriage)?

Sexual Harassment

As you work to understand your host culture, don't forget to listen to your inner voice. There are times when a situation feels dangerous or not quite right. Follow your gut reaction at these times. It is better to err on the side of being culturally insensitive than to be unsafe.

Safety is an essential part of an experience abroad. If your internal alarm goes off, it is not a time to be polite. You need to be in charge of the situation and not be timid.

That said, keep in mind that catcalls or street talk are much more common in many other countries than in the U.S. In such cases, responding to the person making the comments will only exacerbate the situation.

The best indicator of what is appropriate behavior between genders in your host country is to look at how the women of that country interact with the men. Do they spend time alone with men? Is it appropriate to be in a private setting with a date? This is what one student had to say about being in a private space with her host brother in Mexico:

> *My host brother wanted to talk to me when I was in Mexico and he stood in the door and he said, 'Susan, can I talk to you?' And I said, 'Sure, come on in.' And he said, 'No, I can't.' And I said, 'Sure, come on in.' But, he refused and wanted to go down to the kitchen to talk. He literally couldn't physically move past the door because he felt so uncomfortable going into a girl's room.*
> *~ Susan, Mexico*

Thinking of the situation from the perspective of those around you will not only help you understand the culture, but can make a lasting impact on those hosting you and befriending you.
(Adapted from C. Anderson, 2002.)

Love and Marriage

> *You need to tell people that they can fall in love. And that can have real consequences. ~ Dan Jakab, Spain (upon reviewing a draft of this guide)*

Giving advice on love and dating is a bit tricky in a study abroad guide. Two of the authors are in intercultural marriages. Although you would think we would have something valuable to say, we are a bit stumped on giving specifics in writing! However, one author collected a few pieces of advice she has received over the years:

- Trust your instincts. If someone's character seems a bit questionable, question it.
- Don't try to be someone you know you are not—or someone you are not ready to be (like a parent!). While you are overseas, it's a wonderful time for exploring who you really are. Just be careful. Heartache has no mileage limitation.
- Be careful not to send the wrong messages. This means learning the cues for seriousness in a relationship. In some cultures, what is a casual friendship to you might be taken much more seriously.

And if you are serious:

- If at all possible, make sure that you both get a chance to visit the other's culture and home before making a commitment.
- Be honest with yourself about whether or not you could live permanently in your partner's culture.

Being a Visitor

Whether or not you have a homestay, you will hopefully have an opportunity to visit the home of a local person or family during your travels. Although you may have some experience that will help you know what to expect, we encourage you to consider the following before you spend a great deal of time with your hosts.

Take a mental tour

Before visiting, imagine bringing a guest to your own home. What are the unwritten rules that this guest might be expected to follow? Is a gift expected? If so, what is appropriate? Does the guest help prepare the meal? Is there assigned seating or chairs that are always reserved for the parents? Is the guest expected to help clean up after the meal? If staying overnight, can the guest help himself or herself to breakfast in the morning? If the guest is staying for several weeks, in what ways might your expectations change?

Understanding unwritten rules that you have seen guests follow at your home can help prepare you for the assumptions that you carry with you about visiting in your host country.

Preparing for a visit

Now that you have had a chance to think about your own personal and cultural expectations of guests, take a few moments to focus on the following questions. While some of these considerations may be very minor, feeling prepared and comfortable will help increase your confidence that you will make fewer mistakes and lessen the chance of offending your hosts. Make sure to consider how your age, status, and the host's experiences internationally and with U.S. Americans may affect the responses to these questions. If you don't know the appropriate answers to some of these questions, get help from a local person.

Greetings and arrival

- What is the expected greeting? A handshake, hug, bow, or simply words?
- What is an appropriate time to arrive? At exactly the invited time, early, a few minutes after the stated time, or hours after the stated time?
- Should you take your shoes off at the door? If so, are you expected to bring indoor shoes to wear? Go barefoot? Or wear something provided by the host?
- How should you be dressed?

Gift-giving

- Is a gift expected? If so, what is appropriate?
- What can you bring from your home culture that would be a nice gift?
- Are certain numbers or colors considered especially good or bad luck?
- Does a gift need to be wrapped? If so, should you encourage your hosts to open the gift in front of you?
- What is the appropriate way to thank someone for a gift?

Food and meals

- If invited for a meal, should you bring something? If so, what is appropriate to bring?
- Are you expected to help prepare the meals? Set the table?
- Do you sit down or wait to be invited to sit in a certain place?
- What signals the beginning of a meal—an invitation to eat, a saying, a prayer? Are you expected to participate? Initiate?
- Are you supposed to serve yourself or wait to be served?
- Are you expected to eat everything on your plate or leave something?
- Are there certain rooms or areas where food and drink are not allowed?
- If you are a long-term guest, is it OK for you to buy food for the family? What about food for just yourself?
- How long does a meal last and how long is it appropriate to stay after a meal is completed?

Departure

- If you are a long-term guest, are you expected to do something special for your family upon departure, such as give a gift, take the family to dinner, or prepare a meal?

Making the Most of Homestays and Host Families

My friend from the U.S. and I were assigned to the same host family. My friend did not like the arrangement because we were so far from school. She moved closer to school and lived with other students. I decided to stay. I came to cherish my time on the double decker buses of London and going home for evening meals. These were great opportunities to be involved in daily life in London. My friend was equally happy to be close to school and to meet other internationals and students from all over the U.S. She ended up traveling in Europe with these newfound friends. We both knew what we wanted going into the experience, and this helped us decide what was the best living arrangement for us. ~ Barbara Kappler, England

Some programs require that students live in a homestay. For others it is optional. A homestay can provide you with a learning experience like no other: the opportunity to gain firsthand knowledge of what family life is like in another culture. Homestays often provide you with the chance to get to know people from the host culture on a much deeper level than you would in your daily encounters.

Angie Schmidt Whitney's experiences in Germany highlight the specific insights she gained about how to use the language in an informal setting, how rules may vary among families, and how it felt to use the language across age groups:

I remember the first time my German was corrected by my host brother. It wasn't that he was correcting me. It was the fact that he was three. I was humiliated to realize I was learning the language from a 3-year old. I also DISTINCTLY remember the first time I was allowed to use 'du,' the informal version of 'you,' with my host mother. For all of my friends and everyone I talked to, their host families and quite a few other Germans gave almost instantaneous permission. The same was not true for me. It took me almost six weeks to finally have this permission. We lived in the same apartment, ate meals together, and I was still a formal guest. When she told me I could use 'du,' I wanted to cry. I felt like I had finally gotten through the first test and first layer into her German world. ~ Angie Schmidt Whitney, Germany

It is a good idea to take some time to think about the homestay in terms of your own expectations, particularly before you meet your host family. Take some time to answer the questions below.

ACTIVITY: Homestay expectations

What are my expectations for the homestay? What do I hope to gain from my homestay? (Rank from 1 to 5)

____ Get support in adjusting to the culture
____ Improve my language skills
____ Participate in family life and learn the culture
____ Make new friends
____ Other:________________________________

What will be my responsibilities as part of the homestay? Although this will vary, typically you will be expected to engage in the activities of the family and to abide by the rules of the household. This could include respecting any curfews and doing family chores. A few questions that you might ask yourself are:

- Is the homestay smoking or non-smoking?
- Am I prepared to adjust my diet to accommodate the homestay family?
- Am I expected to be home for all meals? If I'm going to miss a meal, what should I do?
- Is it OK to bring a guest to a meal?
- Will I be expected to help take care of small children in the family?
- How will my gender affect my host family's expectations of me?
- How will my family's social status affect me?
- Will I be expected to pay for things I took for granted at home (such as telephone bills, groceries, etc.)?
- Will I be encouraged to treat any household staff with respect and distance?
- Will I be asked to adhere a curfew?
- Is my room considered private and my own, or can others enter and use my things, even when I'm not there?
- Does my host family expect to know where I am each day and what I'll be doing?
- Are there any special rules about using certain areas of the home? For example, are there areas that are open only to the family or to servants?
- Are there certain items I should ask permission to use, such as the phone or television?

Regarding the toilet, bath, and shower: Our experience is that this one room (or two, if the shower/bath is separate from the toilet) can be the biggest source of irritation in a homestay. Misunderstandings typically are centered around how often the student bathes (often criticized as too often) and how long he or she takes in a bath or shower (too long). Spending a few minutes talking to your hosts and others can help you prepare for your hosts' expectations. Consider discussing these questions:

- What is the best time to take a bath or shower?
- How much time is appropriate to spend in the bath or shower?
- How does the faucet work?
- If the bath is viewed as a family tub or communal place, should you wash up before you get into the bathtub? Are others expected to use the same bath water after you've finished?

Potential homestay conflicts

As you might anticipate, any number of conflicts can occur during your homestay. Problems could arise due to cultural differences as well as personal differences between the homestay family and student. In some cases you will be in a position where you can decide what kind of homestay you prefer. Although the homestay is bound to be an incredibly enriching learning experience, you are going to be confronted first-hand with the culture on a daily basis. Having reasonable expectations of your homestay is one way of easing the adjustment to your new surroundings. Finding out as much as possible about how the host nationals live before you get to your country is another way. You will still likely need to make adjustments during the homestay visit itself, as these examples suggest:

> *Over Easter, my host family and I were going to celebrate outside with a picnic. As I was helping get the table set up, I reached for the wine bottle and wine opener. My host father promptly stopped me, saying, 'That's men's work.' Throughout my time with the family, I was aware that their conservative views did not always match with mine, and I typically kept my feelings somewhat quiet. For some reason, his statement really hit me wrong and I found myself responding that, 'There is no such thing as men's work.' This clearly wasn't what he hoped to hear and suggested, 'But there is. It's something you should learn.' I remember feeling I had nothing else I could say. I was a guest in their house, but so many of their traditions were so far from my core values.*
>
> *When I asked permission from my host mother (a different host family in Germany) to have two friends over, she agreed it would be fine. When she found out one of them was male, she very clearly told me I could have him over this one time but never again. She was Hungarian and had lived through unfortunate circumstances in her home country and throughout much of her life living in the German Nazi era. She said, 'What would the neighbors think I am doing with this young man in my apartment?' I was so confused by her statement until I put it into her frame of reference. To her, neighbors were constantly watching, ready to report anything you did wrong. It became so clear to me that we came from different worlds.*
> *~ Angie Schmidt Whitney, Germany*

In these two cases, Angie was able to consider how gender and community rules varied within not only the broader culture, but by personality and specific life experiences. She was also able to accept the situations as ones that taught her about differences between herself and her hosts and to continue to live in these environments without significant behavioral changes.

Another study abroad student describes a scenario in which he realized he needed to change his behavior:

> *When I was 19, I spent time living with an Ecuadorian family who was very traditional. They took American students in to make a little extra money for the family. Well, the mother of the family (my 'ecuamami') was always home. One day after university I brought home a friend of mine (female) to hang out and listen to CDs. She was in a serious relationship, living with her boyfriend at the time, so it was not romantic. I think we closed the door to my bedroom, though. After she left, my ecuamami sat me down for a serious talk about how I was a bad influence on her daughter, bringing girls back to my room. It was difficult for me to deal with that, since I had already gone off to college in the U.S. and had been living on my own. The apparent lack of freedom in Ecuador exasperated me as a young man, yet I realized it was a cultural barrier. Many Ecuadorians simply don't go to each other's homes until they are married! I eventually apologized and did not bring anyone by the house again. I am sure there were other cultural faux pas that I committed during that year, and I was not even aware of most of them. ~ Daniel Cohen, Ecuador*

Both Angie and Daniel describe incidents of conflict and disagreement in which the study abroad student adapts to the environment. But what if you cannot adapt to your hosts? For example, what do you do if the family simply ignores you? How do you respond if you are served food that you tried but absolutely cannot eat? Or, as has happened for some students coming to the U.S., what if you are required to do more chores than you can get done and still go to school? Since conflicts can occur because of culture or personal characteristics, it may be very difficult for you to figure out whether something is happening because you're not used to the culture yet or because this family is not a good match. Your relationship with your homestay family is likely to affect your attitudes toward the host country in general. For problematic homestays that cannot be readily resolved, you might want to try the following:

Give the homestay some time

- Remember that finding common ground and developing relationships does not happen overnight.
- Talk to other students to see how their homestay experiences compare with yours.
- Ask for help from program staff or faculty in interpreting things in the homestay that puzzle you or in developing strategies to deal with conflict or problems.

Explore the alternatives

- Is there the chance to change homestays? What are the consequences of doing so?
- Are other forms of housing available to students in the area, such as dormitories or private accommodations? If so, what is the best way to negotiate the move with the host family? What kind of notice do you need to give, and should someone be present to assist you in giving the notice?

If your first homestay doesn't work out for one reason or another, try not to take it personally or let it detract from your overall study abroad experience. A successful homestay will have a positive effect on your attitude and view of the country, while a negative experience could have the opposite effect. What is important is to keep an open mind, have reasonable expectations, and to give the homestay a decent try. In most cases you will discover that the rewards are well worth the effort.

Conclusion

Your study abroad can be an amazing experience. By thinking carefully about how to become involved and interact with people in the host culture, you can actively make a difference in the quality of your stay and in the amount that you learn. Remember, it's one thing to be in the vicinity of events and another to actively participate in them.

IN-COUNTRY CULTURE STRATEGIES PART II: ADJUSTING

I know that I made a lot of mistakes, some I probably did not even realize at the time, but I am sure that others did. Nevertheless, I think the positive thing about this was the way that I reacted to the mistakes I made. I did try and accept them as part of cultural learning. I knew that it was unrealistic to expect myself to do everything correctly or customary the first time I did it. This does not mean that I was always comfortable with making mistakes. At times it became very hard to always have to be watching others and, in a way, to depend on them in order to do things correctly.... These mistakes made me more aware of cultural differences and more motivated to learn about the culture, ways I could adapt to it, and how I could grow as a person from them. ~ Jessica Novotny, Spain

Jessica was effective in crossing cultures because she knew how to learn about culture. People who are effective purposely create learning opportunities, immerse themselves in the culture, and learn from their mistakes and from insiders. Effective travelers have also learned to manage stress and handle their emotions. They are not afraid to take risks and try out new behaviors. They never think they know it all because cultures, people, and situations are always changing. To stay on top of things, effective travelers are always learning and challenging themselves. This section focuses on some common processes of adjusting to the host country so that you can better understand how to manage your stress and emotional reactions in order to make the most of your experience.

Understanding Cross-Cultural Adjustment

When you are overseas, it's exhausting. There needs to be a chapter on naps, 'A Guide to Taking Naps Abroad.' ~ Suzanne Hay, Greece

Being able to adjust to the new environment and culture is perhaps one of the most important facets of your experience abroad. Not only will your cross-cultural adjustment help your learning and development in the new country, it will make your international life more rewarding and interesting.

Nearly everybody goes through an adjustment when starting a new job or moving to a new city, so in some ways, adjusting to the host country is like other transitions; however, when you start your life in a foreign country you can encounter many cultural and language differences that you didn't need to contend with when you started a new school or job.

According to anthropologist P. K. Bock (1974), there are three kinds of adjustment that someone who goes into an unfamiliar environment must make: physical, societal, and internal. A well-adjusted traveler should have a pretty good handle on all three.

- ***Physical adjustment*** involves getting used to the more obvious differences: a new transportation system, the foods that you don't have at home, the system of education at the host university, etc.

- ***Social adjustment*** involves deeper acknowledgement and acceptance of the host country's values, beliefs, and ways of doing things. Note that it is possible for you to maintain your own belief system while at the same time integrating some of your host culture's.
- ***Internal adjustment*** involves coming to terms with your own intercultural identity and being able to integrate both cultures with a minimum of discord.

Two kinds of people avoid difficulties with cultural adjustment and culture shock:

- Those who are extremely flexible and are naturally comfortable with making physical, social, and internal adjustments. (These types of people do exist, but they are rare.)
- Those who re-create "home" while abroad. They surround themselves with their native language, foods, and peoples. The question facing these individuals is: Why? Why go to all the work to leave home and then end up taking it with you?

Our advice? Go get a bit of culture shock. Explore and challenge yourself to really learn about the cultures surrounding you.

Understanding Culture Shock and the Stages of Adjustment

> *The confusion is a cliché; any American, any foreigner, who has lived or worked here will tell you how the cycle goes. Step one, arrival. Step two, This place is so different! Step three, This place is really just like home! Step four, formation of conclusion: 'Now I think I understand this place.' Step five, collapse of confusion; too many exceptions. Step six, repeat from step two. ~ "The Outnation: A Search for the Soul of Japan," Jonathan Rauch*

No doubt you've heard of culture shock and you may be thinking, "I know enough about the country, so the cultural differences won't present a problem for me." And indeed, it's often the case that the more you know about your host country, including the language, the easier it will be to adjust; however, while expecting the differences is helpful, keep in mind it's the actual cultural confrontation that brings about physical and emotional reactions.

In most cases, culture shock is caused less by one single incident and more by the gradual accumulation of anxiety, frustration, and confusion from living in an unfamiliar environment. Some prefer the terms "culture fatigue" or "culture bumps." And while not everyone experiences some kind of "shock," everyone does go through some adjustment to their environment.

Many people who have been abroad discuss their experience in terms of stages. Often times these stages resemble a "U-curve," which represents the traveler's well-being throughout the experience of living abroad (Lysgaard, 1955). Take a minute to acquaint yourself with the four stages of culture shock and the diagram of the U-curve.

The U-curve of culture shock and cross-cultural adjustment

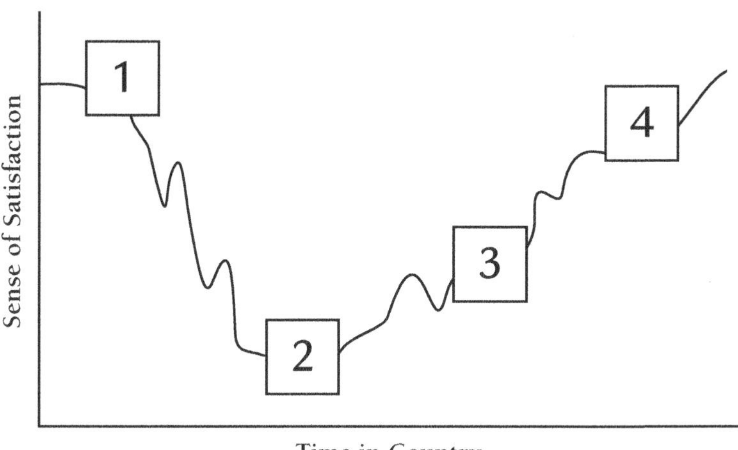

Stage 1: Cultural Euphoria

At the start of your study abroad, there is an initial excitement about being in a new culture. This is often called the "honeymoon stage." Everything is new and wonderful, and you are eager to explore it all. This phase seems pleasant enough, but there are some drawbacks involved. You tend to see the culture through rose-colored glasses, and your interpretations aren't necessarily realistic. You also focus more on all the visible aspects of the culture (e.g., food, scenery, clothing) and ignore the more complex and less obvious cultural aspects. In addition, you tend to focus on similarities rather than differences in the early stage of the visit. Most tourists who travel for a short period of time remain in this stage for their entire stay.

Stage 2: Cultural Confrontation

In the next stage (typically one-third to one-half the way through an experience), the initial excitement you felt when you arrived diminishes and the process of cultural adjustment begins. This stage is typically characterized by confusion and frustration and, as such, is the most difficult stage. Your feelings can shift from very positive to extremely negative. You may view both the home culture and host culture in unrealistic terms; one is superior while the other is lacking. This is because everything that you used to do with relative ease in your home country appears much more difficult due to the culture and/or the language. Homesickness may also contribute to your feelings of discomfort. You feel discouraged and begin to doubt whether you can learn the language or adjust to the culture. Despite these feelings, you are making critical progress in expanding your cross-cultural awareness and, whether or not you are aware of it, you are developing your own strategies for coping with cultural differences.

> *When I was in Malaysia doing an independent research project, I definitely experienced many cultural differences. One was that you bartered for products. No prices were fixed, except the prices of pewter and cultural*

pewter artifacts, which were fixed by the government. I had my eye on a set of pewter carvings that depicted the various ethnic groups of Malaysia, but they were quite expensive and I was really on a shoestring budget. One day, the government announced the price of pewter dropped. Thrilled, I went to the local store and asked about the new price. They politely explained that while it is common to barter in Malaysia, one does not barter for pewter. I politely explained that I knew this, but that the government had just reduced the set price. They politely explained again that pewter was not something one bartered for. I did not respond politely and started yelling that I knew this about Malaysia but that the government had lowered prices. Entirely frustrated, I left the store. I had lost it. Yelling is not a normal strategy for me, even when I'm convinced I'm right. However, the stress of always running into new situations got to me. That's culture shock. When the price in the store was lowered several days later to reflect the new government policy, I sent a friend to purchase it. I wish I would have also apologized so the store owners knew that U.S. Americans don't usually do this!
~ Barbara Kappler, Malaysia

Stage 3: Cultural Adjustment

This stage represents the transition out of culture shock into significant cultural adjustment. You feel increasingly comfortable and competent in the culture, and these feelings prevail over the times you have felt frustrated or out of place. Homesickness may still be an issue for you, but you are interacting more effectively with people from your host country, leading to an increase in self-confidence. You start to look forward to further interactions in the host country and what you can learn throughout the remainder of your experience.

Stage 4: Cultural Adaptation

In this stage, you have reached a point where you have a great deal of confidence in your ability to communicate and interact effectively. You have a deeper understanding of the influence culture has in peoples' lives. You have acquired considerable cultural knowledge, but you also recognize that there is much you still don't know or understand. You have integrated many of the values, customs, and behaviors from the new culture into your daily life. You now possess the ability to examine and comprehend a wide range of cultural norms, values, and beliefs.

relax. comfort. ride. chill.
After being here and having gotten used to the systems and customs and safety and unwritten rules and street knowledge and language, you know you're adapting well when getting into a matatu isn't a three-hour ordeal. you know you're adapting well when people don't try and cheat you with a high price after you barter with them in kiswahili. you know you're adapting well when you bribe your way into a cricket game for seventy shillings instead of eight hundred. you know you're adapting well when you can eat your food with ugali and chapati using your hands like a pro…you know you're adapting well when you can take down eleven glasses of chai in one day. riding the wave. feeling the rhythm. chilling and hoping that things will stay this way

for a bit; but really knowing that they won't, and you will be confronted with new challenges and new opportunities and new feelings of discomfort and alienation and disconnectedness and fear. and the cycle continues—but this time at a different level, with a different understanding, and a different person emerges. and that's the beauty of life. and that's what we are here for—to discover our personalized truths as we find balance and pleasure…in our own struggle to survive… ~ Free verse by Spencer Cronk, Kenya

ACTIVITY: Statements of adjustment

The goal of this activity is to give you the chance to think about adjustment and how you would react or help someone going through the process.

CULTURE: *In-Country*

José and Steven are both juniors in college from the United States who meet in the same chemistry class while studying at a foreign university. Their class is taught in the host country's language, and because they are both unfamiliar with the difficult science vocabulary, they begin meeting at a local coffee shop to study together and help each other understand the material. One evening, they find themselves in the midst of several tables of students, all speaking English. As the night winds down, they become immersed in a conversation with six other students around them, all of whom are from the United States. Although everyone is attending the local university, they did not all arrive in the host country at the same time. The amount of time in the host country for each of them falls between one and seven months.

Read the following statements and try to determine how long you think each student has been in the host country and how well you think that student is satisfied with his or her experience in the country. Place your answer on the graph on the next page, indicating where you think each student falls. Refer back to the U-curve chart on p. 93, if needed.

Kiersten: The people here are so wonderful. I'm having a great time!
José: They always take so long to complete something that could be accomplished much quicker. It's not very efficient.
Steven: Some days I'm frustrated with my language skills, but then I'll have a conversation where I understand everything and I can see how far I've come.
Kurt: I love it here. I can't imagine being anywhere else!
Amira: It doesn't bother me anymore when people stare at me. I would be curious about the strange-looking foreigner, too, if I were them.
Maggie: I can't believe I'm eating raw fish. I couldn't stomach it when I first arrived.
Gretchen: I can barely stand the smell of the cafeteria. Give me McDonald's any day.
Martin: I feel like when I return to the U.S., a part of me will remain here in this country.

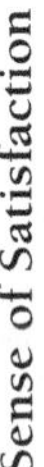

See answers on p. 98.

Reflection questions

- Why is Kurt's comment listed in both stages 1 and 4? (Hint: This was not a mistake; we feel that while overly positive comments are common in stage 1, they can also reflect a deep connection to the culture that is found in stage 4.)
- What reaction did you have to each of the students' comments? What advice would you offer each student?
- What would your U curve look like if your study abroad is two months? One year?
- How has your own emotional experience changed since arrival?

Knowing these eight characters' timelines can be very helpful in understanding how your own experience will change over time and for recognizing when you may be experiencing challenges in cultural adjustment.

ACTIVITY: Personal highs and lows of study abroad

Think about your own timeline and what issues or events might trigger some low points or create some high points for you during your time abroad. Write those down in the space below. You might want to consider keeping a graph in your journal throughout your study abroad stay to record your own experience.

Potential Low Points	**Potential High Points**
•	•
•	•
•	•
•	•
•	•
•	•
•	•

Here are some things other students have shared about their high and low points while studying abroad:

Low Points

- I got on the wrong bus back to my apartment because I misread the sign and ended up on the other side of the city.
- No one here knew it was my birthday—it really made me miss my friends at home.
- My host mother got angry with me for using too much hot water.
- The cash machine wouldn't allow me to access my account, and I ended up yelling at the bank teller because she couldn't understand what I needed.
- I missed my friend's wedding, and she never got the gift that I sent for it.
- My parents canceled their trip to see me here because it got too expensive.
- My girlfriend from home broke up with me over e-mail.
- My roommates went home for the local holiday, and I ended up in the dorm alone because I couldn't afford to go anywhere.

High Points

- I told a joke to the grouchy fruit vendor at the market and made him laugh. After that, he always smiled and talked to me.
- I dreamed in the language of my host country.
- I went to a holiday festival in another village and learned a traditional dance.
- I traveled alone—something I never would have done before. Because I was by myself, I ended up meeting and becoming friends with travelers from other countries.

- I got invited to a classmate's house for dinner.
- I read the newspaper and discussed an article with my host brother.
- My professor actually liked the essay I wrote on World War II.
- I went on a weekend trip with three new friends to a nearby town.

Some helpful coping strategies

What can you do when you are hit with the culture shock blues? Here is some advice from recent returnees:

- **Find ways to relieve stress:** Understand your language and culture limits—if things get overwhelming, take a break.
- **Do what you do at home or something close to it:** What worked for you at home when you were feeling down? Reading? Listening to music? Watching a funny movie? Give it a try in the host country as well.
- **Express yourself:** Find someone who understands to talk things over with, such as another U.S. American or international student. Singing, playing an instrument, or dancing can also be wonderful means of expression you can do by yourself or with others.
- **Connect with family and friends back home:** Write letters home, send emails to friends. Writing can be a valuable way to reconnect when things aren't going so well. But set a limit. Too much time sending e-mail can make you feel you never emotionally left home. And that's not what you want, either.

Answers from p. 96

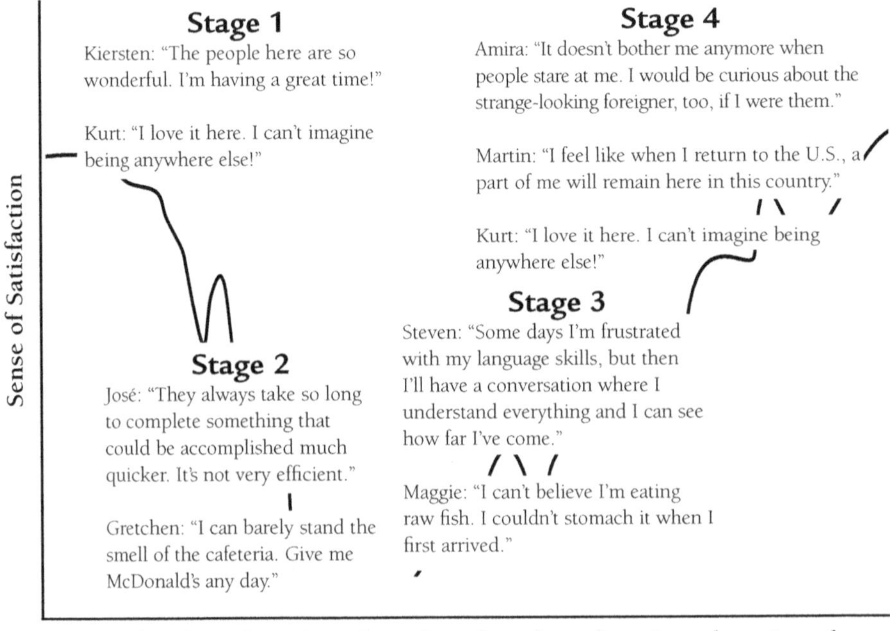

- **Keep a journal** (see p. 119): Writing down your experiences can be a great way to vent, to process your experience, and to gain insights into the cultures surrounding you.
- **Stay active:** Take walks, bike, swim, or engage in other kinds of physical activity. A good workout can be calming and therapeutic.

ACTIVITY: My personal coping strategies

The above are examples to get you thinking about how you might alleviate the symptoms of culture shock. By now you should be able to come up with a few coping strategies of your own. Think about what helps you feel relaxed, valued, and comfortable when you are home. Then adapt these strategies to your new environment in the host country.

1.____

2.____

3.____

4.____

5.____

Going Beyond Surface Adjustment

Although most study abroad students go through stages of cultural adaptation similar to those just described, there is no set time frame during which each stage occurs. When and how each person goes through the confrontation or adaptation stage, for example, depends largely on the individual, degree of cultural differences, and other situational factors that may be beyond control (poor weather, health, etc.).

Unfortunately, many students during their time abroad do not have the degree of contact with host nationals that is essential for complete cultural adaptation to take place. Students who have adjusted only superficially have not become very involved in the host culture. In short, surface adjustment may be easier for you in the short term, but in the long run you are apt to lose out on opportunities for personal growth and significant intercultural learning. It may require a conscious effort on your part to take advantage of immersion opportunities in the host culture. (Later chapters will outline some strategies for immersion and for effective interaction with host nationals.)

Another thing to remember is that while you are making attempts to adjust to your host culture, the hosts may be making just as much effort to adjust to you and your "peculiar" ways of doing things. In most countries throughout the world, the hosts will have the expectation that people from abroad who come to live in their country for a decent length of time will make an attempt to adjust to the manner, customs, and lifestyle of the country. After all, learning these aspects of the country is one of the reasons you decided to study abroad in the first place, right?

There are some things that you may not be able to change, perhaps certain eating or religious customs. These will need special attention and negotiation skills:

> *We hosted a Moroccan student for a few weeks one summer. The first thing he said to us was, 'Hi. I am Rahid. I do not eat pork.' Rahid, as a devout Muslim, had many dietary restrictions—from my point of view. So, I took Rahid to the grocery store with me so he could help me pick out what he could eat. We did try to accommodate his cultural needs so that he could be more comfortable. I also learned a lot about his culture this way.*
> *~ Karin Larson, Coordinator, Center for Advanced Research on Language Acquisition*

Despite your best attempts at adjusting to the new cultural milieu, you still are going to confront differences that you don't understand or that might upset you, you will still make mistakes in your use of language, and at times you will feel like giving up because you think you aren't making any progress. At these times it's important to stop, give yourself some positive affirmations, and do something that gets you back into a better frame of mind. The following scenarios will help you consider how to best cope with these challenging moments.

ACTIVITY: Coping scenarios

A study abroad experience can be the highlight of an academic career. It's an adventure that is anticipated, sometimes for years in advance—a journey we expect will contain few or none of the commonplace problems of day-to-day living in the U.S. It's hard to imagine having normal concerns such as turning a paper in on time or arguing with your roommates about whose turn it is to take out the garbage. Instead, you are envisioning yourself walking along the Great Wall of China or witnessing an active volcano on a remote Indonesian island. When planning a study abroad trip, it's easy to envision an experience free from the bureaucracy and small troubles of "ordinary" life.

But just as life in the United States can be occasionally complicated and unpleasant, a study abroad experience will contain its fair share of problems and complex issues, some of them unique to the culture where you are studying. Read the following scenarios from two study abroad students:

Scenario 1

Jerika is a 21-year-old student from the U.S. studying in Slovenia. In mid-November of her year abroad she begins dating Gregor, a fellow student at the university and a native of Hungary. Since she is not going home to the U.S. for winter break, he invites her over to his family's house in Budapest to celebrate the new year. This would be a large family event and would involve meeting his entire family, including his grandparents, cousins, nieces, and nephews, and spending two days with them. Although she likes Gregor and would enjoy visiting Budapest, she feels anxious that this kind of visit would indicate to his family that she and Gregor are in a more serious relationship than they actually are.

If you were Jerika, what would you do?

Scenario 2

Terry is a 22-year-old student from the U.S. and studying in Bern, Switzerland. Terry is a seasoned traveler and an avid outdoorsman. Part of the reason he chose to study in Switzerland is because he would be centrally located to take long weekend and holiday trips to France, Germany, Italy, and Austria. After his second trip away from Bern, however, his host mother takes him aside and asks him if he is planning on being gone every weekend. She tells him that other students they have hosted in the past spent more time with the family and indicates that she would like it if he became more involved with the family. Terry feels torn. He likes his host family well enough, but he already has plans to leave again in two weeks to go hiking and camping with a friend who is studying in Munich. Additionally, there are a number of other trips he'd like to make before his year abroad is over.

If you were Terry, what would you do?

Here's some advice other students had for Jerika:

- Tell Gregor that for you celebrating the new year with his family indicates the relationship is pretty serious. Ask if he thinks it means the same thing.
- Ask Gregor if there is a cultural meaning to this kind of family visit. Explain that you want to know what this may mean to the family and to Gregor before you go.
- If you feel funny making a big deal about this with Gregor, get advice from another friend who really knows the culture.
- Don't worry so much. Enjoy the experience and don't worry about what Gregor's family thinks. You are only there for a short time and you don't know what the future will bring. Even if there are cultural differences, you cannot control what the family will think.
- Ask Gregor what the sleeping arrangements will be. You don't want to be embarrassed in front of the whole family—either way! And you need to know that you'll be comfortable there.

Here's some advice other students had for Terry:

- You need to think carefully—maybe the host family option is not for you.
- Try to plan for the long run. Is it more important to see a great deal of Europe or to form a relationship with the family? Can you maybe come back again to visit friends?
- You need to recognize that you cannot have it both ways. You have to decide which is more important—travel or the family.
- Will you really get to know Bern and the Swiss if you are spending so much time traveling?
- You are only there for a short time. Perhaps you can negotiate with your family and explain that you would like to spend time with them. Be prepared that they may not feel comfortable with you "scheduling them in" on the weekends you are available. Maybe ask them what would work well. What's the "ideal" time to be with them? Maybe you could adjust your schedule and spend more time with them during the week in the evenings, for example.

Some quick tips for going beyond surface adjustment

- Participate in the culture.
- Don't fight the culture; flex with it.
- View culture learning as expanding your skills and knowledge, not as an admittance of failure or that you've done something wrong.
- Learn what is most important to the people in the culture.
- Constantly test your own ideas about the culture.
- Don't assume you understand the culture.
- Learn from "experts" (expatriate and host culture friends).
- Occasionally withdraw from the culture to avoid culture fatigue.
- Explain your culture to your hosts; help them understand you.
- Learn from others, but don't become dependent on them.
- Learn from TV, radio, and the press; these resources are great for cultural insights.
- When you don't know, ask.

Be assertive! You need to take responsibility for getting involved and talking with people. ~ Jacob Dick, Italy

Summary

We can't easily control how we feel in response to certain events, but we can control how we act upon our feelings. Much of cross-cultural adjustment is about getting used to a number of new and unfamiliar stimuli and understanding them. Part of the reason you decided to study abroad is because you want differences. Even after you have adjusted somewhat, you may still feel negatively about something in the new culture. But you now are able to understand the cultural basis for it and can accept it for what it is—a difference. Other things that you didn't quite care for when you first arrived you will eventually learn to like and appreciate. This is all part of the process of feeling more at home in your host country.

Study abroad challenged me and reinforced my sense of independence. I found that I was able to do things that normally wouldn't be a big deal, but I did them in a completely different country and a completely different language. Things as simple as buying train tickets, using the phone, and traveling became successes to me. I learned that I was stronger than I thought I was and a very capable person. I now feel that if I were set down anywhere in the world I would be able to make my way and be fine. ~ Sarah Parr, France

Phases of Cultural Awareness

When you are in the host country and are surrounded by differences on a daily basis, it's especially important to work on increasing your degree of cultural awareness and building competence in your new culture.

William Howell (1982) has divided cultural awareness into four categories or levels. These can also be considered developmental phases a person goes through when abroad. While you read over the four stages, keep in mind the three different categories of adjustment discussed earlier: physical, societal, and internal. To advance to the next stage of cultural awareness, it is important that progress be made in all of these categories. One of the main goals of this guide is to provide information that helps you progress through the early stages so you build competence faster and make your experience more rewarding as a result.

I. Unconscious Incompetence

In this phase you may be aware of some cultural differences between you and your host country, but you do not know how this translates into the functioning of society or how you should interact with people in the country. In this stage you are likely to make many mistakes but will be relatively unaffected by them because of your lack of knowledge. This is a difficult stage for someone to discern, since it is very difficult for first-time travelers to know what they do not know. They say that ignorance is bliss, after all.

II. Conscious Incompetence

Although it is not always possible, it might be a good idea to start by thinking of yourself as being in this phase. If you assume that you are likely to make mistakes, you may be more careful about making cultural assumptions or rashly evaluating your surroundings. As a whole, adopting a mindset where you lower your expectations of your abilities in the new culture is probably a very good idea and will make your relationships with host nationals easier. As you may realize, you are not really incompetent, you just happen to lack knowledge and skills important in the new culture. This tends to be a difficult stage for many, as people are not used to being culturally incompetent until they go abroad. One positive way to view this phase is to think about how much you are learning and absorbing every day based upon your studies and your interactions with host nationals. These interactions will take you into the next phase, which may feel more comfortable as you begin to build confidence in your cross-cultural skills.

III. Conscious Competence

In this phase you have reached a certain level of awareness of cultural differences and have discovered ways to understand, accept, and integrate them, although perhaps not fully. You have built up some confidence from numerous successful interactions with host nationals, and you are able to shift your behavior so that it is culturally appropriate. You are still learning and deepening your knowledge of the culture, but now you have a solid basis for how you view and interpret the culture. You are glad to make efforts toward cultural appropriateness because you know that this strategy will be effective for achieving your goals.

IV. Unconscious Competence

The final phase of cultural awareness is one in which you no longer need to think much about cultural differences because you have built up an instinctive understanding and you know automatically what works and what doesn't in the host culture. How do you know you are in this stage? In certain countries the hosts may stop telling you how good your language ability is, or will tell you that you are more "Chinese" than the Chinese. But a better measure is to look at the effectiveness of your interactions with hosts. Are you achieving your goals without cultural-related stress? Are you feeling more comfortable about how the host nationals perceive you and how you perceive your new intercultural identity? If the answers to these questions are yes, then it's likely you are in this phase of cultural awareness.

ACTIVITY: Differentiating the phases of cultural awareness

For the following statements, try to determine which phase the traveler is in. Suggested answers are found on the next page.

I. Unconscious Incompetence
II. Conscious Incompetence
III. Conscious Competence
IV: Unconscious Competence

Alexander: *I'm exhausted after I get home every day. It seems I never can do anything right.*
Phase ______

Mee: *I'm feeling very comfortable in the culture. It's become a second home for me.*
Phase ______

Karenna: *It surprised me to realize that I could have an entire conversation on the phone without getting stressed out.*
Phase ______

Shane: *I notice that people here do funny things when they greet one another.*
Phase ______

Ingrid: *It sometimes embarrasses me when other foreigners complain about the culture and act inappropriately. I often feel like I don't want to be associated with them.*
Phase ______

Norio: *I feel like people are watching me all the time. I'm afraid of making mistakes.*
Phase ______

Lia: *Now that I can eat almost anything using chopsticks, it really makes sense to use them as much as the locals do.*
Phase ______

Aaron: *As long as you can speak the language, there will be few problems in navigating the culture.*
Phase ______

Maria: *I am able to learn so much by being able to interact with people here on their level. I can often understand what they are going to say before they actually say it.*
Phase ______

Answers:

Alexander: *I'm exhausted after I get home every day. It seems I never can do anything right.*
Phase II (very aware of his own cultural inadequacy)

Mee: *I'm feeling very comfortable in the culture. It's become a second home for me.*
Phase IV (could also be Phase I if she has no recognition of cultural differences)

Karenna: *It surprised me to realize that I could have an entire conversation on the phone without getting stressed out.*
Phase III (also seems like Phase IV, but then she wouldn't be surprised at her own competence)

Shane: *I notice that people here do funny things when they greet one another.*
Phase I (finds host behavior unusual, oblivious to his own behavior)

Ingrid: *It sometimes embarrasses me when other foreigners complain about the culture and act inappropriately. I often feel like I don't want to be associated with them.*
Phase IV (it can require a lot of patience for a culturally aware traveler to be around those of significantly lower cultural competence)

Norio: *I feel like people are watching me all the time. I'm afraid of making mistakes.*
Phase II (expresses more than usual self-consciousness at his own ineffective behavior)

Lia: *Now that I can eat almost anything using chopsticks, it really makes sense to use them as much as the locals do.*
Phase III (expresses awareness of her own competence development)

Aaron: *As long as you can speak the language, there will be few problems in navigating the culture.*
Phase I (attributes all cultural differences to language alone)

Maria: *I am able to learn so much by being able to interact with people here on their level. I can often understand what they are going to say before they actually say it.*
Phase IV (expresses a high level of intuitive cultural empathy and sensitivity)

Take a moment and consider which stage describes where you are at today. Which character can you most easily relate to?

As this exercise demonstrates, where you are in your ability to understand and manage cultural differences is going to have a direct effect on your ability to adjust to the culture and achieve your academic and personal goals. The next section will provide ways for you to make sense of the plethora of cultural phenomena you encounter in the host culture.

IN-COUNTRY CULTURE STRATEGIES PART III: STRATEGIES FOR DEVELOPING INTERCULTURAL COMPETENCE

It took me a long time to feel competent in Italy. Certainly I mean my language skills, but I also mean almost a change of attitude—an acceptance that things really run differently here. My hard work and the difficulties I faced did pay off, and I learned to really enjoy the culture at a deeper level.
~ Jacob Dick, Italy

What, you may be asking, is intercultural competence? It's when you feel effective in the host culture and others see you as effective. The things that you did at home you are able to do well in the host country, too. For example, you are doing well academically, you have friends you can count on, you work part time, and you have the same (or more!) confidence.

This section focuses on the cognitive skills that you can develop to help you manage differences between cultures and achieve intercultural competence. Understanding how to move through Milton J. Bennett's (1993) developmental model of intercultural sensitivity is one way of gaining these cognitive skills. Bennett examines attitudes toward cultural differences—intercultural sensitivity—and how they relate to intercultural competence. Intercultural sensitivity is viewed as occurring along a continuum consisting of six different levels described below. The greater one's intercultural sensitivity, the easier it is to become knowledgeable about the host culture and function effectively in it. Intercultural sensitivity isn't something we are born with. It is only through experience and reflection upon cultural differences that people begin to view cultural differences as being positive, interesting, desirable, and as having their own internal logic within a certain culture.

A Model of Intercultural Sensitivity

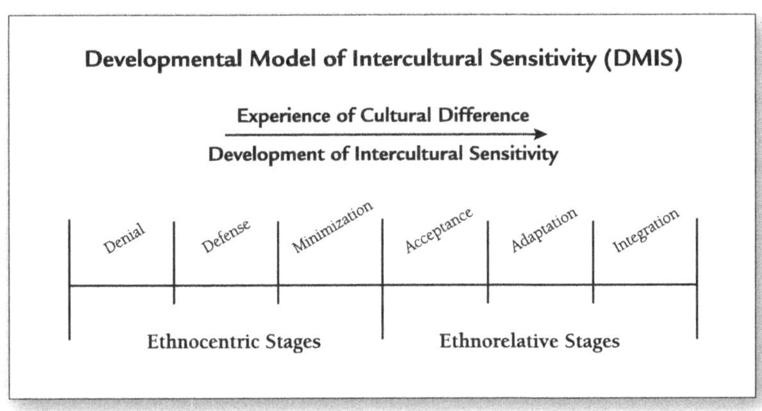

Ethnocentrism and ethnocentric worldviews

Chances are that most of us grow up being ethnocentric. We do things the way we do because we believe it's the best way—or we would do it some other way! Ethnocentric has two meanings: believing your own culture is superior to others and having the tendency to view other cultures in terms of one's own. The second meaning, while seemingly more benign, is still potentially damaging. It may seem OK or even natural to view other cultures by comparing them to your own, but the danger is that you might view your own culture as the central or mainstream culture against which others should be compared and judged (e.g., they are not as modern, they are too liberal). The following stages reflect ethnocentric attitudes toward others.

Denial

People in this stage are not aware that cultural differences actually exist. They also probably only understand culture as visible things (the way people dress, languages) and not as different values or beliefs. Most people in denial have had little contact with people who are culturally different. If they encounter problems in communicating or interacting with people from different cultures, they are likely to attribute the cause to personal reasons rather than cultural. Generally, they interpret these so-called "differences" as being wrong or inappropriate ways of thinking or behaving. People in this stage may say things like, "We should have no trouble interacting in the host culture as long as we can speak the same language." This person is unable to acknowledge cultural differences.

If you identify with this stage of the scale, try these things to move forward:

- Try to meet as many people as possible from the host country and really be open to their points of view.
- Read the local newspaper. Compare the coverage in the local newspaper with an international or U.S. newspaper. Do you see different perspectives offered on the same event?

Defense

People in the defense stage also think of cultural differences as being wrong or inappropriate, but they have acknowledged that differences do exist. These people may encounter more difference in their daily lives, but they feel threatened by it and often make efforts toward justifying the correctness and superiority of their own cultural values and beliefs. Statements like "Why don't they just act more like us?" or blatant stereotyping of groups are indicative of people in defense. Also, statements such as "When I travel abroad, it makes me realize how much better things are in the U.S." still probably reflect defense because the person is making a blanket statement about the superiority of everything American.

If you identify with this stage of the scale, try these things to move forward:

- Search for common ground. What interests do you have in common with people in the host country? Do you watch or play the same sports? Listen to the same music? Celebrate the same holidays?

- Challenge yourself to find something, no matter how small, that you prefer in your host country to your home country. Maybe there is a certain saying that captures your feelings in a way that cannot be done in English. Maybe you've discovered a new angle on a topic you've been studying that has given you insights you did not learn in the U.S. Keep adding to this list so that you can enjoy the differences of your new, but temporary, home.
- Explore cultural events in the country—go to movies, visit museums, watch sports. Dig deeper into what is unique about this place.

There is an interesting version of defense where the person positively evaluates and feels more a part of the new culture than his or her own culture. This is called *reversal* and is also characterized by a negative evaluation of one's original culture. But it is still defense in that one culture is seen as superior to another.

Minimization

In this stage, people minimize cultural differences and instead prefer to focus on similarities between groups of people. They might say something like, "We're all human beings after all," or "Why do we always have to emphasize what makes people different? People are people." What makes this minimization is that the person typically perceives that others are "like me" and does not recognize how others are different. What makes such statements ethnocentric is that the frame of reference is "me" or "my culture." The key point is not that we should ignore similarities, but rather that similarities *and* differences need to be understood in order to truly understand the culture.

If you identify with this stage of the scale, try these things to move forward:

- Challenge yourself to get more involved with your host country. Join a club or sports team and notice the similarities and differences in how the group operates compared to teams at home.
- When talking with your new friends from the host country, try to suspend any thoughts such as "Yes, that's exactly how I feel," or "Yes, it's very similar in the U.S." Instead, try to push those thoughts aside and really listen to your friends' views and make sure that you don't miss key differences.
- Read more local newspapers, books, and magazines to learn how people in the host country really view the world.
- Listen to news talk shows and go to forums and lectures to find out the historical and contemporary perspectives on current issues.

Ethnorelativism and ethnorelative worldviews

Ethnorelative is a term coined by Milton Bennett to characterize those who no longer view their own culture as a center from which others should be judged, but rather as a state of mind in which cultures are respected, compared, and contrasted according to the perspectives of the cultures involved. Read on to discover more about the ethnorelative stages.

Acceptance

This is the first ethnorelative stage, and it involves what might be described as a significant shift in cultural awareness and understanding. In general, people in this stage have ceased looking at cultural differences as negative, but simply as existing. There is a good deal of awareness of cultural differences, and respect is given to groups who are culturally different. There may not be a lot of deep understanding of individual cultures, but there exists the interest and capacity to learn about other cultures. A statement such as "My life is enriched by my relationships with people from different backgrounds and experiences" signifies acceptance because the person is interested in others from different cultures.

If you identify with this stage of the scale, try these things to move forward:

- As suggested in earlier stages, challenge yourself to get even more involved in the culture. You need to be immersed in conversations not only to recognize behavioral and value differences, but also to figure out how to adapt to these new behaviors and values.
- Invite your new friends over for dinner and host a conversation on a timely topic. Give yourself a chance to see your friends relaxed and conversing so that you can learn and join in!
- Try out the journaling methods discussed in this guide (p. 119). You can revisit key events—either because they were initially confusing, exciting, or overwhelming—and try to dig deeper into the cultural nuances. You could even try sharing some of your journal entries with others to see if together you can come to a deeper understanding of key behavioral and value differences, as well as sort out what is personal and what is cultural in any particular incident.

Adaptation and Integration

In these stages, people have incorporated differences in cultures into their own value and belief systems. People in these stages see the value of adjusting their behavior to accommodate cultural norms, and they are more able to empathize with people from other cultures and see things from their perspectives. People in these stages still maintain many of the cultural values of their original culture, but they have integrated others and, more importantly, are able to use at least two different cultural frames of reference for perceiving the world. Lastly, they also may consider themselves bicultural or multicultural. These two statements reflect adaptation and integration: "I usually try to behave appropriately in intercultural situations, but I also can still maintain my values and beliefs," and "When I examine a problem, I usually think about it from more than one cultural point of view."

While adaptation and integration are listed as the final points on the continuum, it certainly does not mean that the learning is over. There are always deeper understandings to familiar cultures, as well as new host cultures and perspectives to explore!

If you identify with these stages of the scale, try these things to continue the learning:

- Spend time reflecting or journaling about situations that are politically or personally troubling to you. How can you apply multiple perspectives to these situations? What do these multiple perspectives suggest about resolving the problems?
- Pursue readings from multiple cultures on particular topics. Your multiple perspectives may be further broadened and deepened by such readings.
- Ask yourself, "What might you need to do to further develop a particular perspective on a topic?"
- Take an active role in helping friends who might be struggling with various stages along the continuum. Sharing your own worldview and ability to take multiple perspectives not only helps others, it helps you to develop your own thinking about multiple perspectives.
- Seek out intercultural role models—people who seem to be very fluid about how they fit in with the host culture. What qualities do you admire about these people and how might you gain experiences to develop such fluidity?

Reflection

Now that you have had an overview of the Bennett model of intercultural sensitivity, you probably have given some thought to how these stages apply to you. Keep in mind that you are likely to have a dominant worldview, one that organizes your way of thinking about difference, but that other elements of the model can also be a part of your intercultural sensitivity. This is the case because intercultural sensitivity is developmental and constantly changing.

So, which aspects of the Bennett model apply to you? One way to answer that question is to think about an intercultural experience you have had and how you reacted. Were you uncomfortable in the situation? Did you find yourself becoming judgmental? Did you want to focus on your similarities and avoid mention of your differences? Were you intrigued with the cultural differences, finding that you wanted to learn more? Did you enjoy adapting to the situation?

Intercultural experiences provide us with the opportunity to develop new understandings and skills, as well as the chance to reflect on what we already know and can do. The more exposure we have to people from other cultures, the greater the opportunity to develop our intercultural skills.

This model is intended to help you become more aware of cultural differences that can lead to deeper learning, of your attitude toward cultural differences, and of your ability to look at things from multiple perspectives. It may sound easy enough, but in reality this type of personal development usually requires a substantial amount of intercultural contact, knowledge, and experience.

IN-COUNTRY CULTURE STRATEGIES PART IV:

STRATEGIES FOR MAKING CULTURAL INFERENCES TO ENHANCE YOUR CULTURE LEARNING

You didn't sign up for study abroad just to learn about yourself—you signed up to learn about others. As you've come to realize, this can take a bit of work. The fact that you are reading this guide suggests that you are interested in going beyond simple and sometimes judgmental comparisons that are easy to make. This section discusses how to dig deeper into your reactions to come to a fuller understanding of your host country.

The Role of Inferences

A U.S. American student studying in a European country observed all the other students in a class immediately rise to their feet when the professor entered the room. She guessed that this was a sign of respect. Later, the students explained the importance of standing when a professor entered the classroom and gave reasons for doing it (it was the way things had always been done to show respect and signal the start of class). Through what they said, she made additional inferences about the importance of hierarchy and ways to be respectful to those with higher status. Thus, when she later encountered situations in which she was on time for a meeting and her professor was not, she assumed that this might also be a part of the role of status in the culture. She checked with other students and her assumptions were confirmed; it was important for students to be on time, and it was acceptable for professors to be 10 or more minutes late.

This student was successful at making inferences because she was able to use observation and conversation with people from the host culture to gain insights about the accuracy of her initial assumptions. To increase your own cultural knowledge, you need to "get inside the heads" of the host nationals. Although this is difficult to accomplish, it's not impossible. Whether or not you are aware of it, you will constantly be making various inferences about the host culture.

In your day-to-day life, you make inferences based on what people say, the way they act, and the objects they use. At first, each cultural inference is only a hypothesis. These hypotheses must then be tested over and over again until you become relatively certain that people share a particular system of cultural meanings. The forming of such hypotheses is a tricky business when moving from practice (described on pp. 57-59) to real situations. Part of gathering information is knowing how to balance insider information with your own observations. A large part of culture consists of tacit, or unspoken, knowledge that host nationals will be aware of but that you, as an outsider, may not. Host nationals know instinctively what subjects they can or cannot talk about or express in explicit ways. On the other hand, cultural informants may be limited in the type and depth of information they can or will provide because they may never have had to articulate their own cultural rules—they just live by them. Being observant and drawing conclusions on your own, based upon your observations of behavior, artifacts, and language, will enable you to gain valuable insights into the host culture. The next section will provide you with some tools for making sense of cultural experiences.

Using debriefing to make inferences

It is important to process fully the cultural information that you gain as a result of your experiences. One way that allows you to accomplish this is often called "debriefing." Debriefing is a process that facilitates discussing, conceptualizing, clarifying, and summarizing an intercultural experience. The following scenario is an example of how you can conduct your own debriefing of intercultural encounters and phenomena, using inferences to enhance your culture learning.

Brick Lane

Maiya is traveling for her first time in London. She has been very surprised by the diversity; there are so many people from the Caribbean, India, and from around the world who have come to live in London. One night, she went out with some friends and ended up at a place called Brick Lane. Here is a conversation she had with her roommate, Beth, about her night. Beth is in London for her second study abroad experience.

Beth: Where did you guys end up going last night to eat?

Maiya: We went to a place in East London. I didn't like it much.

Beth: Really, what didn't you like?

Maiya: I don't know—it's just not what I wanted to do last night.

Beth: What didn't you like—was it the food? Did your friends not have a good time?

Maiya: Actually, my friends seemed to have a really good time. As for the food, I have no idea what I was eating. The whole experience was just kind of weird.

Beth: How did you not know what you were eating?

Maiya: Well, it was in the Indian part of town, and when you walk down the street these guys from India come up to you and hassle you about coming into their restaurant. My friends were laughing with these guys, but I didn't like it. I just wanted to walk along and pick a restaurant on my own without being hassled. When my friends did pick one, we went in and I did not know one thing on the menu.

Beth: Could you have been in Brick Lane?

Maiya: Yes, that's the name of the place.

Beth: Hmm...I've been there before and I know what you mean about feeling like you are being hassled. I went back a second time, though, and tried to just soak it all in. I found out that it's a neighborhood of Bangladeshi residents, many who have been here since the early 1900s. I think we should go back and maybe just walk around together. If you are up for it, you might get a sense that the hassling is really part of the entertainment and bargaining that's part of the social element of attracting customers to Brick Lane. We could bring my friend Oliver, who knows the food really well, so he could help us pick some good food.

Maiya: I think you're right—it would be good to give this place a second try.

Reflection questions

- What are the specific questions that Beth asks Maiya? What helps to make these questions effective at keeping the conversation going?
- How does Beth go about teaching Maiya about the culture? In what ways does she try to create common ground?
- For those who have studied abroad before, how might you be able to help your fellow travelers understand their experiences by using debriefing?

In the previous example, Beth used debriefing to help Maiya understand a confusing experience. This next section will give you a model for debriefing your own encounters.

The Description-Interpretation-Evaluation (D-I-E) Model of Debriefing

Without having a lot of experience in the host culture, it is relatively easy to jump to conclusions about what you observe. Since we are usually looking at the new culture using the same lens we use back home, it's likely we don't fully understand the reasoning behind some cultural practices or norms and thus, our inferences are flawed. The following process of Description-Interpretation-Evaluation (D-I-E) can be a helpful tool in coming to a new understanding of the culture.

Step 1: D - Describe

- Describe the object or situation in concrete, observable terms.
- What happened in the interaction?
- What was said? What did you see? What did you feel at the time?

Notice that Beth's first questions to Maiya asked for more description. (Really, what didn't you like? What didn't you like—was it the food? Did your friends not have a good time?)

Step 2: I - Interpret

- Think of possible explanations (interpretations) for what you observed or experienced.
- From your cultural perspective, try to explain why you think this situation or experience occurred.
- Try to find at least three different interpretations of the interaction or occurrence. What cultural information have you used to produce these interpretations?

Notice that Beth explained to Maiya why the restaurant staff may have acted the way they did and provided historical background about Brick Lane. This information may help Maiya come up with a different interpretation of her experience than "weird."

Step 3: E - Evaluate

- Evaluate what you observed or experienced. What positive or negative feelings do you have regarding the situation?
- Consider how you might have felt if you were a member of the host culture and held the dominant cultural values and beliefs.

Notice that Beth did not directly ask Maiya to re-evaluate her assumptions about the night. Instead, she found common ground by sharing that she was uncomfortable the first time, too.

The D-I-E model of debriefing can help you consider multiple perspectives and interpretations for intercultural encounters. By listening to and understanding varied interpretations, you will become more open to differing perspectives. You will be able to switch to alternative perspectives that are required in different cultural settings in order to make more accurate inferences. D-I-E will also help you to deal more effectively with emotional reactions to differences that often result in a lack of understanding or a rejection of the new experience.

After you have made an evaluation using D-I-E, you may come to realize that even though you understand the cultural reasoning behind an event, you still evaluate it negatively. In short, you may need to recognize that you have to accept certain situations. The D-I-E process will help entitle you to your evaluations—positive or negative—because you have taken the time to reason through them and have worked to try to understand the occurrence from others' perspectives.

(Adapted from J. M. Bennett and M. J. Bennett, n.d.)

Asking questions using D-I-E

Along with learning the D-I-E process, it's helpful to learn what kinds of questions to ask. Descriptive questions are usually the best place to start with difficult-to-understand cultural phenomena. Descriptive questions start a dialogue without injecting your own values into the mix. Through descriptive questions you may find out much more information that will assist you in forming interpretations and subsequently evaluating the event. In the following sample questions, notice the great differences in the evaluative, interpretive, and descriptive approaches.

Evaluative: Why are these people so rude?
Interpretive: The people here aren't very trusting of foreigners, are they?
Descriptive: Why do so many of the villagers follow me around when I go to the market?

If you were to start with the evaluative question, you risk offending others or, at the least, revealing that you have been judgmental. The interpretive question, while potentially less offensive, appears to be less of a real question and more of a solicitation to confirm a negative impression you have formed. As a result of asking either an evaluative or interpretive question, you may alienate yourself from those you are trying to understand. The third question, from a descriptive approach, is more concrete (you are asking about a specific behavior you've experienced) and more open-minded (you have not, at least in the words selected, and hopefully not in your tone, revealed a negative evaluation of the host culture). Our advice is to use descriptive questions as much as possible to demonstrate that you are interested in truly understanding the world around you.

(Adapted from Kappler and Nokken, 1999.)

ACTIVITY: Revisiting the iceberg

When you are well immersed in your host country, it is likely you will have one or more incidents that will leave you scratching your head and wondering, "What just happened?" Perhaps you arrived for a party at a friend's house promptly at the designated time of 8:30 p.m., only to find yourself alone with the host for an hour and a half before the other guests arrived. Or perhaps your host brother became angry when you tried to pay for your own meal at a restaurant. Think about your experiences in the country so far, and take one situation that has left you confused. Write this event in descriptive terms above the line on the iceberg. Now think through the possible cultural explanations that may lie below the surface that could help explain this event. Write these below the line. (Need a refresher on the iceberg? See pp. 46-51 of the pre-departure section.)

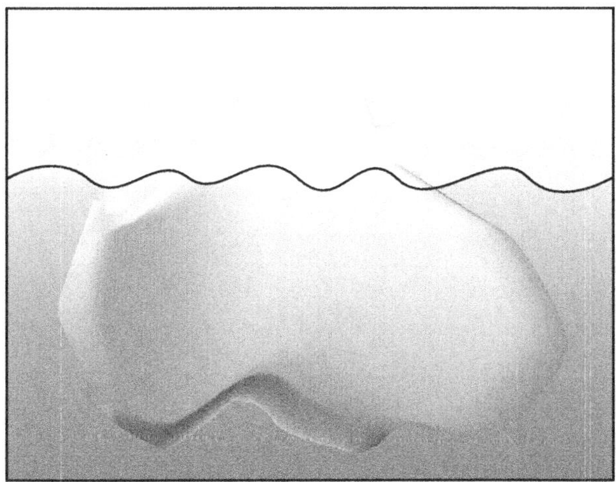

Your approach to making inferences can be greatly enhanced by using D-I-E, the iceberg, hypothesis testing, or other methods you develop. The time spent is truly worth it. These understandings don't get packed in your suitcase; they are a part of you.

The following chapter on journaling gives even more examples of how to put D-I-E and culture learning into action.

IN-COUNTRY CULTURE STRATEGIES PART V:
STRATEGIES FOR KEEPING A JOURNAL

Keep a journal. It will become a treasure and a link. ~ Joy Wildermuth, France

The importance of journaling

One of the things many travelers regret most upon their return is that they neglected to keep a journal while they were abroad. As mentioned earlier, one of the most valuable and relatively painless activities you can do to enhance your experience is to keep a journal. No matter how amazing and unforgettable your experience abroad may seem, it doesn't take long before your memories begin to fade. Who was that guy on the bus in Thailand? What was the name of that quaint pension I stayed at in Paris? Keeping a journal can not only help you remember the details of your experience, but it can help you process and learn the most from it.

What are the functions of a journal?

The journal could have many functions: to serve as a record of experiences, to provide a reference for culture and language learning and development, or to help you cope with your emotions while going through cultural adjustment. Journaling may already be a main component of your academic curriculum abroad, in which case your journal entries will already have a specific focus. Whether or not this is the case, the following journaling ideas are intended to help you make journal writing a regular part of your study abroad experience.

Keep in mind...

Making periodic entries into your journal will take some time and energy. Whether you make daily entries or write only when the urge hits will be up to you. Most people find that once they start making regular entries and get into the journaling habit, it's something they actually look forward to doing.

The Traditional Way to Keep a Journal

I went to Malaysia for a study abroad research program, and I love to pull my journal off the shelf and go through a few pages, reminiscing about the trip. I have an entry for each day that I was there, and I recorded pretty much the details of, and my reactions to, the day. As I read through, I can close my eyes and feel like I am back there again, even though it was years ago. ~ Barbara Kappler, Malaysia

Keeping a journal the traditional way—writing about daily events and your reactions to them—can be extremely effective. If this method works, then use it. We encourage you to record not only what happened, but also what you are learning about the situation, the culture, and yourself. For example, imagine a friend from your host country mentions that she is surprised you are not married yet. You are surprised at the question because you think age is not the key factor in determining when someone marries. The following are some questions you could address in your journal about this scenario. Of course, you could adapt these questions to any situation.

1. Culture-learning questions

What are ways you could learn more about marriage in this culture? How are age and status viewed in this culture, and how is marriage related to age and status? What might be signs you have seen that the host culture is age-conscious and status-oriented (or some other value or trait)?

2. Culture-specific questions

What are the societal rules around marriage? How do people date? Who initiates the marriage proposal? Are the rules the same for men and women?

3. Culture-general questions

What values are influencing how you view this situation? What other phenomena might impact this situation (family history or cultural adjustment)?

4. Problem-solving questions

How does this difference between the two of you impact your relationship? How might this situation have been avoided in the first place? Was it necessary (or even possible) to avoid or has the discovery of the difference been meaningful? If a problem has occurred, what can be done now to help solve the problem?

5. Affective questions

How do you feel personally about this situation?

(Excerpted and adapted from Paige, DeJaeghere, and Yershova, 1999.)

An Alternative Way to Keep a Journal

Keeping a journal while you are studying or traveling abroad seems like a good idea at first, but then you get bogged down with the whole experience. Many people simply give up on the idea, but the funny thing is: though almost everyone regrets not keeping a journal!

One of the main reasons people give up on journaling is that they find the process of writing down every detail of their experience overwhelming and sometimes quite boring. Many journal entries go something like this: "We got up in the morning, ready for a day full of sightseeing. First we went…and then we saw…and then we went…and then we…and then…and then…and then…." This type of journaling can stifle your creative juices and take too long to record your entire day on paper.

So what's the answer?

Consider changing the structure of your journal. One avid traveler began keeping a different kind of journal during her third study abroad trip to India and Malaysia.

It took a little getting used to at first, and I admit I was a little skeptical, but once I became familiar with the technique I was hooked! Now when I travel or live abroad, this is the only type of journaling I do! ~ Kristi Nokken, India and Malaysia

This type of travel journal, developed by Nancy Taylor Nicodemus, involves dividing your journal into four different sections:

- Impressions
- Descriptive
- Narrative
- Expressive

What is unique about this type of journaling is that you do not make chronological entries. Instead, you may make several entries in one day, or none at all, although it is not advisable to go too many days without writing.

You may choose to add other sections to your journal that make sense for you. For example, you can add a Miscellaneous section where you can write entries that don't seem to fit anywhere else. You can also add a Personal section, which you can use more as a diary to write things that you wouldn't want other people to read.

Impressions section

This is the only section of your journal where entries will be made chronologically. The impressions section is for jotting down the places, people, events, concepts, ideas, smells, signs, and other things you remember. You write words, phrases, or sentences that will spark your memory. Be detailed in this section with dates and the names of people, places, events, cities, etc., because this is the only section where you could re-create your itinerary if you needed to do so.

Look at the following example from Kristi Nokken. It is complete gibberish to everyone else, but to her it brings back loads of detailed memories.

8 August — Universiti Sains Malaysia, Penang, Malaysia

Awie's birthday party! Two crazy uncles. A game of lucky draw. Chatting with Winda and her cousin. Dinner with Bernard and Irene. AIESEC meeting with Sow Yee—what a great group of people. Elections—paper everywhere—an environmentalist's nightmare!!! Gloria lost…

Descriptive section

This section is divided into chapters in which you can write entries that are purely descriptive in nature. You will not elaborate on what you think about what you are writing. Instead, you will use your descriptive abilities to create a vivid picture of what you experienced. Entries in this section should be written so that someone who has not visited the culture you are describing would be able to read your words and create a mental picture of what it was like.

Possible chapter titles in the section could include People, Customs, Places, Architecture, Religion, Transportation, Food and Drink, Art, Festivals, Ceremonies, Campus, Life, and Stereotypes.

Example: Descriptive section, "Religions"

13 September *Universiti Sains Malaysia, Penang, Malaysia*

The women who wear tudungs (which is the head covering worn by some Muslim women) take them extremely seriously! They wear them when they are playing sports; they wear them under baseball hats and graduation caps. I've seen a woman or two swimming—perhaps not with a tudung but at the very least wearing a knitted cap that holds all their hair underneath. Around the dorm, I've seen women covering their hair or head with a towel. They do this when they step outside to collect their laundry from the clothesline. They do it when they go down to make a telephone call even though the telephones are in the dorm—there is a glass door down there, which a man could walk by and quickly peek in.

Narrative section

This section is to satisfy the storyteller in you. There's no doubt you will come home with stories—good, bad, funny, and otherwise. Write about them in this section before you forget.

Possible chapter titles in the section could include Good for a Laugh, Stories, Jokes, Embarrassing Moments, Too Good to Be True, and They'll Never Believe This at Home.

Example: Narrative section, "Stories"

30 March *Penang, Malaysia*

Naomi and her husband were taking the night bus down to Kuala Lumpur but made the mistake of going on the night that the World Cup finals were playing. When the game started, the bus driver pulled over to the side of the road and informed everyone that they were stopping so he could watch the game (most buses have TVs in them). So, for however long the game took, a whole busload of people were stuck somewhere between Butterworth and Penang—just a few miles from where their journey began!

Expressive section

This is the section where you get to vent, debate, praise, hypothesize, and evaluate. Where you may have described an event in one of your descriptive sections, you may then make an entry in this section to record what you thought and felt about that event. In the descriptive example earlier, Kristi Nokken described how careful Muslim women were about wearing their tudungs. In the following example from the Expressive section of her journal, she talks about tudungs and comes up with an analogy that helped her personally to come to terms with value differences across cultures. It's a good example of the culture-learning process that you may go through while you are studying abroad. This learning process wouldn't necessarily come out in a typical chronological journal because too much time is spent concentrating on daily activities instead of the larger picture.

Possible chapter titles in the section could include Cultural Adjustment, Religious Awakenings…or Not, Reversals (where you assumed one thing but now realize what it really means to people from the culture), Conclusions, Language Learning, Unanswered Questions, Enigmas, Quotations, and Revelations.

Example: Expressive section, "Religious awakenings…or not"

20 October — *Universiti Sains Malaysia, Penang, Malaysia*

I've been thinking a lot about women wearing tudungs—or more specifically why some women do wear them and some don't. After all, from everything I've been told and taught about Islam, it is a sin for a woman not to wear one.

I think perhaps a good comparison would be to compare the tudung in Islam to birth control in Catholicism. I have many Catholic friends who use birth control. Although their religion strictly says (I believe) that sex is for procreation, many people find this part of their religion outdated and simply choose to ignore it.

Perhaps it is the same with the tudung. Some women may simply see the tudung as outdated and simply choose not to wear it (unless in the mosque or during prayers), despite the fact that their religion views it as a sin.

Keeping a journal in this way may seem a little overwhelming at first, but give it a try. What follows are some tips that will hopefully make it a little less intimidating, a little more manageable, and a lot more fun!

(Adapted from Taylor Nicodemus, 1991; and Kappler and Nokken, 1999.)

Tips to keep journaling fun and easy

- Number your pages and divide your sections early on—preferably before you go.
- Decide which section you probably will be writing in more than others, then divide the rest of the journal somewhat equally among the other categories.
- Give some time and thought to developing the chapters in each section. Think about what interests you most about the culture you are visiting.
- A hardcover book is the best. A loose-leaf binder could work, but it's not as sturdy and may not survive your travels.
- Make it your own: tape memorabilia to the cover or inside, and attach articles, photographs, or other special mementos.
- Try to write at least one entry every day.
- Carry around a little notebook to write things down that you want to remember—names, places, quotes, descriptive words as they come to mind—and transfer them later into your Impressions section.

IN-COUNTRY CULTURE STRATEGIES PART VI: STRATEGIES FOR INTERCULTURAL COMMUNICATION

Being in another country provides you with a range of experiences—sometimes boring, exciting, exhausting, confusing, educational, and interesting all within the same morning. Even knowing the host language well may not prepare you for some of the communication issues that you encounter on a daily basis. In the following two chapters, we integrate culture and language learning to focus on ways you can become more effective intercultural communicators in the host country.

Here are some experiences the authors have had in communicating across cultures:

> *When I first arrived in Turkey, I couldn't believe how emotional people seemed when they were having a conversation. Half the time I honestly thought they were going to punch each other out. It took me awhile to learn that for Turks, a good conversation is one where people show their feelings. If you're not into it, then people think you're cold and insincere. When I went to Indonesia, even though I had a great deal of intercultural experience, it took me months to figure out if someone was telling me yes or no. Once my wife and I invited an Indonesian friend and his wife to join us for lunch at a nearby restaurant specializing in soto ayam (a delicious chicken soup). When we got to their house to pick them up, it was obvious they weren't expecting us. Talk about a breakdown of communication! I eventually learned that being straightforward wasn't the East Javanese way. Communication was much more subtle. ~ R. Michael Paige, Turkey and Indonesia*

> *When my host family told me on the very first day that 'they didn't like Americans', I thought I was in for a terrible experience. It was hard not to take it personally, as their statement felt so direct and blunt. It took me awhile to realize that what they did not like was the President and that they felt things were being portrayed as being better in the U.S. As we got into debates about U.S. politics, I realized I had to work hard not to take things personally. They never meant it that way. They simply wanted to debate and to share their views. In the end, it was a wonderful family stay. ~ Barbara Kappler, England*

> *I learned the Aymara's way of dealing with the gringo the hard way, as would be expected. Shortly after I arrived at my site, one of my counterparts, who was supposed to be working with me, getting me oriented and taking me around, announced that he was going to a market up on the mountain in order to get straw mats for me. The mats were to hold some potatoes so that I could inhabit the room where the potatoes were kept. I waited around all day for my counterpart to return. Actually, as it turned out, he had had no intention of getting mats at the market. Mats were not*

sold there! Instead, he had some other purchases he wanted to make, but he didn't want me to think that he was going for that reason. When he finally appeared in the evening, he informed me that they were out of mats that weekend. ~ Andrew Cohen, Bolivia

As these experiences show, communication isn't something we can take for granted. People communicate in many different ways, and it takes awhile to figure out communication styles—how people are giving and receiving messages. One of the most difficult things about recognizing communication styles is that they aren't just about language. Gaining language fluency doesn't automatically mean you have gained communication competence. So in this section, we want to give you an initial understanding about different communication styles.

Low-Context and High-Context Communication

Like many Easterners, Indians don't like to say 'no' outright. Sometimes the lack of an answer is tantamount to a 'no.' In other instances, a 'yes' without a follow-up is a 'no.' ~ "Passport India," Manoj Joshi

Manoj Johshi's quote reminds us how complicated seemingly simple acts of communicating truly can be when communicating across cultures. This section delves into the nuances of communication style, or how we prefer to give and receive information in a particular situation. We begin with two broad categories for processing the messages we receive: low- and high-context communication.

Low-context communication (low reliance on cues from the context)

You are probably familiar with this category of communication because if you grew up in the U.S., it is quite likely you've been using low-context communication all your life. This communication tends to be more verbal and explicit, that is, we tell people what we think they need to know in order to understand us. We fill in the blanks. We write detailed contracts. We do not assume that understanding will come automatically from the situation, the context, or the person we are speaking with. In the U.S., because people do come from many different cultural or ethnic backgrounds, the tendency is to rely heavily on verbal communication and to be explicit. The goal is clarity of communication. In this communication style nonverbal communication is important, but the verbal or written message is even more important.

Scenario: You find the room cold and would like someone to turn the temperature up. If you are a low-context communicator, you might say something like, "It's getting cold in here. Could you please turn up the heat?"

High-context communication (high reliance on cues from the context)

In contrast, people from cultures using high-context communication pay a lot of attention to the situation, the environment, and the people with whom they are communicating. Things don't have to be spelled out as much as they are in low-context cultures. You don't have to worry so much about explaining everything since people will have a good understanding just from the context. Perhaps you can think of it as communicating with your family members or friends who know you well; in these situations, you don't have to say as much to get your ideas across. In addition, nonverbal cues are much more important for conveying meaning in high-context cultures.

Scenario: You find the room cold and would like someone to turn the temperature up. If you are a high-context communicator, you might wrap your arms around yourself and vigorously rub your upper arms as a way of communicating that you are cold and trying to warm yourself up. You might also say something along the lines of, "Brrrrr. It's a bit chilly in here, isn't it?" The goal of these messages would be that someone take in this information and understand this to be an indirect request to turn up the heat.

When high meets low and vice versa

What happens if you are a low-context communicator and you go into a high-context culture or environment? It might be difficult for you to know what's going on. Let's look at this scenario using an example of a family being a high-context culture. You have had a bad day, and you come home to your family or roommate. How long does it take for them to figure out you've had a bad day? Only a few seconds! They know how to read the cues from how you say hello, shut the door, or simply how you look without your saying a thing. But what if someone who does not know you well is there? It will take that person awhile to figure the clues out. The advantage for low-context communicators is that they often are skilled at asking questions to try to gain more information, and they are very good at processing a great deal of verbal or written information. The challenge is that they may not always know how to read the environment to pick the best time to ask questions.

What happens if someone who is a high-context communicator goes into a low-context culture or environment? This person knows how to read nonverbals in his or her own environment, but how about in the new one? Quite often high-context communicators who are out of their environment feel overloaded with communication cues and may simply shut down in a new environment. Eventually, the skills that high-context communicators have for reading the environment and people will serve as an advantage for sorting out when it is appropriate to ask questions in order to clarify what is happening around them. It is also possible that high-context communicators will feel that they are being treated like children when they are in a low-context environment where everything is so overtly spelled out.

ACTIVITY: Identifying low- and high-context communication

If you are coming from the U.S., chances are you are either a low-context communicator or you are very familiar with this environment. Knowing how to distinguish between high- and low-context messages can therefore help you learn how to "read between the lines"—a skill of high-context communicators. This exercise will help you become more familiar with the differences between low- and high-context communication. For the following 10 statements, decide whether the communication is low context or high context, and then circle the statements that exemplify your own communication style.

L = low context
H = high context

1. A friend emails you about going to a party and you reply, "Things are busy with my exams, but I would like to go." You know that you won't be going and you trust your friend knows this from the email. **Answer:** ______
2. Your professor asks, "Do you have time to meet after class?" You interpret this to be a request to come after class, rather than a question about whether or not you are available. **Answer:** ______
3. Your professor asks, "Do you have time to meet after class?" You interpret this to be a question, and you respond yes or no based on whether or not you are available. **Answer:** ______
4. When you disagree with someone, you use questions to suggest that you have a different opinion. **Answer:** ______
5. You feel good when you are honest with your co-workers and tell them that you are upset about something they did. **Answer:** ______
6. You feel it is all right to say "I disagree" to your professor in class. **Answer:** ______
7. If you have a problem with someone, you won't go to them and say that you are upset. Rather, you will ask another friend to help work out the problem. **Answer:** ______
8. If you want something, you feel it's best to come out and ask for it. **Answer:** ______
9. You feel that hinting at something is an effective way of getting what you want. **Answer:** ______
10. In a job interview, you begin by summarizing the accomplishments on your resumé. **Answer:** ______

Answers

1. You are relying on your friend's knowledge of how serious the exams are to understand that you will not be going. You have been polite because you expressed that you would like to go. A more explicit statement of "No, I won't be going" is not necessary and may be considered rude. **Answer: H**
2. You pay more attention to the status of the person communicating than the actual message itself. In this case, even though the professor asked whether or not you have time, the question is treated as a request to stay after class. How you respond will be influenced by several things, including the extent to which hierarchy matters in the culture and to you, the perceived consequences

for denying a request, your availability, and how others might understand you changing your plans to meet with the professor. **Answer: H**

3. This situation is the reverse of #2 in that the focus is on the words (the question) the professor asked. Although his status may influence your response, it does not lead to a different interpretation of the words used. If you are not available, your response may take the professor's status into account by being more formal or polite and requesting to meet soon, but at another time. **Answer: L**
4. At times it's best to save face (your own and others involved) and be vague so that you do not embarrass others by contradicting them publicly or privately. Questions are used to explore a topic further (even when a firm opinion is held). However, as the topic continues to be discussed, clues are given to help the listener understand that you hold an opposing view. **Answer: H**
5. While it may be hard to hear or say, great value is placed on being open and truthful with others. **Answer: L**
6. Learning is deemed to take place, at least in part, through conversation and dialogue with fellow students and with professors. A debate approach in which ideas are presented and openly critiqued is valued and practiced throughout one's education in high school and college. **Answer: L**
7. Use of intermediaries or go-betweens is common and can be a signal that you care a great deal about those involved in the situation because you made the effort to involve others. **Answer: H**
8. The question "How will they know if you don't tell them?" emphasizes that it is the speaker's responsibility to request what he or she wants and not the listener's job to figure it out. **Answer: L**
9. The listener is given credit for being able to figure out what you may need. There's no need to be forceful or self-absorbed when asking for something. **Answer: H**
10. "Selling yourself" is viewed as the purpose of the interview, and it is up to the interviewee to make sure that all accomplishments are discussed that are relevant to the new job. It is not viewed as demeaning (as it might be in high-context cultures) to repeat in the interview what has already been presented on a resumé. **Answer: L**

Reflection questions

- Did you circle the statements that seem to match your style? How many high-context responses did you circle? Low-context responses?
- Can you think of situations where you have misunderstood someone due to a difference in high- and low-context communication?
- In your host culture, do you think there is more emphasis on high-context or low-context communication? Based on your response to the first reflection question, how might you need to adapt your own approach to better understand the host culture? For example, if you are studying in a higher context culture, what kinds of things have more emphasis than you are used to? The status of the people talking, their age, their experience? What kinds of communication are considered unnecessary? Repetition? Asking small talk questions?

Specific Communication Styles

In addition to high- and low-context communication, research and experience have uncovered other varieties of communication behaviors: direct/indirect, linear/circular, detached/attached, and idea-oriented/relationship-oriented.

ACTIVITY: Contrasting your communication styles

Below, eight communication styles are grouped into pairs, each of which represents the end points of a continuum. Between each pair on the line, mark an X to indicate your personal communication style. On the second line place another X for how people generally communicate in your host country. Then, if you wish, indicate on the third line how people in general communicate in your home country. Remember, we are asking you to state generalizations, not stereotypes. Use your interactions with people in the host country as the basis for evaluation or ask a cultural informant.

Situation 1: You are cold in your apartment. You sent your landlord an email and she has not replied. On your way out of the apartment the next day, you see your landlord. What do you say?		
Direct Communication *Communication is done using explicit verbal statements and represents exactly what the speaker means. There is very little 'beating around the bush' here.* Possible response: "I emailed you about the heat and I did not hear back. It's too cold in the apartment and I need you to do something about this right away."		
Indirect Communication *Meaning is communicated using indirect means, such as suggestions, body language, or pauses. This style often uses other people to resolve conflicts in lieu of direct contact.* Possible response: "Did you get the email I sent you yesterday?"		
You	direct ————————————————	indirect
Host Country	direct ————————————————	indirect
Home Country	direct ————————————————	indirect

Situation 2: Your roommate asks, "How was your exam today?"
Linear Communication *This style is similar to direct communication as it gets to the point without going off on tangents. The communication progresses systematically along a straight line until the point is made. As such it is considered faster and more economical to those who use it.* Possible response: "Pretty good. The professor had told us about the main areas to study, so I was pretty prepared. I had a hard time with the last question, but I think overall that I did just fine. Might even have aced it!"

Circular Communication		
In circular communication, the person rarely states the point directly. Instead, a discussion proceeds in a roundabout way and incorporates many details until the point is reached. This way of communicating is similar to how stories are told. Possible response: "The tests tell you a lot about the person giving them. This professor is quite interesting. She seems to have a philosophy that tests should be mostly transparent. The last question was challenging. She had taken time in class last week—a whole week to prepare—and had told us what to expect on the test. Yet she kept that one trick up her sleeve on that last question."		
You	linear ———————————— circular	
Host Country	linear ———————————— circular	
Home Country	linear ———————————— circular	

CULTURE: *In-Country*

Situation 3: You are really angry that your friend went ahead and booked a weekend trip without including you.	
Detached Communication *In detached communication, issues are discussed with calmness and objectivity. Emotion is kept at a minimum, and objectivity is preferred over subjectivity. People who use detached communication think that they are being rational and fair.* Possible response: You know that you are mad, and you pick up the phone to call your friend; however, you decide to put the phone down and wait awhile to call. You don't want to say anything you might regret later on.	
Attached Communication *This communication style is characterized by a high level of emotion. People communicating this way think that they are showing sincerity or personal concern for the topic and the person with whom they are interacting.* Possible response: You call your friend right away. You don't want to wait too long, otherwise your emotions will dissipate and your friend will not understand that your feelings have been hurt.	
You	detached ———————————— attached
Host Country	detached ———————————— attached
Home Country	detached ———————————— attached

Situation 4: A faculty member has asked you to give a one-hour presentation to his class about your culture. You take a long time to prepare the presentation. The day before, the professor tells you that you have just 10 minutes for the talk. You are really frustrated.		
Idea-Oriented Communication *In this form of communication, disagreement with ideas is stated directly, with the assumption that only the idea, not the person from whom the idea came, is being attacked. Responses such as 'No offense, but I don't agree with you,' or 'We'll have to agree to disagree' are indicative of this style.* Possible response: "I don't understand—you stated it would be an hour. I don't see how I can cut this down to 10 minutes. With all due respect, this seems very unfair. I would not have agreed to 10 minutes."		
Relationship-Oriented Communication *In this communication style, disagreeing with an idea is viewed as being the same as disagreeing with the person who originated it. Intellectual disagreement in particular is handled more subtly and indirectly. This communication style emphasizes interpersonal harmony and strives to maintain relationships between people.* Possible response: "Is there another time I could speak for one hour? If not, is there something I could cut out to make this a shorter presentation? Do you have some flexibility with the time—could there be 30 minutes?"		
You	idea ————————————————	relationship
Host Country	idea ————————————————	relationship
Home Country	idea ————————————————	relationship

(Communication style categories adapted from Bennett, Bennett, and Allen, 1999.)

Reflection questions

- Did you see any patterns in your responses? Many of these styles can be said to support one another. For example, a direct communication style could support a linear style, as both can have a preference for getting to the point quickly. (However, it's also possible to be linear and to take a long time to get to the final point.) Also, an attached communication style can often coincide with a relationship-oriented style since both emphasize paying attention to the feelings of others.
- Do your answers change based on the situation you are in? Go back to the diagram and make notes about situations where you might tend to use the opposite style of what you marked here.
- In which styles are you and your target culture most alike? In which are you most different? Will you need to modify your communication style to be more effective in the host culture?

IN-COUNTRY CULTURE STRATEGIES PART VII: NONVERBAL COMMUNICATION

A smile, a simple wave, an affirmative head nod, the universal sign for 'check please'—all are examples of gestures that I took for granted before my study abroad experience. Because the motions we use in the States are inherent to me and come automatically, it had not occurred to me that there would be such a difference in the gestures that are used between countries. This was one thing I did not learn much about before my study in France.

One example that came up during my stay in Paris shows the frustration that can develop due to miscommunication because of incorrect gestures. One day I was having a discussion with a native French speaker, so I was trying to take great care with choosing my words since I knew he would be able to pick up my mistakes very quickly. As the discussion continued, it grew into an argument. I was arguing my point and trying to clearly explain my position in French when I slapped the palm of my hand for emphasis on a point. Since I was by no means done talking I continued. Once again, I slapped my hand while debating.

The second time I made this gesture my friend started laughing at me—something you don't want to happen when you're arguing in a foreign language! I started to think, 'What did I say? Am I making no sense?' So I asked him, 'What?! Why are you laughing?' He explained to me that in France when someone slaps their hand as I had done, it means that the conversation is over. He was amused that I had, by his standards, terminated the conversation twice, yet I kept on talking. ~ Tammi Brusegaard, France

Obviously, there is more to communicating than just the words you use. How you say something or what your body or face is doing when you say it has meaning, too, and that meaning of course is very dependent on culture. The language strategies section on speaking later in this guide will discuss intonation and the notion that how words are stressed can significantly alter the meaning of what is being said. For example, the nuance of "Is THIS your bag?" is much different from "Is this YOUR bag?"

Similarly, there is in every culture a whole realm of nonverbal communication that consists of things we aren't usually conscious of such as gestures, eye contact, physical distance between people, facial expressions, and touching behavior. As Tammi found out in France, other cultures will often have very different meanings for these nonverbal behaviors from what you are used to.

Communicating Nonverbally

Nonverbal communication is often not discussed in the language classroom, but it is an important aspect of intercultural communication nevertheless. Most of us, if we have not been abroad, will not be very aware of the various ways we gesture with our hands, and we take our facial expressions for granted. Various studies of facial expression have shown that many cultures around the world have similar ways of expressing emotions such as anger, sadness, and joy. But they also show that the same expression can have more than one meaning; for example, in some cultures a smile can mean the person is embarrassed. In addition, the extent to which facial expressions are used varies across cultures. The Japanese, for example, tend to display much less facial expression than people in the U.S. or Latin America.

Most students who go abroad are not going to be aware of all the nonverbal language of the host culture before they get there. The longer you are in the host country, the more naturally you will be able to use the nonverbal behaviors that are appropriate for various situations.

You can use two basic strategies for picking up the nonverbals more rapidly: ***observation*** and ***practice***.

- **Observe:** Make a conscious effort to watch carefully how people communicate with each other nonverbally. How close do they stand to each other? Do they maintain direct eye contact? Is there a lot of vigorous gesturing when they are speaking? What gestures do they use? Make note of whether these patterns change between friends versus casual acquaintances.
- **Practice:** Make attempts to perform the nonverbal behavior with groups of host nationals you feel comfortable with and who will let you know tactfully whether you are doing the behavior appropriately.

Both of the above strategies require spending a great deal of time with people in your host country. The second strategy, while very important, may be more difficult than the first. Much of the difficulty of nonverbals is that, even if they are learned and understood, actually performing them may seem unnatural or uncomfortable to you.

Despite these hurdles, making attempts at using the appropriate nonverbals will be appreciated by people with whom you interact. For example, a student in Japan who does not know to bow slightly when greeting someone of higher status will come off as disrespectful. If you stand too far apart or refuse to touch casually in many Latin American countries, the hosts might think you are cold and unfriendly. To engage in these nonverbals properly demonstrates your sensitivity to the other culture, as well as your willingness to adapt.

ACTIVITY: Observing gestures and understanding their meanings

These five gestures are common in many countries throughout the world. This exercise is designed to give you some practice at recognizing nonverbal behavior in both your home and host cultures and to become aware of where the differences lie. It should also help you make interpretations based upon your own observations in the host country. You are asked to interpret the meaning of these gestures based upon how most Americans perceive them and how you think they might be perceived in your host country. Refer to p. 136 for suggested answers and explanations.

A.	What might this gesture mean to most people in the U.S.?
	What could this gesture mean in your host country?
B.	What might this gesture mean to most people in the U.S.?
	What could this gesture mean in your host country?
C.	What might this gesture mean to most people in the U.S.?
	What could this gesture mean in your host country?
D.	What might this gesture mean to most people in the U.S.?
	What could this gesture mean in your host country?
E.	What might this gesture mean to most people in the U.S.?
	What could this gesture mean in your host country?

(Excerpted from Morris, 1994.)

Suggested answers

A. Although in the U.S. this is typically the sign for "OK," it doesn't mean the same thing in most other countries. In Japan this is the sign for money. In Belgium and France it is interpreted as "zero." In Greece, Russia, and other countries, it could be considered a sexual insult.
B. Most U.S. Americans might interpret this gesture as someone praying or begging, as in "I implore you." However, this is a common greeting in India and Thailand and also means "thank you" in many parts of Asia.
C. To many U.S. Americans this might mean "I don't know," even without the shrug of the shoulders that sometimes accompanies this gesture. In other areas, such as the Middle East and in South America, it is more clearly a sign of trying to show one's sincerity, as in "I swear."
D. This sign, which for most U.S. Americans means "all right!" or "good job!" does have similar meanings in many other countries. But in Japan, it is used either to indicate the male gender or the number five.
E. Probably all U.S. Americans have crossed their fingers for good luck at one time. In many Christian countries this has a similar meaning, but this sign is even more commonly interpreted to mean "friendship," except in Italy and Turkey, where it could be understood as "a threat to end friendship."

Note: Age or generation can impact the nonverbals used. As one student who went to Costa Rica reminded us:

> *My professor, who is about 60 years old, explained to the class that holding up your middle finger is not offensive and can be used to point at something. However, some friends I have met here who are my age told me that it has the same meaning as in the U.S. and is offensive.*

Summary

The above examples were intended to help you think about the nonverbals used in different cultures. The longer you are in your host country and the more you observe, the more you will learn about nonverbal communication in that culture.

Three Important Forms of Nonverbal Communication

Even if you are familiar with many of the physical gestures of your host culture, there is more to nonverbal communication. Gestures are the more obvious form of nonverbal communication. Learning them is important, but they are not the only nonverbals to be aware of. We will now look at three other forms of nonverbal communication that exist but are different in every culture: eye contact, physical space, and touching norms. Many people may not realize these behaviors actually differ from culture to culture and will not make attempts to modify their own behaviors or to adopt those appropriate to the host culture.

As you read through the following nonverbal trouble spots, note your own preference for the behaviors covered. Take time to jot down how common the behavior is in your host country and for which contexts.

Eye Contact

In the U.S., particularly in the business culture, direct eye contact is standard procedure. While eye contact can imply sincerity and honesty in other cultures just as it does in the U.S., in many Asian countries, including Japan, looking straight into someone's eyes could be considered intimidating or a sign of aggression. The degree of eye contact can also sometimes be based on gender, status, age, and other personal characteristics. In some cultures, direct eye contact is permissible for members of the same sex but not proper when communicating with the opposite sex.

ACTIVITY: Eye contact survey

Think about how much eye contact you generally prefer and then consider the different situations listed below. For each situation indicate if you would use ***direct***, ***casual***, ***indirect***, ***peripheral*** (sideways glances), or ***none***. Then find out the same information for your host country.

Situation	How much eye contact do you prefer?	What is the preferred form of eye contact in your host country?
1. Chatting with friends		
2. Talking with a professor		
3. Interviewing for a job		
4. Giving a presentation		
5. Placing an order with a waiter		
6. Talking to your father		

Did you discover many differences between you and the host country? In which situations are they most pronounced?

Sense of Personal Distance/Space

The concept of our own space, or the space between ourselves and others, is another important factor in intercultural communication. Standing too close to people with whom you're interacting may make them uncomfortable, while standing too far away may give the impression that you're cold and unapproachable. Although people have their personal preferences, there is also a cultural basis for the appropriate amount of personal space. People from Arab cultures, for example, tend to stand very close to each other when they are talking, while the amount of personal space given to one's communication partner is much greater in both the U.S. and Japan.

ACTIVITY: Personal distance survey

Think about how much personal distance you generally prefer and then consider the different situations listed below. For each situation indicate whether you would prefer to keep the ***normal*** amount of distance, ***greater than normal***, or ***less than normal***. Then find out the same information for your host country.

Situation	How much personal distance do you prefer?	How much personal distance would be considered normal in your host country?
1. Chatting with friends		
2. Talking with a professor		
3. Interviewing for a job		
4. Giving a presentation		
5. Placing an order with a waiter		
6. Talking to your father		

Did you discover many differences between you and the host country? In which situations are they most pronounced?

Touching

As with personal distance, the degree to which people use touch to communicate varies greatly from culture to culture. Even in the United States there are differences based upon ethnicity and cultural background. In many collectivist cultures like India and Thailand, it is considered natural for people of the same sex to touch each other publicly, so you will often see men with their arms around each other or holding hands. But in many other countries, physical contact with someone of the opposite sex is considered inappropriate and carries a sexual connotation.

ACTIVITY: Touching behavior survey

Think about how much touching behavior is appropriate in your culture, under what circumstances, and with whom. Then consider the different situations mentioned below. For each situation indicate whether some kind of touching would be appropriate. Then find out the same information for your host country.

Situation	Is touching appropriate in the following situations?	Is touching appropriate in these situations in your host country?
1. Chatting with friends		
2. Talking with a professor		
3. Meeting with your boss		
4. Speaking to a child		
5. Talking to your father		

Did you discover many differences between you and the host country? In which situations are they most pronounced?

One of the best ways to learn what touching is appropriate for a certain culture is to observe how people greet each other. Do they hug or kiss? How many times? In France, people who are close kiss each cheek twice. In Latin America, hugging and sometimes kissing are more common. A handshake is more common in Germany and northern Europe. In Japan, touching or other public displays of affection, even among close acquaintances, are generally not very common.

ACTIVITY: Nonverbals used in host country greetings

Try to figure out the most common nonverbals, including touching, for the following situations. You may have more than one answer. Ask someone from the culture if you're not sure of the answer.

Type of encounter	Common type(s) of nonverbal greeting in the host country
Meeting someone of the same age and sex for the first time	
A man greeting his wife at home	
Two professional women meeting for lunch	
Two adult male friends meeting at a bar	
A brother greeting his sister at the airport	
A child greeting his father as he arrives home from work	
A young woman meeting her boyfriend in the park	
Two women seeing each other at a high school reunion	

Was there a lot of variation in the types of possible greetings based on age, gender, or relationship? What differences do you notice in how people greet each other in the U.S. and in the host country? When you greet someone in the same situation, what do you tend to do?

Pauses and Silence in Communication

Pauses and silence in communication are nonverbal patterns that people take for granted and rarely think about. The role that silence has in communication is not often discussed even when learning a foreign language. Research has shown, however, that different languages have very different patterns and meanings associated with silence and pauses. Even in English these differences are widely apparent, whether the person speaking is from Australia, India, or the southern region of the United States.

In general, U.S. Americans don't have a lot of tolerance for lengthy periods of time during which not much is said. Silence is more often than not considered uncomfortable in the U.S. and should be avoided at all costs. Try it out sometime by pausing in the middle of a conversation, particularly when you are in a group situation, and watch how long it takes before someone else says something. It will rarely be more than a couple of seconds when U.S. Americans are speaking.

In many cultures there is a much higher regard for silence in communicative encounters. The saying, "Those who know do not speak; those who speak do not know," is actually a second-century Chinese proverb by which many Asian cultures abide. In these cultures, what is not said is regarded as important, and lulls in conversation are considered restful, friendly, a time for reflection, and appropriate. For those of you going to such cultures, your challenge will be learning to balance verbal expression with silence.

> *A survey of 3,600 Japanese people's attitudes toward speaking obtained data indicating that 82 percent of them agreed with the saying, 'Out of the mouth comes all evil.' ~ 'Skills in Self-Expression,' Inagaki, 1985*

ACTIVITY: Journaling—making sense out of nonverbal communication

Previously in this guide, you covered materials on participant observation and journaling. Now it's time to practice these skills by observing how people communicate nonverbally with each other in your host country. Select any setting, such as a coffee shop, where you can safely and unobtrusively observe a small group of two or three people. Focus on how they communicate with each other nonverbally rather than only verbally. Use the following questions as a guide and then make entries in your journal using the instructions below.

- Is there a lot of gesturing? What sort of gestures are used? Who makes them?
- Is there eye contact? Is it frequent or infrequent? About how often do people make eye contact?
- Is there touching? In what contexts and how often?
- How much time elapses between when one speaker stops and the other begins?
- How do people show pleasure/agreement versus displeasure/ disagreement?

CULTURE: *In-Country*

Journaling questions

- What is the setting?____________________________
- Who are the speakers (male, female, approximate age)? What can you know or guess about them (e.g., they look like students, businesspersons)?

  Speaker #1:__________________________________

  Speaker #2:__________________________________

  Speaker #3:__________________________________
- Use the chart below to record your observations of their nonverbal behaviors. Watch for gestures, eye contact, physical space, touching, pauses/silence, and paralanguage (tone, pitch, loudness, etc.). One way to organize your observations is to look for patterns or recurring behaviors.

Description of nonverbal behavior	Interpretation

After completing the observation part of this activity, check your interpretations with someone from the host culture.

Additional suggestions for this activity:

- Try this same exercise again at another location with a different group than the first time and see if you notice some commonalities or new patterns in how people communicate.
- Try this activity with another study abroad student and compare the results of your observations.
- Try this in a situation where you can also hear what the people are saying and then make notes on things you noticed about verbal and nonverbal communication together. For example, you can observe what people say and do when they greet each other.

Summary

The last two chapters were intended to give you some insight into the world of intercultural communication, where culture, language, and behaviors combine to affect how we interact with each other. Hopefully you have developed an appreciation for communicating cross-culturally and have learned some of the cues to pick up when interacting with others who are culturally different from you.

IN-COUNTRY CULTURE STRATEGIES PART VIII:
PREPARING TO RETURN HOME

During the final days in your new country, the last thing on your mind might be taking time to think about "home." These next few pages invite you to do just that—because it can make a world of difference in your entire experience!

> *I had two very different study abroad experiences and two very different departures for home. The first was in England. My host family had decided to go on a family vacation right at the end of my stay. Since they were not going to be at home for my last days in the country, they took me out for dinner at an Indian restaurant. I can still picture my host mom pleading with her husband Ron not to eat so many hot peppers. After they left, I finished final papers and exams. The last hours were a whirlwind—I was leaving England with just barely enough time to make it home for Christmas. I ran from monument to monument, shop to shop, grabbing mementos to bring home. I stayed up so late the night before I left that with just two hours of sleep, I did not hear my alarm. The taxicab driver luckily pounded on the door, and I finally awoke. I left England in a blur, panicking about catching my flight. When I left Malaysia I was a bit wiser. I walked to my favorite places and sat and absorbed the sights, smells, and sounds of that amazing country. I spent an evening with my Malaysian friends having a relaxing dinner and talking about the past few months. I felt I was just getting to understand this tropical place of contradictions. Even though I was not ready, I left in peace, having said my goodbyes, promising myself and others to return. I have traveled some since these adventures, but interestingly enough—despite my convictions—I have never returned to these places. This is OK, too, as I knew that saying 'I'll be back' was not a replacement for 'goodbye.' ~ Barbara Kappler, England and Malaysia*

CULTURE: *In-Country*

ACTIVITY: Leaving the country

You are near the end of your study abroad experience. Undoubtedly, you are feeling a range of emotions: regret, bewilderment at where the time went, excitement about seeing family and friends, numbness, concern about what's next, satisfaction about all you have seen and enjoyed, and even a sense of loss. We encourage you to take a moment to record how you feel about leaving your host country:

Acknowledging your range of emotions can help you prepare for saying goodbye to the country, your friends, and the experiences you have come to love (or not) in this new, but temporary, home of yours.

Now think back to Barbara's two very different stories of leaving England and Malaysia. What is your ideal way of leaving your new country? You may need to plan carefully, as the days before departure can easily become a blur of activity, leaving you little time enjoy one last crêpe, lager, or look at the Rhine. Take a minute to record the things you want to experience before departing:

I plan to come back, so I don't really need to say goodbye....

> *Make sure you tell students who read this guide to say their goodbyes.*
> *~ Sarah Sonday, Spain*

Many people do return to the countries where they studied abroad. But life's unexpected twists and turns lead others, no matter their intentions, to either remain in the U.S. or to explore new destinations. We don't say this to discourage you; we say this because we don't want you to leave the country with a fantasy that you will return and do the things you did not get a chance to do this time. If it's important, do it this time. If that's not realistic due to lack of time or money, still make sure you say your goodbyes in a way you can live with…possibly for the rest of your life.

What's ahead

> *I came back from 4-1/2 months in Mexico and was immediately thrown into a whirlwind of visits with every relative I had ever known as I had missed Christmas at home to experience it in Queretaro. The following week I moved to a new dormitory as school started again. The week after that I moved, again, into an apartment. Life was back to 'normal.' What I wouldn't give to have time to myself to reflect—and breathe! ~ Julie Chi, Mexico*

ACTIVITY: A thoughtful return

Some of you may experience exactly what Julie did. It's the reality of the fast-paced world in which we live. Since time upon re-entry may be scarce, we encourage you to record here or in your journal your thoughts on these questions to prepare you for returning home:

1. In what ways have I changed?

2. In what ways might my friends and family have changed?

3. How would I like my family and friends to treat me when I return home?

4. What am I looking forward to the most? The least?

5. What are the lessons I have learned that I never want to forget?

6. What are some skills I have learned?

7. Many say that re-entry shock is more challenging than initial culture shock. What are some things I might do to make the transition easier? (See the next section for suggestions from other students.)

8. What have been the important things about this study abroad experience that I want to share with family and friends?

9. What do I want to do with the experiences I've had (e.g., continue studying the language)?

Coming home is for many much more of a challenge than going to a foreign culture. Students need to be aware of this. I don't think it is emphasized as much as the culture shock going over, and I think it should be, at least as much if not more so. This is where it all falls into place, or begins to. My suggestion? Keep writing a journal—a lot of reflection is necessary to truly get the most out of it all. ~ A. J. Fleming, Spain

POST-STUDY ABROAD CULTURE STRATEGIES:
CONTINUE THE LEARNING

If I had culture shock while I was in England, it passed quickly. The same is not true with returning to the U.S.A. There were many things I had to get used to again, like going back to my university and finding a job. However, after six months of being home, I see something now that I cannot get used to —American politics and business. ~ Seth Lengkeek, England

I remember getting off the plane after three months in Malaysia. My family took me to a Mexican restaurant for a long-awaited margarita and a salad. I spent the next four days on the couch. My parents, worried I had contracted some tropical disease, called the doctor in my small town for a house visit. He suggested my parents call the restaurant and find out if food poisoning had been reported. Sure enough, my worst case of illness on this adventure happened after safely returning home. My mom, delivering the news, said, 'Welcome home. Aren't you glad you are sick here and not thousands of miles away?' The irony was that coming home was what made me sick. Yeah, I was glad to be on her couch, but where I really wanted to be was in Kuala Lumpur. I was not delirious enough to tell my mother this. ~ Barbara Kappler, Malaysia

Coming home isn't easy. For some, the return is more difficult than adjusting to the host culture. How could this be? Isn't home what you know best?

Culture shock is the expected confrontation with the unfamiliar; re-entry shock is the unexpected confrontation with the familiar. ~ R. Michael Paige, co-author

"Home" can have a difficult time competing with the thrill—even in its darkest moments—of the continual adventure and discovery of self in the world of study abroad. As returned student Seth Lengkeek said, "When talking about re-entry, a good subject to discuss is boredom. I found that I had the hardest time dealing with being home when I was bored."

Moreover, having seen new parts of the world, you have undoubtedly changed. That means that re-entry should not be a time simply for getting back into the swing of things. Instead, re-entry is really the time to maximize your study abroad experience. You did not go there to stay. You went knowing you would come home. This chapter is intended to help you make your re-entry experience meaningful in the long term.

You may not want to do this chapter in a linear fashion, so here are topics to choose from:

Dealing with the Emotional Challenges of Study Abroad

When I first came home my parents had a surprise welcome home party for me and invited all my friends. Some of my friends asked the customary 'How was Spain?' and didn't ask anything else. They really didn't care…or at least that's how I felt. I noticed that many of my friends I no longer have a relationship with because I feel like I can't relate to them and they can't relate to me. We both changed in different directions while I was gone.
~ Sarah Sonday, Spain

I have found when I've returned from working and studying abroad that each time my family and friends wanted to know how it was, but what they wanted was a bunch of short and funny stories about my experience. I needed time to process my thoughts and feelings about such rich experiences because I came back with lots of contradictory thoughts about my time abroad. When I wasn't able to give my family and friends the short 'sound bite' they seemed to want, they stopped asking questions, and I didn't tell them very much at all about my experiences. It was something that I could only share with others who had also studied abroad and understood the complexity of an experience in a different culture. ~ Karin Larson, studied abroad in France, worked in Taiwan and Indonesia, and interned in Malaysia

ACTIVITY: Reacting to the changes

Returning to one's home environment isn't easy for a number of reasons, including how much you have changed, how much you understand these changes, and how much your friends and family accept these changes. It's important to take time to consider what your particular frustrations are. Either in this guide or in a separate journal, record your reactions to the following statements.

1. I know that I have changed as a result of my experience because…

2. My friends do seem to understand ____________________ about me, but they don't understand…

3. My re-entry experience would be better if…

4. Now that I am home, I worry most about...

5. The one thing I know I have learned about myself is...

6. I wish I could explain to my family and friends that...

While your home may have remained fairly unchanged in your absence, it's possible that there have been some significant changes—a move, a divorce in the family, or a change to a new university. If you have changed and home has changed, it's almost like you need to learn how to dance together again. Will you vary the music to adapt to the new rhythms of your life or play the same tune?

Several returnees collaborated to develop the following chart of common emotional challenges encountered upon re-entry and possible strategies to cope with these challenges.

Read through these entries and remember—you are not alone. Many study abroad returnees experience the same challenges.

Challenges	Strategies to help you deal with re-entry
Friends and family at home don't seem interested in hearing about aspects of your experience that you feel are important.	• Realize they may be adjusting to changes in you. Allow some time for this adjustment. • Plan a special time for you to share photos, souvenirs, or food from your experience. • Don't assume the opportunity for meaningful conversation will happen—make room for it to take place. Without a comparable experience, your family and friends may have difficulty understanding the depth of your stories. Be patient with them. • Write down your thoughts and feelings. It will help you to process them even if you can't talk about them. • Seek out others with similar experiences. • Give presentations to community organizations. Write an article for your local or school newspaper. Be active!
Friends and family may treat you as the same person you were before leaving. You want your relationship to change as a result of your changes.	• Your family and friends may be feeling uncertain about how you have changed. Discuss your feelings about yourself and others with them. • Encourage positive changes in old relationships. Don't expect your friends to suggest seeing a new international film—especially if they never did before. Take the initiative and invite them. • Seek out relationships with people who are compatible with the new you.
You may be anxious about your academic situation because the subjects you enjoyed studying abroad, including language, appear to have little relevance at home. You might also be confused about your educational future and career plans in light of new or uncertain goals and priorities.	• Take advantage of the wide range of educational opportunities available to you by finding informal and nonacademic ways to continue the study of your favorite subjects. • Take time to consider educational and career plans that include your new areas of interest. • Seek out the advice of your counselors and mentors.
If you find that your attitudes and opinions have changed considerably during your stay abroad and are not widely shared in your home community, you may feel highly critical of your home country because you have new perspectives on it. Others might be critical of your "negative attitude."	• Try to keep your feelings in perspective; remember that your opinions and ideas may initially be greatly influenced by the host culture and may not represent your final balanced viewpoint. • Share your feelings with others but carefully choose situations in which to bring up controversial issues. • Continue to foster your ability to look at the world critically by reading and seeking out a diverse range of information, rather than falling into the trap of just thinking of things (politics in particular) negatively.
You may become frustrated because people at home are uninterested in other peoples and cultures. Faced with this lack of concern, you might feel there aren't ways for you to take an active role in helping solve the problems of the world community.	• Attempt to generate local interest in other peoples and their concerns. • Use your special status as an intercultural traveler to educate others through private conversations or by public speeches and presentations. • Look at problems in your own community now that you have a new perspective. Become a change agent.

(Adapted from Kappler and Nokken, 1999.)

Examining What You Have Learned While Abroad

Seeing the U.S. and the world in a new light

> *I took a class on international management with a Canadian professor. A few of us were joking that when we were overseas and ran into people who did not have a favorable attitude toward U.S. Americans, we would pretend to be Canadians. One even sewed a Canadian flag on her backpack. My instructor's response completely amazed me. He said, 'Why do people have allegiances to countries? The concept of nation-status is an outdated mode.' Years later, I understand the comment. I married someone from another country. It was frightening to have the governments be involved and to have a say in the sanctity of the marriage and in where we might live. I never forgot the Canadian professor's comment. I don't have an alternative, but I now feel I understand this Canadian's view. ~ Barbara Kappler, co-author*

Barbara's comments aren't intended to fuel anti-American sentiment or to slander someone for taking pride in one's own country. Rather, the story's purpose is twofold:

1. To recognize that like many other study abroad students, you may return feeling more aware of U.S. dominance on the world political scene and feel overwhelmed and ashamed—even if you return appreciating toilet paper!
2. To acknowledge that studying abroad can result in challenges to core personal or societal beliefs. For example, before studying abroad, the following comments often make little impact. After, they may take on a whole new light:

> *If an extraterrestrial committee of experts in planetary management visited our Earth, they would not believe their eyes. 'You are insane!...You were given one of the most beautiful planets in the cosmos...and look what you have done with it: You have divided this planet into 160 separate territorial fragments without rhyme or reason—without geographic, ecological, human, or any other logic. All these fragments are sovereign; i.e., each of them considers itself more important than the planet and the rest of humanity.' ~ Robert Muller, former assistant secretary-general, United Nations*

In short, your view of the U.S. and the world may have changed. For some, this is the most profound experience of study abroad.

> *It's difficult to live overseas and then come back to this country. You carry within you a perpetual ache, a sense that we need to know more, to do more. ~ Jim Malarkey, world traveler*

Specifically reflecting on the impact of world events surrounding the attacks on the World Trade Center and Pentagon, Malarkey remarked:

> *If I think of myself as primarily an American, then I see the world a certain way. I become concerned about America's enemies. But if I think about myself as a world citizen, then I worry about different things. Then I become concerned about imbalances in the world and about how to fix those imbalances.*

In addition to struggling with notions of world imbalances, a returnee may face contradictions:

> *I thought very differently about the U.S. when I returned from Turkey. People seemed so concerned with things like shopping that seemed quite trivial to me. It was like 'Didn't they know there was poverty in the world? How could they consume so much?' And I was also very critical of my government's policies regarding other countries. In retrospect, it seems contradictory because many times when I was abroad I would curiously find myself defending my country's actions. The term 'contradiction' nicely summarizes the conflicting thoughts I had about many things. ~ R. Michael Paige, Turkey*

And finally, it's OK to appreciate the physical and mental comforts of life in the U.S.:

> *I would assume that many returnees come back appreciating much of what the U.S. has to offer. Just take the university setting—toilet paper in the bathrooms, large structures, good heating, ample seating, free daily newspaper, easily available computer terminals, and on and on. We could make a litany of all the wonders of the U.S. This is to counter the somewhat assumed position that things are far better abroad. ~ Andrew Cohen, co-author*

ACTIVITY: Seeing the U.S and the world in a new light

You have probably changed your views on a number of things since you came back. Many students have a new awareness of politics and the interpretations they get from the media of different countries and cultures. Some people feel either more highly critical of their own country or very grateful for the things that they enjoy in their own country—or both. To sort through your new perspectives, jot down a few ways in which your views have changed. Here are a few questions to get you thinking. Write your responses in the following chart:

1. What new experiences did you have while abroad that shocked or surprised you about the world?
2. How do you feel now about those experiences after returning home?
3. Are there certain stereotypes that you have let go of? Kept? Modified?

How my views of the world have changed	How my views of my own country and culture have changed

Understanding Yourself Differently

Positive gains

Re-entry is a transition and, like all transitions, has the potential for both pain and growth. Here is what returnees said about how they've grown from their experiences:

I now...

- have a new sense of autonomy. If I can figure out the subway in Paris, I can do anything! If I can enroll in a course in Spanish by myself, I can surely tackle my home institution's bureaucracy! If can travel around a tropical island myself and be in a place where I didn't understand all of the language around me, I can be comfortable and confident almost anywhere.
- feel more responsible about my lifestyle choices and their global consequences.
- feel more focused about my career interests.
- feel more self-confident.
- have more concern for international politics.
- have a greater awareness of other eating patterns.
- know that dating can mean different things, and I now know about different patterns of male/female relationships.
- have a genuine feeling of breaking the language barrier by studying a content subject (such as economics) in another language.
- am more in sync with the real world and the harsh reality of life (professors not showing up for class because of societal forces and events)—not the U.S. American "ivory tower" phenomenon.
- have a greater sense of what it is like to watch out for personal security.
- am less consumer-oriented.
- am more interested in social issues.
- know that I can hit emotional rock-bottom and come back up.
- feel connected to people across the world.
- have a new appreciation for the number of opportunities and material things that I enjoy at home and at the same time a keen awareness of how much more I have than people in other countries.
- have a greater sense of connection to family and friends (even if they don't always understand me and my new experiences).
- have a greater view of the possibilities in the world and in my life. It is like the doors and windows to many things were opened.
- feel like a "global citizen" and care more about what happens around the globe.
- am interested in a greater concept of justice and injustice as it is manifested differently in other countries.
- have a higher tolerance for ambiguity in situations. Now I can be in situations in which I don't understand all that is going on and still feel comfortable in trying to communicate.
- am able to suspend judgment about people and their actions because sometimes you just don't have all the cultural and language background that you need.
- have the ability to think more critically about political events and take a look at multiple sides of current issues.

Whew! That's quite a list. Which of the preceding statements describe you? Take a moment to write down ways you have changed as a result of your study abroad experience:

Possible outcomes of an international experience

This next section provides a handy list of skills and qualities you may have developed as a direct result of your experiences abroad. Use this to spark ideas for creating a resumé, preparing for an interview, and reflecting upon your experiences.

Skills

- Understand cultural differences and similarities
- Adapt to new environments
- Learn through listening and observing
- Establish rapport quickly
- Function with a high level of ambiguity
- Take initiative and risks
- Utilize time management skills
- Identify problems and utilize available resources to solve the problems
- Accept responsibility
- Communicate despite barriers
- Learn quickly
- Handle difficult situations
- Handle stress
- Manage and organize
- Lead others in formal and/or informal groups
- Conduct research despite language and cultural differences
- Cope with rejection

Qualities

- Self-reliance
- High energy level and enthusiasm
- Appreciation of diversity
- Perseverance
- Flexibility
- Open-mindedness
- Assertiveness
- Inquisitiveness
- Self-confidence
- Self-knowledge
- Independence

Identity challenges

As mentioned at the beginning of this section, the changes you go through while studying abroad don't always feel good. Change can be painful—even if it turns out to be rewarding in the long run.

> *Within four days of arriving back in the U.S. from my first study abroad experience, I turned around and drove 800 miles to spend the summer working as a lifeguard at a resort in the Rocky Mountains. As I crossed over the Iowa border, the song 'Convoy' came on the radio. I burst out crying—sobbing really. I remember driving by myself that day, listening to the radio with tears streaming down my face. 'This is so American,' I thought bitterly. It makes me laugh now—that a '70s pop song about truckers and smokeys and CB radios could have such an intense effect on me.*
>
> *Anyway, the whole idyllic summer that I imagined while I was in Greece turned out not to be like that—really charged and emotionally discordant. I didn't know anyone at the resort, and the other staff members from the U.S. all seemed really young and superficial to me. I had a hard time relating to them, so I spent a lot of time alone, taking hikes, and trying to understand why I was feeling so strange. Eventually I became friends with Liza, another lifeguard from Australia, and Stuart, a guy from England, both of whom were working at the resort on student visas. I think because they were also 'international,' I could relate to them on a level that I couldn't with the other staff members.*
>
> *I had heard of culture shock before I went abroad, but I didn't really understand how difficult it would be to return to the U.S. In Greece, my identity had been so thoroughly 'American,' and yet now that I was back in the U.S., I felt so un-American. I knew I hadn't become 'Greek,' but I certainly wasn't the same 'me.' Eventually the struggle abated, but the struggle didn't fit neatly on a curve or a timeline. And, to be honest, there really is no end result. As one of my Greek professors said to me, 'The only thing certain in life is change, and the more you can accept change in your life the happier you will be.' The more experiences I have, the more I realize how true that really is. ~ Suzanne Hay, Greece*

How can leaving home and coming back lead to such struggles? Exposure to different cultures—to different ways of behaving, of problem solving, and of perceiving the world—leads us to question beliefs and values that were once taken for granted. It is almost like trying to sort out two versions of you. This sorting out is a process. The first step in this process is to be aware of the changes that have occurred within you and to embrace your new "intercultural identity." Although this should be a liberating and developmental experience, it may also be accompanied by a sense of loss because you aren't exactly the same person you were when you left home.

Some who return to the U.S. after study abroad experiences sometimes no longer feel "American" in the same way they did when they first left the country. They also don't feel fully a part of the culture that they just experienced, either. In a way, they are emotionally in cultural limbo. This identity conflict can feel overwhelming, and words such as "insignificant," "lonely," "restless," and "agitated" have been used to describe this internal upset. These feelings are very normal, and the majority of students are able to come to terms with their conflicting identities. Students who continue to feel this way very intensely should seek help from counselors, friends, and family.

Some returning study abroad students come back with a strong sense of their own unique cultural identity. For example, instead of feeling like they need to be "American" or "French," they can just be themselves—a definite mixture of U.S. American and French beliefs, values, experiences, and language. People who are able to integrate their sometimes conflicting sets of experiences can develop a sense that they have found two places to call home.

> *The mark of a successful sojourner is not that he has finally come to appreciate fully the true meaning of home, or that he may have relinquished one home for another more suited to him, but that he has found two places 'where he can go out and in.' ~ Lewis and Jungmar, 1986*

You may feel in between these two "poles," and for a few months following your return you might experience a feeling of "cultural identity crisis." Indeed, you might feel like creating a new identity for yourself. Be patient and take time to reflect upon how you can incorporate all of your cultural identities into your own unique perspective on the world. For now, take a moment to reflect upon these questions:

- What values, beliefs, and behaviors have I learned from my host country that I want to try to maintain while back in the U.S.?

- In what ways might these values, beliefs, and behaviors conflict with U.S. culture?

- How can I find support for these new values?

> *Keep a journal still. It is a full circle experience—and helps to develop a more thorough experience. ~ Joy Wildermuth, France*

Appreciating Different Styles of Successful Re-entry

Active re-entry

When I came back from Italy I knew the transition back into my former life would be hard, but I decided that it would be better to be proactive rather than get overwhelmed. Everything that had seemed so familiar before was suddenly completely foreign. But my experience didn't just cause a feeling of alienation; it completely changed me and inspired me. When I got back, I chose activities to participate in that resounded with all that I had now become.

I gave private Italian lessons, taught a community education course in Italian (I just called and asked if they needed any Italian teachers—they were hesitant, so I said I could volunteer…they said it would be great and gave me the teacher's name. It's not much commitment but gives you good reason to keep up with your language), began a research project on study abroad (the deadline for some funding was close, so I looked for a professor in my area of interest and asked what research he knew of and how I might get involved), got more involved in the Italian department, and started working at a homeless shelter. Through these activities I obviously found plenty of opportunity to strengthen my language skills, but I also was able to see more clearly where Italian was going to fit into my career. The last thing on my mind was whether or not I had some post-study abroad stress disorder—I just didn't have time to sit home and worry; I was having too much fun. ~ Jacob Dick, Italy

I found that I had the hardest time dealing with being home when I was bored. Being occupied, whether it be at school or work or just hanging out with friends you have not seen in awhile, will help with the re-entry process. ~ Tammi Brusegaard, France

Don't put your study abroad experience on the shelf; the experience should not end when you return! Consider some of the following "action steps" to make the most of building on your study abroad experience:

- Join conversational groups to keep up your language skills.
- Volunteer in a community where you can use your new skills in being culturally flexible and, in some cases, where you can use your language skills or be exposed to yet another language.
- Make presentations for school and community groups about the country or countries you were in and the cultures and languages you experienced.
- Sign up for academic or language classes that will build on your experiences.
- Select topics on various political, historical, and social aspects of your study abroad experience for papers that you have to write in your classes.
- Volunteer for programs that address some of the new values that you've adopted as a result of your experience. If you are more aware of hunger in the world, for example, volunteer at a food shelf. If you are now more politically aware, join a political campaign.

Reflective re-entry

If you aren't the kind of person who wants nonstop action, that is OK. You might want time to reflect on your experience and let it soak in. For you, purposely reflecting on your experience is sometimes more valuable than a lot of activity that doesn't lead you anywhere. Take a look at what these returnees have to say about taking time to reflect:

> *Getting the most from study abroad takes time and reflection. Asking me what I got out of it is like taking a survey in a magazine—the answer is superficial and doesn't really convey the internal shift that's occurred. There's something about being completely out of your normal context that turns everything upside down, and it's both exciting and scary. My experience really did change the concept I have of myself. I am generally a thoughtful, self-aware person, but while I was gone I found myself thinking, 'Who the hell am I?' ~ Suzanne Hay, Greece*

> *Don't look at things as better or worse. Accept your home culture as an entity that you can look at from an outsider's perspective. This could help cause a harmony from the blending of your two cultural identities.*
> *~ Dan Jakab, Spain*

> *Re-entry is much more difficult than people anticipate. Many people feel that they can no longer relate to their old life, but people should be warned not to get a condescending attitude toward their old life. ~ Elizabeth Hook, Australia*

> *I did not attend the re-entry dinners planned by my study abroad office—I thought they were just for those having problems adjusting. I was fine emotionally, so I did not think I needed to go. However, what I did need and missed out on was a way to connect my coursework in economics and communication to my career interests. I definitely could have made the path a bit easier and more fulfilling—rather than pursuing an initial path that was so clearly wrong for me. After working in a career for over two years that was not connected to my international and intercultural interests, I finally took time to fully reflect upon my study abroad and changed career paths, selecting to attend graduate school in intercultural communication. ~ Barbara Kappler, England*

It's critical to take time to reflect upon your study abroad experience. Stop and ask yourself questions such as:

- How has your study abroad experience changed your values or identity?
- Are my current activities "in sync" with my new sense of self?
- Do I feel like I am using new skills, making new friends, strengthening former relationships, and gaining new knowledge?

Study Abroad Leads to Lifelong Learning

You've heard it so many times: "Study abroad was the greatest thing I did." This statement typically is not just wistful reminiscing about an adventurous time. Rather, it reflects a turning point, a fork in the road, or a pinpointable moment of a critical life lesson.

> *I am a big reader of World War II history. When I went to England, I took a history class specifically because it covered World War II. I know it sounds naïve, but I was surprised to learn from my Scottish professor that the U.S. armed forces were not necessarily viewed as coming to the rescue (a view I had read about repeatedly in the U.S.), but rather with some disdain—'Why didn't you come earlier?!' I have never forgotten this lesson—that history has multiple views. ~ Barbara Kappler, England*

> *After I came home from being in Taiwan, I was looking for some kind of volunteer activity to get plugged into here at home. I didn't have a great job and really needed something to make my life more meaningful. Since I had already taught English overseas, I decided that it would be interesting to sign up to be a volunteer English tutor with the then very new Hmong refugee population. What I didn't realize was being here in the U.S. with a group of people who had a more radically different culture than even what I experienced in Taiwan would be life-changing. I got drawn into being involved with a number of Hmong families with whom I still have a strong relationship 20 years later. One of my Hmong friends let me stay at her house for a month as my own special 'homestay' here in the U.S. I lived with the family for a month and ate Hmong breakfasts of watery rice, helped with the kids (six of them), and had a bird's eye view of their life in a crime-ridden neighborhood. I can tell you I learned so much in that one month, and that experience helped shape my values and my sense of what is important in life.*

> *I think if I hadn't studied abroad, I would never have had the courage to reach out and try to get to really know people from another culture. Though I learned a lot from being in Taiwan, I think that particular experience was most valuable in preparing me to participate in an even more powerful experience in my life. I think study abroad affects each person so differently and leads them down any number of paths—all worthwhile and mostly more enriching. ~ Karin Larson, Taiwan*

> *I was in the grocery store the other day, and there was a woman at the head of the line whose first language was not English. She was having a lot of difficulty understanding how much money the cashier wanted, and I could tell that the people directly behind her were getting impatient. Eventually she figured it out and gave the cashier the correct amount, but the whole thing made me feel for her. I have a hard time understanding numbers when they are spoken in Greek, and it made me think of all the times I tried to pay for something when I was in Greece but wasn't able to 'hear' how much it cost. One time I tried to buy a bus ticket and, after having the price repeated to me*

several times and still not getting it, I just stuck out a handful of drachmas for the vendor to take what he needed. It can be embarrassing not to be able to understand such simple things, and it makes you feel very vulnerable, childlike. Anyway, I think that if I could go back and 're-do' my recent experience in the grocery store again, I would make the decision to go up to the woman and try to assist her, even if it meant making the people around me feel uncomfortable for 'disrupting the line.' It's weird to think how rigid our culture can be about certain things, like standing in line, or making sure that things are running quickly and efficiently. We get so worried about time and keeping our 'place' that we become paralyzed to help out those around us.

Although the experience at the grocery store is a tiny example, I think that overall I have a lot more empathy for people who are new to this country and are English as a Second Language learners. My experience abroad continues to make me appreciate what I have in this country, to remember to have patience with others, and to try to extend myself to those around me, strangers or not, when I can. ~ Suzanne Hay, Greece

Strategies for Long-Term Maintenance of Language and Culture Learning

Here are some suggestions from veteran returnees on how to transform your study abroad experience into lifelong learning.

Continue your language and intercultural education

Whether through formal or informal instruction, there are many opportunities to continue studying your language and culture of interest after you've returned. Colleges and universities offer many choices for foreign language instruction, and many offer some of the less commonly taught languages as well. Private language schools also provide opportunities to practice and brush up on language skills through noncredit classes. Also, many schools offer language exchange or "tandem" programs that match a native speaker, usually an international student or scholar, with someone interested in that student's home language and culture. In exchange, the partner can tutor the native speaker in English.

Involve your friends

Your friends will want to learn more about your time abroad and can benefit from your experience. Invite your friends to an international-themed dinner or to an international potluck party. Use this as a chance to learn not only about the food, but to have your friends share any of their experiences with other cultures. Lots of colleges and universities have student organizations that help get international students and U.S. American students together. If yours doesn't, you can start one!

Write about your experiences

Magazines and newsletters, both on campus and off, will be interested in reviewing and possibly publishing accounts of your international experiences and the unique perspective you now have. This is an excellent way for you to share with others what it's like living in another country. Most of your audience will not have experienced what you have, so by sharing your stories, intercultural encounters, and travels with them, you allow them to enter into your world. Perhaps you may even inspire them to take steps toward their own journey abroad!

Keep the international connections alive

Many returnees report regretting that after returning home they did not keep in touch with their new friends they made in their host country. You will feel torn, like your heart and mind is split between two countries. The good news is that with the Internet, it is easier now more than ever to maintain contact with people halfway around the world. Writing letters and e-mail is also an excellent way to maintain your newly acquired language skills. In addition, as more and more nations have Internet connections, the amount as well as the variety of information available via the Web has mushroomed. Online newspapers from your host country can give you immediate access to news on current events that often is not reported in U.S. newspapers.

Make new international connections

Most universities and colleges have active international student organizations that tend to be organized and attended by both international students and U.S. Americans. Many professional and community organizations also exist that have cultural exchange and learning as one of their goals. If one of these organizations interests you, find out when its next meeting is and check it out.

Seek out international volunteer and employment opportunities

There are a multitude of opportunities for you to volunteer or find employment that utilizes your bilingual and bicultural skills:

- Become a homestay family to an international student. Agencies and universities are always looking for suitable homestay families for students, and this is perhaps one of the best means of keeping connected internationally. Be willing to accept a student outside of your own experience and expand your cultural horizons.
- Volunteer or intern in a study abroad office. Your international skills and knowledge about living overseas can be put to valuable use by advising prospective study abroad students and by participating in pre-departure and re-entry orientation programs.
- Volunteer at an office for international students. Offices that work with international students tend to be understaffed and can use volunteers to do a number of vital tasks, such as transporting students from the airport, organizing drives to collect used household goods and winter clothing for newly arrived international students, or organizing events or volunteering at orientation for new students.
- Become a buddy or tutor for international students. Because you know how it feels to go through cross-cultural adjustment in a foreign country, you can better understand the needs of international students studying in

the U.S. Use your cross-cultural skills to help others and, in turn, deepen your own learning and make valuable international connections.

- Seek out volunteer or work positions at international organizations located in your area. You might be surprised at the number and breadth of international linkages that already exist in your area.
- Volunteer to work with refugees or immigrants in your community. The needs and backgrounds of refugees and immigrants in this country vary tremendously, but most of these new arrivals do not have access to the kind of resources that international students have. More and more communities around the country have refugee communities that could use the support of culturally sensitive volunteers.
- Many companies now have in-house opportunities for bilingual/bicultural translators and interpreters. In addition, you could offer your services as a tour guide, if the company has visitors from your host country.
- Seek out opportunities through work, school, or other means to go abroad again. Use your cultural and linguistic fluency to accompany a delegation or tour to your country of interest. They do need you and your skills, even if they might not be aware of it yet!
- Seek out a job with an international company, whether you want to live abroad again or be based in the U.S.
- Look for opportunities to intern or volunteer overseas. Some of these experiences are longer term (1 to 2 years) and some are available for a few months or less.

These are just a few of the potential volunteer and work-related opportunities that will allow you to use your study abroad experience. Keep in mind that as more and more connections worldwide are formed, there will be even greater need for your international skills and perspectives. Organizations and corporations are realizing that if they want to be successful, having staff with a global perspective and making international linkages is not optional but essential. As someone who has experienced another culture firsthand, you are well equipped to contribute to the growth in international and intercultural awareness happening at home and throughout the world.

Recommended Reading on Culture-Learning Strategies

Bennett, M. J. (Ed.). (1998). Basic concepts of intercultural communication: Selected readings. Yarmouth, ME: Intercultural Press.

The ideas contained in this collection have been assembled from time-tested classics and more contemporary viewpoints. The carefully selected articles provide a great breadth of perspective of the concepts of intercultural communication.

Gonzalez, A., Houston, M., & Chen, V. (Eds.). (2011). *Our voices. Essays in culture, ethnicity, and communication* (5th ed.). New York: Oxford University Press.

This anthology examines intercultural communication through an array of cultural and personal perspectives, with each of its contributors writing a first-person account of his or her experiences in the real world.

Hofner Saphiere, D., Kappler Mikk, B., & Ibrahim DeVries, B. (2005). *Communication highwire: Leveraging the power in diverse communication styles.* Yarmouth, ME: Intercultural Press.

In this book on communication styles, the authors use real stories to help the reader gain insights into the complexities of communication style differences. The book includes new models for understanding one's own style and tools for understanding others. Expanding upon typologies of different communication styles, the authors present questions and checklists to focus on the behavioral and contextual issues of communication styles to improve our communication skills in everyday events.

Kim, Y. Y. (2001). *Becoming intercultural: An integrative theory of communication and cross-cultural adaptation.* Thousands Oaks, CA: Sage.

This text is one of the best volumes on the topic of cross-cultural adaptation. A more advanced theoretical text, it is particularly useful for the reader with a solid foundation in intercultural communication. The author discusses the processes of adaptation in terms of personal communication, social communication, contextual and environmental issues, predispositions (e.g., adaptive personality), and intercultural transformation.

Lustig, M.W. & Koester, J. (2012). *Intercultural competence: Interpersonal communication across cultures* (7th ed.). Boston: Pearson.

Blending both the practical and theoretical, this text offers students the requisite knowledge, the appropriate motivations, and the relevant skills to function competently with culturally-different others. The text provides a discussion of important ethical and social issues relating to intercultural communication and encourages students to apply vivid examples that will prepare them to interact better in intercultural relationships.

Martin, J. N., & Nakayama, T. K. (2010). *Experiencing intercultural communication: An introduction* (4th ed.). Boston: McGraw-Hill.

This introductory text covers the core concepts of intercultural communication and offers students a basic skill-building framework designed to be used every day for communicating across cultures. By using the "building blocks" of the framework in different ways, students will understand the complexities of intercultural interaction and learn about other cultures as well as their relationships with their own culture.

Samovar, L.A.,Porter, R. E., McDaniel, E.R., & Roy, C.S. (Eds.). (2014). *Intercultural communication: A reader* (14th ed.). Boston: Cengage Learning.

This newly updated volume, offers a series of essays that enables students to gain an appreciation and understanding of intercultural communication. The text provides readers with overviews of key concepts (ethics, competencies, context, nonverbals), as well as culture-specific research and reflections (Argentina, Chinese, Egyptian, Korean, Mexican, Germany, gay, elderly, and more).

Storti, C. (2007). *The art of crossing cultures* (2nd ed.). Yarmouth, ME: Intercultural Press.

Adjusting to a new culture and getting along with the local people can be huge challenges for someone who lives and works abroad. This timely new edition focuses special attention on how to deal with country and culture shock and identifies two types of intercultural incidents, giving a more holistic picture of cross-cultural misunderstandings. Learning how to anticipate differences and master positive alternative reactions is at the heart of this book, as well as the cross-cultural adaptation experience.

Ting-Toomy, S. (1999). *Communicating across cultures.* New York: Guilford Press.

Integrated into this text are extensive overviews of intercultural communication theories and research. Concepts used throughout this book (high and low context, verbal communication style, values) are presented in easy-to-understand summaries with many examples.

Ting-Toomey, S., & Chung, L. C. (2011). *Understanding intercultural communication* (2nd ed.). New York: Oxford University Press.

This is a very comprehensive and accessible introduction to intercultural communication. The authors discuss core intercultural communication concepts and issues, including cultural value patterns; cultural, ethnic, and global identities; culture shock; the language-culture relationship; verbal and nonverbal communication; intercultural conflict; intercultural relationships; and ethics in intercultural communication.

Section II
Language-Learning Strategies

INTRODUCTION: MAXIMIZE YOUR LANGUAGE LEARNING

These strategies give you a new container to put information into. ~ Jacob Dick, Italy

I have been studying Estonian for two years. I sure wish I had learned these strategies when I first began my language studies! The strategies make me so much more aware of what works for me—and what doesn't—so I get the most out of my time studying and learning the language. ~ Barbara Kappler, Estonia

This portion of the guide focuses on strategies for improving your language learning and language use. The readings and activities are intended for skilled learners wanting to hone their skills, novice learners slightly unsure of their skills, and everyone in between. In short, if you are learning a language, the following pages have something to offer you.

To begin, make sure you take the Language Strategy Use Inventory on p. 21 to help you focus your learning. After that, you may want to make a list of the strategies described in the guide that could enhance your language learning and use. Then prioritize the most important ones for you.

Going to an English-speaking country or a country where you have easy access to English? Several educators and students have commented that the strategies in this book have helped them—even when the hosts spoke English. No matter your destination, unless you will be entirely exposed to native U.S. American speakers, you will need to learn new vocabulary and a new rhythm of speaking.

ACTIVITY: Do you speak English?

The following are examples of British English. Below each one, write an equivalent sentence in U.S. English. Check your answers on the next page.

1. Ben had been watching the telly since half five and was starting to feel a bit peckish.

2. Evan is in a nark. He thought he was going to get a pay rise at work, but instead he was made redundant.

3. When Alex moved to London, all he could afford was a bedsit.

Suggested answers

1. Ben had been watching the telly since half five and was starting to feel a bit peckish.
   Ben had been watching television since 5:30 and was starting to get hungry.
2. Evan is in a nark. He thought he was going to get a pay rise at work, but instead he was made redundant.
   Evan is in a bad mood. He thought he was going to get a raise at work, but instead he got fired.
3. When Alex moved to London, all he could afford was a bedsit.
   When Alex moved to London, all he could afford was an efficiency apartment.

Like any other language you are learning, the meaning of a word that you hear or read in the United Kingdom, Australia, Ireland, or other regions such as India and Kenya (where British English is the norm) can often be discerned from its surrounding context. However, the number of new words or expressions, as well as English words that have completely different meanings outside of the U.S., might surprise you. This guide can help you develop strategies for learning this new vocabulary.

Perhaps language learning comes easily for you, and you feel quite confident in your skills. Perhaps you are just beginning your exposure to a new language, and your study abroad experience is going to be a way to really challenge yourself and immerse yourself in the language. Or perhaps you have selected an English-speaking site and are simply interested in strategies to understand different accents and learn some new vocabulary. Whatever your situation, you can learn much by becoming aware of the strategies you use for learning language so that you can get the most of your time abroad.

Language-learner strategies

While we often talk about learning a language as if it were just one skill, it's really a number of skills. Thinking in terms of strategies for dealing with different elements of language helps to make language learning a more manageable process. Language-learner strategies are conscious thoughts and actions that are usually intended to enhance the learning or use of the target language—that is, the new language you are learning for your study abroad experience. Often such strategies appear in a sequence or a cluster. For example, looking up an unfamiliar word may involve strategies for dealing with the alphabet, removing inflections to find the word in the dictionary, deciding which alternative in the dictionary is the desired one, interpreting the dictionary's abbreviated grammatical terms, determining the closeness of the target language word to the definition in your home language, and perhaps 10 other strategies. Often these strategies are performed in sequence but at times in clusters, with several being used almost simultaneously and sometimes in a back-and-forth manner.

Language-learner strategies have been classified according to both the *language skill* involved (listening, speaking, reading, writing, learning vocabulary, or translating), which is easy to understand, and the *function* of the strategy (metacognitive, cognitive, affective, or social), which is somewhat more difficult to follow. In simple terms, metacognitive strategies have as their principal role that of supervising (i.e., planning, monitoring, and evaluating) your language learning and use. Cognitive strategies are aimed at your learning and using the language material itself (e.g., identifying, grouping, retaining, and storing). Affective strategies help you regulate your emotions, motivation, and attitudes, and are often used to reduce anxiety and provide self-encouragement. Social strategies involve your interaction with others, such as asking questions to clarify social roles and relationships, asking for an explanation or verification, and cooperating with others to complete tasks.

Of course, during any given instant of strategy use, these four functions may overlap and intertwine. Suppose that a learner (Margo) practices in the target language the words she would use to introduce herself to a prospective supervisor for an internship in the host country. At one instant, Margo may be using a cognitive strategy by finding and rehearsing the appropriate language material for introducing herself graciously and without too many grammatical errors. When Margo is consciously planning this strategy, she is using a metacognitive strategy, especially during the moments when she thinks to herself that this is what she wants to do and then quickly plans how to do it. When Margo feels anxious about meeting the person who may become her future supervisor, then practicing is an affective strategy. Finally, if Margo is rehearsing her self-introductions to come across as more socially adept in the target language, then her practicing can serve as a social strategy. Understanding the strategy skills and functions can help you implement the broadest range of strategies to ensure you are doing all you can to increase your language and cultural proficiency.

The language strategy material in this guide is organized according to the following language skills: listening, learning vocabulary, speaking to communicate, reading for comprehension, writing, and translation. Before delving into these skills, take a moment to consider your motivation to learn a language.

The limits of my language are the limits of my world. ~ Ludwig Wittgenstein

Motivation to Learn a Language

As you discovered from taking the surveys at the beginning of this guide, you have preferred learning-style preferences and language-learning and language-use strategies within your repertoire. Another important factor to keep in mind is your motivation to learn your target language. Recently, researchers have begun to view motivation as constantly in flux and influenced by the characteristics of the learner, the personality and style of the teacher, and the nature of the course in the given context (Dörnyei, 2003, 2002, 1994a).

- ***Motivation toward the language itself:*** What is the social dimension of motivation for your learning a given language? What values and attitudes do you attach to this language?
- ***Motivation intrinsic to you as the learner:*** What relatively stable personality traits do you exhibit in the classroom, such as confidence in your language ability and your need for achievement in language learning?

- ***Motivation as related to the learning situation:*** How interesting, relevant, and satisfying do you find the particular language course? Is the instructor authoritarian or laissez-faire? Does the instructor model language behavior, present tasks, and give feedback in a motivating way? How cohesive or competitive is the group of students? Are the goals for the class and expectations for student performance clear and reasonable, with an articulated reward system?

Many situations and factors can influence your motivation to learn your target language, and these factors can change your motivation from one moment to the next. Here are some factors that might influence your motivation:

- How good you perceive yourself to be at learning languages in general
- How much you like the particular language
- Your affinity for the people who speak the language in the given speech community
- The particular language-learning situation in your school
- Your role as a learner enrolled in the given course
- Studying with the given teacher
- Learning with your peer group in the given classroom

The following activity provides you with an inventory to gauge your motivation to complete a language task. You could take the inventory before, during, and after you perform a language task. The purpose is to take your motivational temperature at a given point in time, so you can see how much your motivation increases or decreases depending on your language experiences at the moment.

ACTIVITY: Taking My Motivational Temperature on a Language Task

Andrew D. Cohen and Zoltán Dörnyei

The purpose of this inventory is for you to find out more about your motivation to learn a language starting with the "motivational baggage" that you bring to any given task in the target language. Then, if you are currently taking a language class, you are to indicate your motivation regarding various aspects of the class.

The final part of the measure has you look at your motivation to do a specific task. Ideally, you would fill out this task-focused portion of the questionnaire with respect to different tasks (tasks performed in class or as homework) so that you have an opportunity to see just how your motivation fluctuates while doing a particular task and across tasks. The instrument may prove to be a yardstick for determining the most motivating ways for you to perform certain tasks!

4 = very (much/good/important)
3 = somewhat (much/good/important)
2 = not very (much/good/important)
1 = not at all (much/good/important)

Pre-Task Motivation (to be filled out once, for example, at the start of a course or when starting a new unit):

What "motivational baggage" do I bring to this task?

___ How good am I at learning languages in general?

___ How much do I like this language?

___ How important is it for me to learn this language?

___ How motivated am I in this general learning situation (e.g., learning language at school)?

If you are currently taking a language course:

___ How much motivation does this language course instill in me?

___ How motivating is it to study with this teacher?

___ How much do I like learning together with my peers in this course?

___ How willing am I to do better in the target language than my fellow students?

Motivation concerning the task at hand:

How motivated am I to do this specific task?

___ How beneficial does this task seem to be in terms of my goals for learning the language?

___ How interesting does this task seem to be?

___ How self-confident am I about my ability to do well on this task?

What is it like for me as I begin to do the task?

___ How much does the setup of the task (e.g. physical conditions, grouping) add to my motivation?

___ How sufficient has the guidance been (from the teacher, the textbook, etc.) as I look to completing this task?

___ How much will my being anxious about this task actually facilitate my successful completion of it?

Looking ahead to the completion of the task:

___ How much does the prospect of feedback (praise or grade) contribute to my performance on this task?

After the task is completed:

___ How motivated am I to do other, similar tasks, now that I have completed this one?

Authors' note: This instrument was developed at the University of Minnesota by Cohen, with input from Dörnyei at the University of Nottingham, England. Many of the dimensions in the instrument were inspired by Dörnyei's book, *Motivational strategies in the language classroom*. Cambridge, UK: Cambridge University Press, 2001.

Increasing your motivation

Note that different learners will have more of a self-motivating capacity than others. Even under adverse conditions and without teacher assistance, some of you are more successful at staying committed to the goals you have set for yourselves than others. The good news is that you can increase your own motivation. How do you do this? Here are some suggested strategies:

- Be mindful of your learning-style preferences and, if possible, approach a given task in a way that favors your preferences. For example, if you are more visual in preference, use imagery to help you remember new vocabulary.
- Choose strategies for accomplishing a given task that have proved effective for you in the past. For example, if you have understood an academic text in the target language best by reading through it first just to get the general idea before reading it in depth, then make sure you do that. In other words, set yourself up for success on the task.
- Give yourself a mental pep talk from time to time, especially when you sense your motivation is waning. Say things to yourself like, "Come on, you can do it!" or "You did it fine last time!"
- Monitor your motivational level and if you find it is decreasing, ask yourself, "What would I need to do to increase my motivation at this point?"

The important point to take away from this discussion is that motivation is not a constant; it is in flux, so be mindful and take charge of your motivational level. While this won't ensure success at language learning and use, it can certainly contribute to your mastery of the target language over time. The following is a realization that came to one study abroad student about the role of motivation in language learning:

> *...after completing the series of surveys, it has become clear to me just how my learning-style preferences, strategies, and motivation all work together to help me as a unique individual on my journey in language and cultural learning. ~ Ashley Martens, Mexico*

LANGUAGE-LEARNING STYLES AND STRATEGIES: LISTENING

Pre-Departure Listening Activities

To me, the number one project for pre-departure would be EXPOSE YOURSELF TO THE LANGUAGE (which I did not do enough)! Rent movies. Go to conversation groups. Figure out how to get a host country radio station over the Internet. Order books on tape in the target language through interlibrary loan. (Or better: ask your language teachers. They probably have stuff.) I'm sort of ranting because the one aspect of my German that is the most frustrating is the inability to understand speech. ~ Molly Zahn, Germany

In getting ready to go to Malaysia, I had great plans to study the language before leaving. But working to pay for the trip and studying for the heavy course load I had were all that I could manage! Before leaving, I did review some basic grammar and pronunciation. People had told me that I would be able to get by with English. They were right, I could get by with English. But even better than getting by, I was also able to learn some Bahasa Malaysian and some Cantonese from friends I met in-country. Being open to the language and the basics that I reviewed before departing made a big difference. ~ Barbara Kappler, Malaysia

Improving your listening skills doesn't have to wait until you are in your host country. Try some of these ideas to get started:

1. Listen to radio from your host country over the Internet. You can find good sites simply by launching a browser and searching for keywords such as "international radio" or the language you are interested in and the word "radio."
2. Form a group to watch foreign films (ones that are not dubbed into English) in the target language. Listen to the movies while taking into account the strategies suggested in this section.
3. Find CDs of songs recorded in the target language and try to understand them not only for their words, but also for their meaning. Being familiar with popular music and musicians from the country also gives you something to talk about with new friends.
4. If possible, go to a local market where the customers speak your target language and eavesdrop on conversations about the prices of meat or the quality of the produce. Listen to the grocer give directions to someone about where to find a particular item in the store.

It can be difficult to gauge your skills in some of these areas while still in the U.S. For example, I had NO IDEA how bad my comprehension of conversational-speed German between Germans was until I got here—I had simply never been exposed to it before because, of course, my teachers and classmates at my university didn't talk like that. However, if you begin to recognize your strengths and weaknesses before you go, you can focus on improving your skills. This will make your life drastically easier when you get there! ~ Molly Zahn, Germany

Strategies to Become a Better Listener

What does a competent listener do? In this section we will talk about the skills or abilities that are needed in order to be a successful listener in your host country. You may already have partially developed some of these skills. This section highlights how you can use language strategies to develop your skills, either before you leave for the country or after you've arrived.

Check which of these you feel you can do now when you listen to native speakers of your target language:

- ☐ Distinguish separate words from a blur of sounds
- ☐ Distinguish one sound from another, like the vowel sounds in the English words "sit" and "seat"
- ☐ Comprehend the message without understanding every word
- ☐ Understand the entire message
- ☐ Decipher fast speech
- ☐ Figure out the intention of the speaker
- ☐ Listen to a conversation between two or more people
- ☐ Recognize different types of speech according to the speaker (e.g., age, status, relationship) or setting (e.g., in school, at dinner, at a nightclub)

Now, go back and circle the items you would most like to work on. See the following list for specific strategies to develop these skills.

(Adapted from Mendelsohn, 1994.)

1. Distinguish separate words from a blur of sounds

Increase your exposure to the language. For example, tape what someone says to you and play the tape over a few times. Or, go on the Web and listen to radio or voice segments in the target language.

Have a friend say a sentence slowly, then quickly. Count the number of words you can identify in each sentence. Try to separate out more words each time you practice.

Visualize. When you hear something said, see in your mind the chunks of language it consists of, perhaps looking for the subject and the verb.

2. Distinguish one sound from another (like the vowels in "sit" and "seat")

Practice aloud. Repeat the major vowel and consonant sounds in that language to yourself.

Practice with a friend. Have the friend repeat challenging sounds and vocabulary for you to identify which sound is being spoken or what word is being used.

> *To become more familiar with the sounds in Japanese I practice speaking the Japanese sounds that aren't found in English. I try to imitate the way that native speakers speak. I pay attention to the way they pronounce sounds and also to the rhythm they use in their speech. When I listen to conversation in Japanese I listen especially for the key words, but I also pay attention to what is stressed, keep in mind the context, and try to understand as many details as possible. If don't understand what someone says in a conversation, I will usually ask the speaker to repeat what they said or ask for clarification of the message. I pay attention to background information about the subject matter and the context to understand the message. ~ Philip Banks, Japan*

3. Comprehend the message without understanding every word

Listen for key words. These are sometimes signaled by stress or by a pause.

Practice "skim listening." Tap into the key topics, and pay particular attention to these while ignoring others.

Play the game of probabilities, inference, and educated guessing. You can guess what is most likely being said, given the following:

- The topic and your prior knowledge
- The context
- Who is speaking
- The speaker's tone of voice and body language
- Cues from prior spoken words or phrases

For example, when one of the co-authors, Barbara Kappler, traveled with a friend to Estonia, she could only speak a few phrases of Estonian. However, during the first 10 minutes of visiting friends, she understood the gist of what was said because there was a ritual to the conversations: "How was the flight? By what route did you travel? How is your family? Your work?" She understood by hearing *Amsterdamis*, *Minnesota Ülikool* (University of Minnesota), family member names, etc.

Try to predict what the speaker will say. If you know something about the topic of conversation, take an educated guess depending on the context and the environment.

Listen for words that are borrowed from English. Words like "computer" and brand names like "Coca-Cola" are quite common.

Use both top-down and bottom-up listening strategies. Bottom-up processing involves taking the items heard and putting them together to create meaning. So, for example, you hear: "Yesterday…earthquake…kill 273 people…Kobe," and you conclude that there was an earthquake yesterday in Kobe that killed 273 people. It is because of the adverb "yesterday" that you assign past tense to the verb. In bottom-up listening, you are finding clues by examining the words themselves as fully as you can.

Top-down processing is a more holistic approach where you look for clues to meaning beyond the specific words you hear. You draw on your knowledge of the world and events. For example, you overhear two people talking. One person says the word "earthquake" and you also hear the word "Kobe." From your background knowledge, you know that they are talking about the earthquake that just happened in Kobe.

The advantage of the top-down approach is it allows you to stay actively involved, especially early on in your language learning, whereas, the bottom-up approach enables you to modify your interpretation as you collect more information.

Identify which style you tend to use while watching a movie, attending class, or overhearing a conversation. Pay attention to how you determine the meaning of the conversation. Once you've identified the strategy you use, try to see if you can also use the other.

> *Having previous experience in the same context has definitely helped me understand loads and loads of Korean speech that I never would have understood a few months earlier. This point became clear to me when I was at a Korean restaurant for lunch with my husband, his Korean friends and their daughter, and an English-speaking couple. The waitress, who was speaking Korean, continued on and on about how Korean children learn so much English but tend to forget their Korean very easily. She also told a story about a man she knew who would get upset with his children when they spoke English and insisted that they speak Korean instead.*
>
> *I already knew the words for 'Korean,' 'English,' 'daycare,' and 'speak' in Korean, and I had recently started attending the Korean church in my city (giving me many opportunities to witness the concerns of the Korean parents). Using the waitress's tone of voice while she told the story and her nonverbal communication, I easily put the conversation together. Ultimately, I was able to reiterate it to the English-speaking couple without any problems. The others stared in amazement! Even though I didn't have the grammar or vocabulary to repeat it back in full, in the end, I was successful in understanding what the speaker said. ~ Julie Chi, co-author*

4. Understand the entire message

Put yourself in a frame of mind to understand the target language. Put aside other thoughts, including what you might want to say in reply, and focus only on what the speaker is saying. Then you should consider your response.

Accept some ambiguity in what you hear, and practice listening. Remember that it is perfectly normal to encounter speech that you do not completely understand. One hundred percent comprehension, even in your own language, is unrealistic. At your home university, one of your professors may use many words that are new or unfamiliar to you, but you use the surrounding context to understand what the professor is saying. You might be able to get the main idea of what was said, but you probably can't repeat it back word for word.

Try these listening activities:

- Tape a commercial on the radio or TV, and play it back a few times. See how well you can identify the words in the message. When you are unsure of sounds in words, what do you do? Can you understand what is being advertised?
- Record a conversation between two native speakers—ideally, friends of yours—who are talking about a topic you are familiar with. Then play it back to yourself several times. See how much of their interaction you can understand. What strategies do you use to get the gist of what they are saying to each other?
- While listening or viewing something (live or recorded) try to visualize the ideas you understand in your mind—or write them down if that suits your style. As you continue to listen, add new information and update your mental picture or notes on your understanding of what the person is talking about.

The strategies I used to increase exposure to the Slovak language were definitely listening to TV because they speak clearly and at a moderate pace. I also found movies to be a great way to increase exposure because I could watch them more than once and because I could always rewind. An added benefit of watching movies and TV is that you can pick topics that you are interested in—cooking, sports, weather, etc. ~ Beth Isensee, Slovak Republic

5. Decipher fast speech

Reduce your expectations. You may need to be exposed to the language for awhile before you will start to understand fast speech.

Try to stay in the conversation. Don't tune out when you feel the conversation is over your head.

Ask questions. The number one advice from returning students: Ask questions! If you don't understand what you just heard:

- Ask for clarification
- Ask for the statement to be repeated
- Try to paraphrase and see if you are correct

I was in Paris at midnight, in the dark, alone, and lost. I went back to a landmark, the Best Western Hotel, and buzzed the night clerk. I explained, in French, my situation. 'I'm locked out of my apartment, but I'm not really sure where that apartment is. I'm sure it's around here, but I can't remember exactly where. I'm an American student, and I just arrived in the city. I know it's stupid, but I seem to be lost.' He agreed about my stupidity but was kind enough to call my hostess, who explained how to get in the building. I made it out of a bad situation by not panicking and not being afraid to ask for help. ~ Tammi Brusegaard, France

Become familiar with ritualized speech. While studying abroad, one of the greatest challenges is that daily life involves so much ritualized language. For example, a student studying in the U.S. talked about how he felt he was doing OK with learning English—then he went to McDonald's. After successfully ordering, he heard the clerk ask "Izat fur hearutágo?" Paralyzed, he stood there, only to hear again: "Izat fur hearutágo?" Finally realizing it was a question, he replied, "Yes." The frustrated clerk simply threw the meal in a bag. After a few more visits to McDonald's the student understood what he was being asked and said, "Oh! Is that for here or to go!" And proudly said, "Here!"

Unclear word boundaries: When speech is too fast, it can be difficult to distinguish separate words from each other and, therefore, difficult to understand the meaning or intent of the speaker.

Weak forms: In English, when a phrase is spoken quickly some vowels become lax, creating words like "gotta" and "gonna," for example. Sometimes initial consonants are deleted in order to make speech more fluid in statements like, "Tell 'em t' meet at the restaurant." You may think of this as "lazy speech," yet these are examples of fast speech, which occurs in all languages. You might not be aware of how much you use this sort of abbreviated speech every day in your native language until you try to figure it out in a foreign language!

Suggested activity: Record segments of fast speech (e.g., when friends are using it or from a TV show) and then replay it several times. You will probably find yourself understanding more each time you listen to it. If you still have problems, ask a native speaker to listen to your recording and explain what the speakers are talking about.

I find myself constantly asking natives to repeat themselves, slow their speaking down, or clarify—use simpler words—when I am confused about something or just don't understand it altogether. So far this has worked extremely well and I have learned so much from asking for help. I also tend to imitate the natives and try to remember phrases and words that they have used repeatedly. Since my grammar is not very good, I try to focus in on key words and getting the gist of what is being said. If conversations are at a basic, elementary level I can understand every word, but when topics become more in-depth I tend to get lost more easily. I believe this is due to the fact that I did not have a conversation-structured high school class. Then when I was in Ecuador, every day was conversation-oriented, but at the same time I was taking in everything around me and did not start to really get a hold on the language until right before it was time to fly home. ~ Erin Leline, Ecuador

6. Figure out the intention of the speaker

Use tone of voice to guess the meaning or intention of what was said. Remember, the meanings of tone can vary across cultures, so your guess might not be completely accurate. How will you know if someone is using an angry or agitated tone, a serious tone, a playful tone, or a sarcastic tone? Anger, for example, may be marked by an increase in volume or intensity. It may help to ask locals how they know if a native speaker is using one tone or another.

Make yourself aware of nonverbal cues. Look at facial expressions, body language, and hand movements. Again, try to guess the meaning, keeping in mind you may be inaccurate in your interpretation, given cultural differences in nonverbals. (For more information, activities, and specific strategies for learning about nonverbals, see *p. 133.*)

Understand the use of stress. Depending on the language, stressed words may often be more important to the meaning of the sentence than words that are not stressed. Therefore, stress may signal the key words that can help you understand the speaker, especially in skim listening. Consider this sentence in English: "The **grass** is **always greener** on the **other side**." The words in bold are the key words. They are also the stressed words. Say the sentence to yourself. How clearly do you really say or hear the smaller words?

The meaning of a sentence can change dramatically when people put greater emphasis on certain words. Consider the difference in meaning/intention in the following sentences:

- Elena bought a French COOKBOOK. (She bought a cookbook, not a magazine.)
- ELENA bought a French cookbook. (Elena, not someone else, bought it.)
- Elena bought a FRENCH cookbook. (She bought a French, not German, cookbook.)
- Elena BOUGHT a French cookbook. (She bought, rather than sold, a cookbook.)

Determine how people signal the key words in your target language:

- Listen to conversations in your target language and try to note the words that stand out more to you.
- Try reading lyrics to songs while you listen to them. Circle or mark the words you hear more clearly.
- Ask your language teacher.

Learn the stress patterns in your target language. Listen for them while people are speaking, whether in a conversation with you, on the radio, on TV, or in class. Identify when stress might change the meaning, as in the above examples.

Understand intonations. Intonation refers to pitch variation or the rising and falling of the speaker's voice. For example, in English, when the speaker wants to ask a question, the listener will generally hear a rising intonation at the end of the sentence. For a statement, the listener would hear a declining intonation at the end. Emotion is also often expressed through one's intonation.

Be aware that intonation can change the meaning of a message, so you cannot pay attention to the words alone. It is important to check out the role of intonation in your target language to see when it could make a meaningful difference in what you say. For example, what may be intended as an apology, "Well, I am so sorry," may come across in English as a snide comment or even an insult if the speaker's intonation falls instead of rises at the end of the sentence. In these kinds of high-impact communications, it's important to know how to convey the meaning appropriately through correct intonation! Here are a few suggested activities to help you:

- Take one sentence and try to convey different meanings by changing the intonation.
- Consider the following two conversations. Say them aloud and listen to your rising and falling intonation.

Keon: Did you like the musical?
Asif: The cast members were interesting.
Shadeen: Oh, they sure were unique. I've never seen a group like them before!

Loann: Hey, guys! What do you think about my new hat?
Aurelio: Wow! I've got to say, Loann...that's quite a hat!
Micheli: Yeah. It's really different. Where did you find a hat like that?

7. Listen to a conversation between two or more people

Expose yourself to a variety of enriching conversations among native speakers. Eavesdropping is easy and generally acceptable on a bus, while waiting in line, on the subway or train, etc. Try to get a global understanding of the message.

8. Recognize different types of speech according to the speaker or setting

Types of speech can vary depending on the speaker (e.g., age, status, or your relationship with the speaker) or the setting (e.g., at dinner or at a nightclub). To really understand these differences, you will probably need to get more involved in the culture so you can be exposed to a variety of speakers and settings.

ACTIVITY: Increasing Your Exposure to Language in the Host Country

The number one goal for the majority of study abroad students is to increase their language ability. The number one regret expressed by students is that they did not do so enough. Why can it be so difficult to learn the language while being surrounded by it? It can be hard to find people to talk to, especially if you are at a beginning level. It can also feel intimidating. Nevertheless, you need to take charge and take advantage of opportunities to increase your language exposure.

Here are some ways to increase your language exposure in your host country:

1. Watch TV soap operas (the dialogue is often understood by the nonverbal communication)
2. Ask for directions—even when you know where you are going
3. Watch children's TV shows or listen to children's radio shows
4. Read children's books
5. Go to movies
6. Listen to commercials
7. Read materials posted on bulletin boards
8. Read the local newspaper
9. Read a magazine on your favorite hobby
10. Ask the grocer how to make a local dish
11. Talk to the bus driver or a fellow passenger during your commute
12. Talk to school librarians about their favorite books
13. Ask your language instructor to suggest novels aimed at your comprehension level
14. Get a native-speaking conversation partner
15. Ask questions about items on the menu (move beyond pointing and nodding as a way to order food)
16. Go to a museum with written explanations in the native language only
17. Spend two nights a week with your host family
18. Eavesdrop on other people's conversations and guess the topic
19. Search the Internet for sites in the language
20. Learn the words to the national anthem
21. Go to a playground and listen to the adults talk to the children

Now make your own personal list of ways to increase exposure to the local language in your host country. Feel free to include items from our list that work for you.

1. ______________________________
2. ______________________________
3. ______________________________
4. ______________________________
5. ______________________________
6. ______________________________
7. ______________________________
8. ______________________________
9. ______________________________
10. ______________________________
11. ______________________________
12. ______________________________
13. ______________________________
14. ______________________________
15. ______________________________

Making the Most of Your Language Classroom

Many of us don't take full advantage of the language classroom. Why not? It's easy to tune out due to language fatigue, get distracted by an instructor's presentation style, or simply take a mental break from rushing between work and classes.

Here are a few tips to help you get the most out of your classroom time both at home and while in your host country:

- Prepare for classroom lectures. If you have been informed of the topic for the following day, prepare a list of possible questions your instructor might ask you.
- Increase your attention span. Note how long you pay attention and encourage yourself to be more active, such as by answering in your mind the questions asked of other classmates.
- Make sure that you are getting enough sleep, exercise, and healthy food. Learning a language takes a lot of work, and you need to keep up your energy level to do it.

I try to predict what will be said next, and often if I know we will be working on a specific topic in class, I will look up words that might be used beforehand. I listen for key words and try to get the gist, but I also try to pick out a few details. ~ Mary Jo Loch, Germany

Avoid Faking that You Understand the Conversation

Perhaps you thought you were the only one who ever faked that you understood a conversation? It's actually common and occasionally necessary to save face and time —or simply to look good—but it will slow you down if you do it too much.

Here are ways to avoid faking it:

- Learn culturally appropriate ways to indicate you are not following the conversation. Don't simply keep nodding or maintaining eye contact.
- Ask questions to make sure you are understanding the conversation.
- When students are reading aloud in class, focus on the reading of your peers, rather than counting ahead to prepare the line(s) that you will most likely be asked to read.

Cover strategies create the impression of having control over material to hide or cover unpreparedness or lack of knowledge (such as using a memorized phrase that you did not understood in a classroom drill). Sometimes cover strategies are performed almost instinctively so that you will not be embarrassed in front of the teacher or other learners. Refer to "Strategies for Intercultural Communication" (p. 125) for more information on the impact of culture on communication.

Understanding Different Types of Speech

In the U.S., your most frequent exposure to your target language is or was from a foreign language instructor. In your host country, you are likely to be exposed to spoken language in at least five ways, and you need to be able to maximize your listening to all these types of talk.

- *Native-speaker talk:* The language of native speakers speaking to one another with no attempt to simplify, slow down, or repeat for your benefit.
- *Foreigner talk:* The modified language that native speakers use with you in an effort to help you understand what they are saying. It may entail simplifying the verb tense, selecting a more common noun or adjective, or slowing the pace of speech.
- *Teacher talk:* "Foreigner talk" that teachers choose to use in the classroom. Sometimes the teacher, perhaps without even being aware of it, may use language that is not exactly grammatically correct just so students will be sure to understand it. Teacher talk can be "sheltered language," because the teacher is making it easier for you to understand and practice the language. This is one of the main advantages of spending time in a classroom.
- *Interlanguage talk:* The version of the target language as spoken by foreign-language learners like yourself. Interlanguage speech is a version of the target language that is influenced both by the way things are said in the native language and by erroneous hunches about how things are said in the target language.
- *Commentator talk:* The language of TV and radio commentators. If you are a beginner in the language, such talk will be most difficult to understand, even if it is in supposedly simplified language, because it is often read from a prepared text so that there are few false starts and little repetition or redundancy.

In the beginning levels of language learning, some forms of language input are difficult and frustrating—such as TV news broadcasts and rapid-fire conversations among native speakers. Repeated exposure could eventually lead to comprehension, but such an approach is not very efficient. A more efficient way would be through listening to input that is understandable, and then gradually increase in the complexity of input.

Understanding the influence of culture on your listening

If your classmate asks, "Is that your cell phone?" what would you answer? Would you simply say, "Yes, it's mine," or would you think the speaker is really asking you to turn it off or maybe asking to borrow it for a short call? This is where interpretation comes into play. You could start by thinking about the way the particular culture deals with cell phones, when they are allowed to be turned on, and when/whether borrowing someone else's phone for a call is appropriate. After considering the specific culture, you could think about the speaker's actual signals. A speaker often gives a variety of nonverbal clues for you to consider. It may be that a given facial expression, a certain gesture, or a particular pause is an indicator of what the speaker intended by asking you, "Is that your cell phone?"

One way to help you understand cultural rules is to understand if the culture seems to be more low or high context (Hall, 1976). For example, in some movie theaters in the U.S., a message is displayed before the movie starts that asks you to turn off your cell phone. That's low-context communication, where the meaning is conveyed directly in written or spoken form. In other high-context situations and cultures, it may be expected that people will just know when it is or is not permissible to have the cell phone on, and there is no need for signs explicitly indicating this. The culture section of this guide also gives you an activity on high- and low-context communication in order to practice your understanding of this important concept (p. 128).

Improve your active listening

The strategies you use in your native language to help you listen have probably become second nature. These strategies are extremely helpful to recall now in order to help you increase your listening comprehension and to practice speaking in the target language (Mendelsohn, 1994). Check to see which of the following strategies you are most comfortable using in your target language, and challenge yourself to use more of those you are less comfortable with.

Recall: paraphrase information, put what you have heard into your own words

- Revise—correct information that you misunderstood the first time
- Check—recall information in order to support or verify something that you previously said

Probe: go beneath the surface of the information presented

- Analyze the topics—try, by asking questions, to glean more information than has been presented to you
- Analyze the conventions of language—focus on specific features of the language system such as definitions of words, pronunciation (noting it or practicing it to yourself), and cohesive ties (how words in the second language link up to other words in that context)
- Evaluate the topics—make comments that are judgments or critical assessments concerning information you hear (i.e., contest what you hear based on what you think you know to be the case)

Introspect: focus your attention inward and reflect on your own experiences as a listener

- Self-evaluate—make comments that show that you are trying to keep track of how well you are doing while engaged in listening (e.g., "This is really too hard for me," or "I understand that completely, but I think I already knew most of it before she explained it.")
- Self-describe—explain how you listen or what you are trying to do as you listen (e.g., "Well, I missed this the first time, but now I remember," or "It all came back to me on the way home.")

Language Shock and Language Fatigue

Some of my worst days abroad were the result of a language barrier.
~ Joshua Bleskan, Venezuela

Experiencing any of these things?

- Getting angry when you can't recall a word in the target language you know that you know
- Sleeping or wanting to sleep a great deal more than you did at home
- Putting on headsets and cranking U.S. American tunes
- Not putting on headsets and cranking U.S. American tunes
- Wishing you were in a country where more people spoke English
- Not caring if you are speaking English to your friends
- Not caring if you perform rude behaviors according to the host culture
- Coming home at the end of a day and feeling mad that your host family is there and you have to talk to them
- Feeling like you are spending hours trying to understand one page of text

If so, you have language fatigue. And you are not alone. Individuals who immerse themselves day in and day out in another language are bound to get tired physically and emotionally.

Here is what others suggest you do about language fatigue:

- Understand what it is. When you go abroad, you may find that language learning is much different than it was when you studied in your home country. Often study abroad students find that they must do much more independent work than they had to in their own universities. Also, in the host country, you may experience a great amount of stress related to the fact that you do not understand the target language and culture. Sometimes your expectations may be set too high, and you do not recognize the mini-steps you take on a daily basis in your language learning. You might even be surprised to find that learning a language can be as arduous and draining as it is.
- Keep a journal so you realize how far you have come. Ask a trusted friend how you are doing. Seek out support from family and friends.
- Give yourself time away from learning and using the language. Read something in your native language, call a friend back home, or take a nap. You may also need time to digest the enormous amount of input you have received during the day.
- Lower your expectations for your language proficiency. Give yourself time to learn at a comfortable pace.
- Praise yourself for the accomplishments you achieve. You are learning much more than you realize.

Here is a quote from a study abroad student about breaking through the "sound barrier":

> *The Spanish language was fairly new to me when I arrived in Toledo, Spain. I simply took the required Spanish to become eligible for a trip such as this. Upon arrival, I was bombarded with new words, a deep Spanish accent, and conversations at an accelerated speed. How was I to learn to speak Spanish stronger when I feel all I learned was not applicable? Within the first month, after some of the initial language fatigue subsided, I was frustrated because I came to my first plateau. I could depict some words but still had trouble following a conversation. By the time I figured out the sentence, my friend or teacher had moved on well past the point I was at. My frustration returned in a more intense way.*
>
> *At that point, a good friend came over to me while I was struggling to follow a native speaker in a bar. My friend said, 'Justin, relax. I know by now you have the understanding of the Spanish language—you're just trying too hard. Relax, listen, it will come to you—you will be surprised.' From that point, I started to loosen up and follow what I could. Learning a language is a process. The kind words of my friend helped me gain confidence and insight into maximizing the whole language experience. ~ Justin Perlman, Spain*

Language shock and culture shock are closely related because of how they both affect your cross-cultural adjustment process. For more information on culture shock and coping strategies, see "Adjusting" (p. 91).

Post-Study Abroad Listening Activities

Keep the momentum going

Here are some things recent returnees did to keep up their listening skills:

- *I did something I was scared to do before leaving. I was much more confident, so I got a language conversation partner.*
- *Once a week I get together with friends and see a French film, have French food, and speak French.*
- *I got a job at a Mexican restaurant so I can use my Spanish.*
- *I bought CDs—from both the U.S. and my host country—on the Internet.*
- *I stay in touch with friends from the host country and continue to build my relationships.*
- *I visited again.*

Keep an open mind to opportunities for target language listening, but proceed respectfully: approaching native speakers of the target language back in the U.S. may not be as easy as it was in your host country. Be cautious about how you approach them, the language you use, and when the right time is to open a conversation.

Do not expect that native speakers of your target language will want to speak anything other than English. After all, they may be in the U.S. specifically to learn English and American culture. Approach them carefully, expressing your interest in their native language and culture; in most cases, they will respond favorably.

LANGUAGE-LEARNING STYLES AND STRATEGIES: LEARNING VOCABULARY

Need to learn more vocabulary? Who doesn't?! This chapter gives you a variety of techniques for expanding your repertoire.

Let's face it. You have a number of things you want to do while in the host country—see the sights, make new friends, visit neighboring regions and countries, and improve your language skills. This section will help you make the most of your time by raising your awareness of the strategies you currently use and suggest new ones to increase your vocabulary-learning skills.

Pre-Departure Vocabulary-Learning Activities

Want to impress your fellow travelers with your language skills? Do you have visions of saying just the right thing when you meet your host family? Or do you just want to know you can hold up your end in a basic conversation? Before you depart for your host country, you'll want to brush up on your vocabulary so that when you arrive you won't be groping around for important words. Here are a few things you can do before you go:

- Make a list of the words you expect to use often. Make flash cards or write them in your journal so you can review them every day.
- Purchase sets of ready-made flash cards available at student bookstores and online (just search for the language you want and "flash cards"). Often the ready-made sets of cards include extra information about the words, such as the forms for the verbs in different tenses.
- Spend time with native speakers and have them provide you with crucial vocabulary you might not know. You will need to tell the native speaker what situation you need vocabulary for, such as calling a museum to get information about hours. Then he or she will be able to walk you through a mock conversation.
- Make a commitment to learn 10 new words a day.
- Discover materials that you can read online. Look for newspapers, magazines, articles about your hobbies, etc., in your target language.
- Think of yourself as a natural topic of conversation and learn how to talk about you. People in your host country may be quite curious about you, or the conversation may turn to you simply as a cultural expression of politeness. Either way, it will be helpful, especially when you first arrive, to know some statements prepared about yourself. Potential conversation topics may include:
  - Your basic activities in the host country: What are you doing there? Studying economics at the local university? Researching the traditional fiber arts of the area? Learn the correct words and phrases needed to describe these activities.
  - Your living situation in the host country: What city or region are you in? Do you have a host family? Are you sharing an apartment with other students? Are you living in a dormitory?

- Your length of stay in the host country: When did you arrive? How long will you stay? Will you travel? What do you hope to see or do?
- Your life in the U.S.: Where are you from? Are you a student? Do you work full time? What do you do for recreation or fun at home?
- Your family: Where is your family? Do you have brothers and sisters? Are you married? Do you have children?

Note: Depending on what country you are staying in, be prepared for some "unusual" questions about yourself (unusual in that they may not be considered polite topics of conversation in the U.S.). For example, one study abroad student was asked on several occasions how much she weighed while she was in her host country. Other students have noted being surprised when asked how much they paid for something or how much money they earned. There may be some other topics that you can prepare for before you go with a little research on the host country or with the help of a host country native.

ACTIVITY: How do you learn vocabulary? Part I, Learning Aymara

The first step in helping you to improve your vocabulary-learning strategies is to recognize how you actually go about learning new words. This activity will raise your awareness of strategies you currently use and suggest new ones to increase your vocabulary-learning skills.

Let's suppose that you are learning the Aymara language, which is spoken in parts of Bolivia and Peru. We picked this language precisely because the odds are low that you are studying Aymara. In the following activity, we are asking you to think about what you do to learn new vocabulary and not just recall words you might already know.

The activity involves learning 10 words from Aymara. It may take you 5 to 10 minutes to complete. If you don't have time to learn 10 words, then try to learn 5—the idea is to practice learning words.

Pretend you have just finished reading a story about a young man who is hospitalized with an infection in his leg. His new girlfriend brought flowers to his hospital bed but found him sleeping, so she wrote him a note and left quickly.

Learn the words on the following page so when given the English equivalent, you can produce the Aymara word. Pay attention to how you learn each word. After you feel you have committed these words to memory, continue reading this section so you separate yourself from the vocabulary for a moment. Do not refer back to the vocabulary list until asked to do so.

The words selected come from Bolivian Aymara and conform more or less to the sound system of Spanish. Aymara belongs to the same language family as Quechua and is spoken by about 600,000 people in Bolivia and Peru.

AYMARA	**ENGLISH**
wayna[1]	young man
usuta	sick
cayu	leg
machaka	new
aca	this
pankara[2]	flower
ucampisa	but
iquiña	to sleep
kellkaña[3]	to write
laka	quickly

Much language learning is unconscious or at a low level of consciousness. If you become aware of the actual processes you use, you will gain insights about the learning strategies that work for you and those that do not.

For example, you may be a person who thinks that repeating a word over to yourself a number of times will fix the word in your memory, yet in reality this approach may not work well for you. Remember that just because you have used an approach to vocabulary learning for awhile, it doesn't necessarily mean that it's the best for you. So it may pay to take the time to see what other approaches are out there to see if something else might work better. For example, you may not be aware of how much you benefit from seeing visual images of words or concepts.

Sometimes you may use a certain approach to vocabulary learning not because it works, but because you think that you should be able to learn that way. Perhaps you use a certain strategy because you know it works for someone else, because a teacher once told you to do it that way, or because you did it that way once and it worked then. For instance, you may once have kept an alphabetical listing of target language words and their native language equivalents, not because this listing genuinely contributed to your vocabulary learning, but because it seemed like the appropriate thing to do since other students were doing it.

---

[1] There are three main vowel sounds in Aymara: a, i, and u. The a is pronounced like the a in "father," as in the Aymara word *laka*. The i sound is somewhere in between the i in "bit" and the ee in "beet." In some Spanish loan words, the i can sound more like an e, which is pronounced like the ay in "hay." The u is pronounced somewhere in between the oo in "boot" and the oo in "look." The u can also sound like the o in "rope." A common Aymara diphthong is ay, like in *cayu,* and pronounced like "eye."

[2] In Aymara, r is pronounced like the middle consonants in "butter" and is not rolled or trilled.

[3] In Aymara, c and qu are pronounced like the initial consonant in "kiss" and k is pronounced like the initial consonant in "cool."

Now, without looking at the original list, supply the Aymara word:

this	________________
flower	________________
leg	________________
but	________________
young man	________________
to write	________________
new	________________
sick	________________
quickly	________________
to sleep	________________

Note that for this exercise you were asked to perform what is considered to be the more difficult vocabulary-learning task: producing a target language word when given the native language equivalent. The intention is to help you understand how you learn vocabulary when it is not easy to do so.

Compare your answers with the original list to see how many you got right. Can you retrace the process of how you learned each word?

Below is the list of the Aymara words, followed by three blanks. If you remembered the word correctly, put a check in the first blank. Next, ask yourself *how* you learned this word: by rote memory or by association. Learning vocabulary by rote memory refers to repeating the word orally or writing it down a few times without attempting to link it to something else. Using an association refers to any relationship you might have made between the word and something else. For example, *usuta* (sick) could be linked to "used up" (someone who is sick is used up). Note that it's common to initially assume that rote memory was used, so think carefully about how you really remembered the word.

	Got It Right	**Used Rote Memory**	**Used Association**
wayna (young man)	______	______	______
usuta (sick)	______	______	______
cayu (leg)	______	______	______
machaka (new)	______	______	______
aca (this)	______	______	______
pankara (flower)	______	______	______
ucampisa (but)	______	______	______
iquiña (to sleep)	______	______	______
kellkaña (to write)	______	______	______
laka (quickly)	______	______	______

So, which strategy worked best for you—rote memory or association?

Learning Vocabulary by Association

Associations can be funny—in fact, the funnier or stranger the better because you're more likely to remember them that way. I used to have great ones when I learned Hebrew. My friend and I remembered the Hebrew word likra't, 'against, toward, to meet' with the phrase, 'Licking rats? I'm against it.' ~ Molly Zahn, Hebrew student

The energy you use to learn new words is energy well spent. Long-term recall is based on your depth of processing—the more intricate the web you create, the longer you will remember the word. This section helps you understand how to create a more intricate web.

Using mnemonic links, or associations, can greatly improve your learning of vocabulary. Here are common associations used by college-level foreign language learners whose native language was typically English.

Note: Certainly rote memorization can work, and you need to use whatever strategy works for you. However, research reveals that using an associative technique, particularly using mental images, is more effective for most people than simple rote memory.

Association Techniques

Technique	Description	Example	Explanation
Native Sound	Link to a sound in your native language	Aymara = *pankara* (flower) English = pancake	Think of a pancake-shaped flower
Target Sound	Link to a sound in the target language	Hebrew = *cosher* (aptitude) Hebrew = *kasheh* (difficult)	Something that is difficult takes aptitude
Another Sound	Link to a sound in another language	Korean = *sulsa* (diarrhea) Spanish = *salsa*	*Salsa* sounds like *sulsa* and *salsa* could lead to diarrhea (the goal is to learn; the means can be some novel link)
Meaning of the Parts	Pay attention to the meaning of part of a word	German = *frühstuck* (breakfast) German = *früh* (early)	Think that an early meal means breakfast
Structure	Take the word apart and make a connection to a word you already know in that target language	Hebrew = *mithalek* (divides up) Hebrew = *mahlaka* (department)	Think of dividing up an academic faculty into different departments
Category	Place the word in a topic group in the target language	Hebrew = *mitsta'er* (am sorry) Hebrew = *mevakesh slicha* (ask to be excused) Hebrew = *mitnatsel* (apologize)	Group these three expressions for apologies together and then you can compare and contrast their meanings and functions
Visualization	Picture the word in isolation or in written context	Spanish = *ojo* (eye)	

Technique	Description	Example	Explanation
Situation Link	Link the word to the situation in which it appeared (e.g., a song or poem you heard it in or some encounter where the word came up)	Korean = *seol-tang* (sugar) English = cappuccino and coffee shop	You remember the word for sugar because you learned it in the coffee shop when there was too much sugar in your cappuccino
Physical Sensation	Associate some physical sensation to the word	French = *triste* (sad) English = feel sad Japanese = *ichi* (one) and *ni* (two) English = itchy knee	You feel sad because of the tone of voice in which the word is said Think of an itchy knee. Maybe you even scratch your knee to recall these words
Mental Image	Create a mental image or picture that you associate with the word through the key word and its meaning	A Korean student remembered "you betcha" in English by thinking of calling someone "cabbage head." *Baechu* = cabbage	Think of agreeing with what that cabbage head has just said
Free Association	Free associations that are specific to your life experiences and reactions to the words	Arabic = *arjuli* (leg) English = your friend, Julie	You think of Julie having long legs in conjuring up the Arabic word, or if you hear the word, it reminds you of Julie and then of her long legs
Enjoyable Sound	You remember a word simply because you enjoy the sound it makes	Estonian = *rõõma* (joy) Spanish = *pupi lentes* (contact lenses)	One learner enjoys the elongated vowels and loves to say this word One learner remembered this because it sounded silly to her

Learning a language with characters

Learning by association can be very helpful. Studying languages like Japanese and Chinese with rather complex characters used for reading and writing may well call for the extensive use of associations. In some cases, the ideographs really do depict the concept being expressed. In other cases, it is up to the imagination of the learner. Some kanji (Chinese characters used in Japanese) symbolize shapes of things. The kanji for a tree looks like a branched-out tree. The kanji for "woods" is made up of three kanji for a tree, so the association here is that woods have many trees. You can also create your own associations. For example, take the kanji for "to eat," which looks a bit like a house with a floor in it, and think of someone eating in the house. Then, the kanji for "to drink" consists of a similar kanji for "to eat" and another component alongside that looks like a person under a little porch roof. A learner could remember "to drink" by thinking of someone drinking out on the porch.

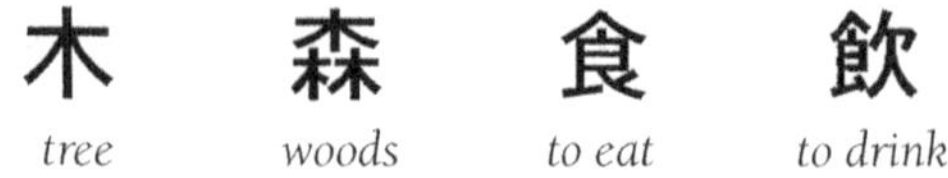

tree *woods* *to eat* *to drink*

ACTIVITY: How do you learn vocabulary? Part II, Using association techniques

Now let's take another look at the Aymara exercise (p. 188). Check if you used an association, and then record which association you used from the preceding chart (native sound, target sound, etc.).

	Used an Association	Which Type?
wayna (young man)	_____	_______________
usuta (sick)	_____	_______________
cayu (leg)	_____	_______________
machaka (new)	_____	_______________
aca (this)	_____	_______________
pankara (flower)	_____	_______________
ucampisa (but)	_____	_______________
iquiña (to sleep)	_____	_______________
kellkaña (to write)	_____	_______________
laka (quickly)	_____	_______________

Now, select 10 words you want to learn from your target language. Record them and their English equivalents here:

	New Vocabulary	English Equivalent
1.	_______________	_______________
2.	_______________	_______________
3.	_______________	_______________
4.	_______________	_______________
5.	_______________	_______________
6.	_______________	_______________
7.	_______________	_______________
8.	_______________	_______________
9.	_______________	_______________
10.	_______________	_______________

Jump ahead and write the English word again on the next page, before you start memorizing. Scramble the order to make sure you haven't simply memorized the words according to their position in the list.

When learning these words, try to use all the association techniques listed in the chart on pp. 191-192. Don't get too frustrated if you can't come up with an association; some words are easier than others. After you have learned these words, keep reading as you did in the last exercise. Again, do not look back at this list until told to do so.

Sometimes successful learning strategies are discovered in unusual ways. Here are two examples of language learners remembering new vocabulary using word association:

> *I had a funny experience when I returned from a weekend in a small city called Fréjus in southern France. Upon returning, I had dinner with my host mother, and she asked me about how my weekend went. I had gone to Fréjus to see a concert of my favorite band and was trying to tell her about it. I told her that there were many people in town and that I had a really good time. She was looking at me strangely and seemed confused. I continued to talk about the concert and suddenly she smiled, stopped me, and explained that I had mispronounced the word 'concert' and was instead saying 'cancer.' The only difference between the two words is in the vowel, and I had not pronounced it correctly. She thought I had been saying there was a lot of cancer in Fréjus and that lots of people were there because of cancer. I was embarrassed about it at first, but we joked about it and I felt a lot better. Of course, now I always remember the word for 'concert' because I link it to the sound of 'cancer.' It's also like using free association because I remember the whole story around learning this word and the correct pronunciation.*
> *~ Sarah Parr, France*

> *When first learning Estonian, I was a bit overwhelmed at needing to remember to add the word 'kas' when I wanted to ask a question. As a result, I found myself a bit obsessed with the word. Instead of asking my future mother-in law 'kuidas elate' (how are you)? I asked her 'kas elate' (are you alive)? After her response of 'ja' (yes) instead of 'haisti' (fine), I realized my mistake. I now remember 'kas' is not the same as 'kuidas' because I picture myself holding the phone and asking the correct question! I think this free association will stay with me forever! ~ Barbara Kappler, Estonia*

Now try to come up with your 10 target language words, using the English equivalents you wrote down earlier.

	English Word	Target Language Word
1.	____________	____________
2.	____________	____________
3.	____________	____________
4.	____________	____________
5.	____________	____________
6.	____________	____________
7.	____________	____________
8.	____________	____________
9.	____________	____________
10.	____________	____________

At this point, check your original list and see how many of the words you got right. Below, indicate how you went about learning each word. See if there is any pattern to how you used associations.

	Got It Right	Used Rote Memory	Used an Association
1.	_____	_____	_____
2.	_____	_____	_____
3.	_____	_____	_____
4.	_____	_____	_____
5.	_____	_____	_____
6.	_____	_____	_____
7.	_____	_____	_____
8.	_____	_____	_____
9.	_____	_____	_____
10.	_____	_____	_____

Reflection questions

- Note the words, if any, for which you did not come up with mnemonic associations. Is there any pattern to these words?
- What do you now know about how you learn vocabulary?
- Did you use more associations to learn this set of words than you did for the Aymara words?
- Did your performance on the memory task improve?

Other Means of Learning Vocabulary: Pre-Departure and In-Country

1. Take a good look at the words themselves

When looking for clues to the meanings of words, you may have been taught to pay attention to parts of words (that is, the word base or root, prefixes, suffixes, or radicals of characters in Japanese or Chinese). Depending on the language you are learning, it may be more effective to look for other clues, including clues in the text surrounding the word you don't know. When in doubt about a word, ask these questions:

- Is it a noun, verb, adjective, etc.?
- What's the relationship between this word and others that accompany it? Consider this sentence in Japanese: *Gakusei wa daigaku de sensei to sodan shimashita* ("The student had a consultation with a professor at the university"). Maybe you know the words *gakusei* (student), *daigaku* (university), and *sensei* (professor), but not the word *sodan*. What are some likely choices? Meet? Discuss? The correct word is "consult," but you wouldn't be too far off with the other choices.
- How is the sentence with this unknown word related to other parts of the text? In the example above, the text might go on to indicate what the student got out of the consultation, such as advice about what courses to take.

If there is still doubt as to the meaning of the word, then it may work to break the unknown word into its prefix, root, and suffix, if possible.

> *Some of the strategies I use when learning new vocabulary include paying attention to the structure of the new word and also breaking the words into parts that I can identify. Because Japanese uses so many compound words, knowing a particular kanji involved can be a great help in remembering what the word means. This is also key for me when recalling words. If I can identify one of the parts involved I can usually get at the point. I also make mental images of words, group them according to parts of speech, and practice writing them out in sentences. To review vocabulary I just go over words first when I learn them, and then periodically afterwards so that I don't forget them. Typically, when I just learn a new word I'll look for ways to use it in class sessions so that it stays fresh in my mind until I have it memorized. ~ Philip Banks, Japan*

> *When I learned new vocabulary words, I would first see if they made any correlation to an English word and then I would break them apart to see if they had any smaller Spanish words within them that I was already familiar with. If neither of the strategies worked I would simply have to memorize them. In some cases I would remember the situation, sign, or phrase that I first saw them in, or I would make a flash card and add it to the pile sitting on my desk! ~ Erin Leline, Ecuador*

2. Use quick and easy cognates

Easy-to-learn vocabulary can be found through cognates—words in two languages that are from the same source, look or sound similar, and thus have the same or similar meanings.

- If words are *true cognates* (e.g., "police" in English and *policía* in Spanish), then it will help your vocabulary learning.
- Be wary of *false cognates* (i.e., different meanings in the two languages, such as "macho" in English and *macho* in Spanish, which is used to describe a male animal). Sometimes the existence of false cognates can actually help you remember the target language word by remembering the discrepancy in meaning between the words in the two languages.
- *Deceptive cognates* have only a partial overlap of meaning, and thus you may erroneously interpret the meaning of the word. For example, the word for "education" in Spanish is *educación*, but the Spanish concept of *educación* is broader than the English concept. For another example, the word for "plumber" in Hebrew is *instalator*. In English, it is possible to refer to a "plumbing installation" but not to an "installer" as a plumber, so there is some overlap of meaning between the two words.

The above are excellent points illustrating that in many languages word-for-word translation is difficult—if not impossible. There will always be nuances in the original language that don't quite transfer into the language being translated to. Even the many "loan words" borrowed from English and used in other languages often mean something very different. For example, the word "get" has now become popularized in Japan, but its meaning is more narrow than in English. In Japanese, "get" is used as a verb, usually with an exclamation mark, to mean "to win something" or "to obtain something good or fashionable." It wouldn't be used as in "to get a job," but as in *konsaato no chiketto wa getto shita,* or "I got my hands on a ticket to the concert!"

3. Use a dictionary, but not as a crutch

Use a dictionary sparingly. It can provide intermediate or advanced learners with a more finely tuned meaning or set of meanings for a word with which you have some familiarity, but as pointed out elsewhere in this guide, a dictionary can become a crutch. A good rule of thumb is to keep the dictionary a bit out of reach so that you stretch your mind a little before you stretch your arm! Of course, electronic dictionaries have increased the speed and facility of looking up words. This still doesn't mean, however, that you will benefit much from what you look up. Often, you will forget the information the dictionary provided right after you put it down. Also, you may not look in the right place or may not understand the reference because the choices are not clear, are too technical, include symbols you don't know, and so forth.

4. Use flash cards

You can use these great tools anywhere—on a plane, a train, or even standing in line.

Tips for creating flash cards:

- To assist with long-term memory, the target language word should be defined using your native language and not the target language. Include on the card a minimal amount of context about where or when the word was heard or read. Write the word in a sentence to help you remember its definition.
- If you have the opportunity, check the cards with a native speaker before you study them to make sure that each word is spelled correctly, that the meanings have been correctly interpreted, and that the words are used correctly in a sentence. Note on the native language side of the card any association technique you created to help remember the word.

Here's an example from Spanish:

New word:
fumar

'to smoke' (verb)

Association keyword:
fumes

El está fumando: "He is smoking."
"I can smell the **fumes** from his smoke."

Try these quick tricks when using flash cards:

- When you get a word wrong, don't put it back at the bottom of the pack. Place it about six cards from the top, giving you a chance to rely on short-term memory. Then place the word farther back until it is well beyond the reach of short-term memory. Learn 10 words at one sitting, reviewing the last two when each new one is learned. Then review the words once the same day and for the next two days.
- Some study abroad students have used Microsoft PowerPoint to create "computer flash cards" that flash characters and vocabulary on the screen.
- For learning nouns, tape flash cards, small signs, or Post-it notes on the objects that correspond with your vocabulary word. Your room can be a visual dictionary with the target language words for desk, lamp, bed, etc.

A note about flash cards: While flash cards can be a great way for you to learn and practice your vocabulary, it is important to try other strategies. If you spend all your time making flash cards, you can miss out on more critical opportunities for learning vocabulary.

> *When I am learning vocabulary, I try to make connections between the word and a word in English I know. It is also helpful for me to write the words down so I can see them in my mind. Flash cards are also very helpful for me, which is obvious by the entire drawer they take up in my desk! When I was in Spain and I learned a new word simply from hearing it, I would try to use the word in later conversations. Sometimes I surprise myself when I know a word that I just picked up. It is fun when this happens because you feel like you are accomplishing so much! ~ Amanda Smith, Spain*

5. Practice writing your new vocabulary words

To help you remember new vocabulary, practice by writing the words in a variety of different contexts. As mentioned above, creating your own flash cards provides a good opportunity for doing this. For those of you who do not use flash cards, here are some other venues for writing the new words in sentences:

- Experiment with new vocabulary words in e-mails or postcards to friends
- Include new words in essays and other class assignments
- Use new vocabulary in a target language diary you are keeping
- Create an ongoing vocabulary log (a personalized vocabulary listing) and add the new words along with meaningful sentences

The main thing is to exercise your knowledge of the new words *in writing* since this helps to fix the words in your mind.

6. Group your vocabulary

Simplify your language learning. Reduce the number of things you have to learn by grouping like ideas together. Groups can be based on:

- Parts of speech—for example, nouns, verbs, adjectives; or function words, including those hard-to-guess ones such as personal pronouns,

determiners, auxiliaries, prepositions, and conjunctions
- A theme or topic—such as words related to banking, dating, etc.
- Synonyms and antonyms—perhaps grouped around themes, such as happy, content, and joyful; sad, dissatisfied, and sorrowful; etc.

7. Create a visual map

You can combine memory strategies through techniques such as semantic mapping, where the key concept is highlighted or centralized and is linked with subsidiary concepts, attributes, and so on by means of lines or arrows showing relationships. Here's an example:

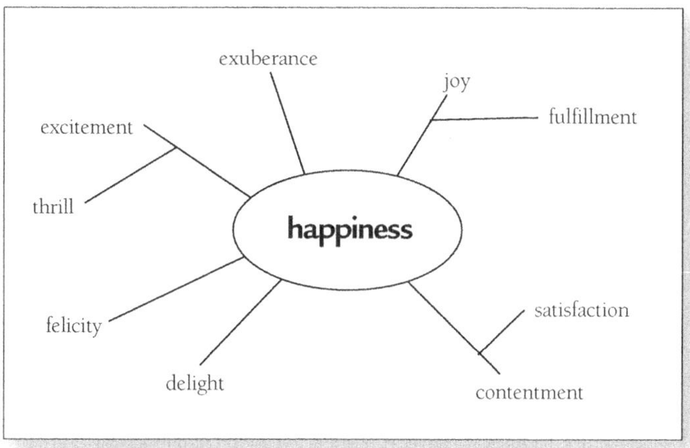

LANGUAGE: *Vocabulary*

Additional Ideas for Vocabulary Learning

Let's face it. Learning vocabulary can be boring! Here are a few boredom breakers:

- Videotape an interesting television show or movie in the target language, or audiotape your teacher or someone else speaking. Listen to the speakers carefully. Write down any unfamiliar words you hear (as best you can) and either talk to a native speaker or look up the words yourself. Try to piece together what the speaker was saying, then watch the video or listen to the tape again to verify if your prediction was correct. Later, try to use these new words in conversations.
- Try putting together target language words into a short, familiar song that you can recall easily, like "Frère Jacques," or the music for your favorite commercial or TV theme song. Whenever you need to remember these words, you can go back to your "key song."
- Find a song that you like in the target language, then try to learn the lyrics and sing along. Note that this is really hard to do if you don't have the words written down, but CDs of popular music usually come with an insert that has the lyrics printed. If you don't know the meanings of some of the words, consult a dictionary or a native speaker. This is a fun way to learn popular words and slang.

- Bring a small, pocket-sized notepad when you go out with your friends so that you can record the "street talk." Ask those who know to explain colloquial phrases and write down these expressions for later reference.
- Develop an ability to describe your feelings and emotions. Ask native speakers for relevant words and phrases, and have them indicate whether the expressions are part of the colloquial or standard language.
- Ask your native-speaking friends or teacher to teach you some tongue twisters, idioms, proverbs, or other language games. Practice these, but also learn the meanings of the words you are playing with.
- Try practicing action verbs by acting them out. You could have a friend give you commands to act out as a way to practice your comprehension, or you could describe what you are doing out loud while you are doing it.
- Listen to songs and see how much of them you can understand. Write down words you don't understand. Guess with regard to the spelling and ask a native speaker later. Write down words you don't understand.

Listening to Japanese music has helped familiarize me with the sounds of the language and has also helped me remember vocabulary. While it is certainly true that conversational language is very different from singing, it has still been a great help to me. If I hear a word in a song, and then later learn it in class, it is far easier to remember the word and meaning because I think about it every time I hear the song.
~ Philip Banks, Japan

These types of activities are especially good for auditory learners and those who learn best by doing, but they can be fun for anyone who is struggling with the monotony of memorizing vocabulary.

What Native Speakers Know about the Vocabulary in Their Language

You've heard it over and over again: Talk to native speakers. Even if you can't, it's helpful to realize what a native speaker really knows about using the language:

- How frequently a word is used and corresponding words (that is, words that can go with it—for example, fruit that is "ripe," "green," or "sweet," but not "stale").
- Limitations on the use of the word: Is the word stylish, artistic, or out-of-date?
- What is the meaning of the word, and is the word used more in speaking, writing, or both equally?
    - Look at the common dictionary meanings of the word.
    - Look at how can you use it grammatically in a sentence.
- In what part of the country or world is the word used? What is its social role?
    - **By class:** Do people of a certain social status use the word more/less?
    - **By situation:** What is the resulting level of formality conveyed by using the word?

- **By age:** Is it more common for elders or the young to use this word?
- **By job or profession:** Is the word restricted to talk within a given profession, such as law?
- **By gender:** Do you use a certain word depending on the gender of the person you are talking to, your own gender, or the grammatical gender of the person or thing you are talking about?

You can see that your host country nationals will know a lot about the words you need to learn. By using these people as informants, you will be able to pick up tips about the language that you wouldn't be able to in the classroom or by practicing with a non-native speaker.

Post-Study Abroad Vocabulary Activities

Vocabulary learning doesn't have to stop when you arrive back home. Here are some tips for continuing to learn new words:

- Write to friends. Challenge yourself to include two or three new words in each letter.
- When reading, keep a notebook to write down words you don't know and review the words periodically.
- Keep using flash cards. Set aside time to review them at least once or twice a week.
- Learn all the words to a new song.
- Rent a movie in your target language and learn new words by listening to the soundtrack while comparing with the subtitles.
- Find a conversation partner who is a speaker of your target language. You help this person with English vocabulary half of the session, and the partner can help you with your vocabulary the other half.
- Tape commercials from a TV or radio program in the target language. See which words you understand and what the words reveal about the culture.
- Volunteer to help in the community with recent immigrants speaking your target language. You may need to think globally here; if your language is French, for example, people from Vietnam, Ivory Coast, and other countries are often French speakers.
- Get involved with your university's language department, or write an article in your target language for a departmental newsletter.

SPEAKING TO COMMUNICATE

Pre-Departure Speaking Activities

You may think that it is best to wait until you are safely ensconced in your new environment to worry about really trying to speak the target language. Guess what? It may be less stressful if you start beforehand to "break the language barrier."

Some of you may be lucky enough to be at schools where there are programs designed to help you meet international or local students who speak the language you are learning. Or it may be that you live in an area that has a community of people who are native speakers of your target language. In either case, you have a great opportunity to spend some time before you leave speaking the language with native speakers. Here are some useful suggestions from students who themselves have prepared to study abroad:

- Spend a day with a native speaker or group of speakers of the target language
- Have regular meetings with a conversational partner over coffee
- Practice the language over the phone if you cannot meet in person
- Offer a language exchange with international students on your campus—the internationals practice their native language with you in exchange for your help in improving their conversational skills in English
- Speak with friends and fellow students who are studying the target language, ideally those who are a bit more advanced than you and possibly with experience in having used that language abroad

If you don't know groups of students who speak the language you are trying to learn, try some of these strategies:

- Contact your school's study abroad office, language departments, or local community groups that are involved with international activities to locate native speakers of the language you are learning
- If you are enrolled in a language class, you could ask if your instructor knows of opportunities outside of class to practice your new language
- At the least, you'll want to speak up in class as much as possible!

The more time that you can spend practicing speaking, the better. Whenever and however you can, try to find opportunities to surround yourself with the target language. When you do this, you are allowing yourself to open up to the new language and lessen the "language shock" you may experience when you are in another country. If you don't have any of these opportunities available to you before departure, read on and discover strategies you can use once you have arrived in your host country.

Advice to Help Improve Your Speaking Skills

Overcome the fear of speaking

The only way to get over fear is to face it—especially with language. The only way to get better is to use it in all situations and to make situations where language skills are pushed to the limit. ~ Mickie Berg, Italy

Here is Mickie's story on how she pushed herself to the limit:

During the five months I spent in Milan, Italy, I not only attended classes but also had an editorial internship at The Italy Daily Newspaper—a four-page section of the International Herald Tribune, a newspaper sold all over Europe.

During the day I had several hours of language class and used my language with my two Italian roommates and at local coffee bars and shops. In the afternoons, I went to the newspaper where many of the employees were English, Australian, or American. We spoke English and the paper was written in English, but the rest of our jobs were in Italian. I translated news from the Italian wire services into English and rewrote the story into correct newspaper style. I helped the other reporters in obtaining information from businesses or whatever else they needed.

I felt comfortable with my language skills in the office with my co-workers or on the telephone. But when I was faced with the prospect of calling strangers in Sicily for interviews on a story, I was terrified. I felt my language skills were not strong enough to go beyond my circle of people who I knew and who cared about me.

I did not do interviews with sources in Sicily, and I did not write the story. However, in the last few weeks of my five-month internship I was forced to do an article of my own for the newspaper. I had story ideas by the dozen through the internship but had too much fear to do the interviews.

Now was the time. I set up interview appointments with the founder of a volunteer civic police. I went to the Stazione Centrale, the location of the story, and hung out, talking comfortably with Italians, Moroccans, police, and homeless. I was shocked to find out that, even though my language skills were not perfect, I was able to communicate. I could understand everything they were saying and was accepted as a respectable journalist.

After I succeeded with the story, I had a twinge of regret for not taking a chance right away and getting out of the office to do more interviews and write more articles. I have regrets but refuse to kick myself for something I didn't do, even though my experience would have been better had I not hid behind my poor language skills. ~ Mickie Berg, Italy

You may read that and think, "Yeah! I can do this!" Or you may think, "There is no way I could work in this language, let alone carry on an interview!" Here's a story for you:

> *On my first trip to Japan I was very eager to get in there and use the minimal Japanese I had learned in my college courses. I knew about the propensity for Japanese to want to use English with foreigners and so I requested a homestay that spoke hardly any English. What an ordeal that was! Not only did I have to deal with a language I could barely speak, there were environmental and cultural factors that I was confronting every day that became overwhelming. My first homestay didn't succeed, but my eagerness to learn the language was not diminished. If anything, I wanted to learn more language to see if I could piece together the factors that resulted in my homestay going awry. Even though my second homestay didn't speak any English either, I was able to develop a close relationship with my 'okaasan' (mother) and 'otoosan' (father) that contributed to my language improvement as well as to my motivation for learning about the language and culture.*
>
> *While I lived in Japan I continued to use a 'Japanese-only policy' with nearly every Japanese I met. Although I met many Japanese who would not recognize I was speaking Japanese to them and who would constantly answer me in English, most Japanese would eventually oblige me by speaking to me in Japanese. Still, this is not an easy task for a Westerner who speaks a language very much 'in demand' by the hosts. It requires some stamina, persistence, and a little stubbornness at times. Nowadays, since I am more comfortable with my language ability, I am more flexible about obliging English conversation. ~ James Lassegard, Japan*

If you need a little push, ask a native-speaking friend to force you to use only the target language when you are together. If your friend is supportive, you will feel even more comfortable speaking the language even if you make errors. Although it may be frustrating, it may be the best way to get past that tongue-tied stage!

Be willing to make mistakes

It is not surprising that errors are made because in order to produce even a single sentence in a target language, you have to perform a mind-boggling series of tasks to plan what to say, figure out the word order, and then say it correctly—at the right time! But if you don't make mistakes, what funny stories will you bring home to share with others?

> *One day in Venezuela, I was waiting for my American friend to meet me and her host brother. I knew my Spanish language abilities were not that great...but I tried to make conversation anyway with her host brother. It was raining a lot at that moment, so I figured why not talk about the weather. I said, 'Esta llorando mucho,' which I thought was 'It's raining a lot.' He looked at me funny and said 'Lluviendo?' 'Oh! Yeah, lluviendo,' I said. What I actually said was, 'It is crying a lot.' But I was able to joke*

about it and say it's kinda like someone is crying a lot! Ha, ha, ha! Even if you make mistakes in the target language, usually people will think it is cute and just correct you. They understand you are learning. Have fun with the language. ~ Tammy Yach, Venezuela

Learn when to talk

You may not know where it is appropriate to pause and how to signal that you have not finished. This usually entails some way of filling the pause, which varies from language to language and culture to culture.

In English, we often use expressions like "um"..."er"..."you know"... and "like," which often fill pauses between phrases when we speak. Below are some examples of fillers in other languages. Your goal is to figure out the fillers used in your target language.

There are two common pause fillers in Japanese, *eto* and *ano*. You extend the final "o" sound in pronouncing them and to signal that you are thinking. It is possible to overuse them as well, which is what happened to co-author Andrew Cohen in his efforts to "hold the floor" (to keep talking so you aren't interrupted) in his somewhat rudimentary Japanese. A Japanese language partner politely suggested he could use *ano* a bit less! Cohen was also oblivious to the fact that while *eto* tends to be used when addressing people of equal and lower status, *ano* is the preferred pause filler with addressees of higher status! Linking filled pauses with status seems to be unique to Japanese, but you may wish to check this out in your target language.

Additionally, people in other cultures accept and even welcome silent pauses far more than Americans tend to. Cohen had an embarrassing experience of chairing a meeting where a Japanese speaker paused so long before continuing that he thought he had finished and led the audience in a round of applause—only to find the speaker still had 10 minutes left of his presentation! Cohen felt so embarrassed he wanted to climb under the table!

In many regional varieties of Spanish, *este* will help to hold the floor for the speaker. *Et* will do the same in French. It's important to know how silence is perceived in the culture in order to regulate speech and the use of pause-fillers.

During my four weeks in Japan, there were many new aspects of communication to get used to that weren't taught to us in class. An example of such communication is some of the sounds that people make that aren't actual words. The English equivalents for the sounds I'm talking about could be things like, 'Oh' and 'Huh.' I arrived in Japan at about 4 p.m. and traveled without speaking much Japanese at all until about 7 p.m. It was at this point that we students met our host families, who were waiting at the high school. By the time I arrived home with my first family, I was already mimicking their sounds. I'm pretty sure I got some of them wrong, but I caught on eventually. I found those sounds useful because they do express meaning to some degree, and they are easy to remember. ~ Philip Banks, Japan

Consider your speaker type: Are you planner or a corrector?

There are two groups of speakers among those learning a new language—the *planners* and the *correctors*. Planners prefer to carefully plan their speech in their heads and are often silent or show signs of hesitating. Correctors just jump into the conversation, preferring to produce the speech in whatever form they can and work on perfecting it after it has been said. These behaviors are also linked to learning-style preferences. As you learned at the beginning of this guide when you took the Learning Style Survey, some learners are more reflective and others are more impulsive. The more reflective ones may like to prepare what they will say carefully before saying it to others. Impulsive learners may be more likely to speak without hesitation and fix mistakes afterwards, if necessary. One strategy is to be aware of your own preferences and behaviors. A second strategy is to try to use a balance of reflective and impulsive strategies, and challenge yourself to try the opposite approach to increase your learning of the language.

> *I never wanted to embarrass myself when it was a simple request or comment, so in an effort to sound intelligent I would say things in my head first before actually speaking them out loud. Rarely did the words come out as well as I had just said them in my head, but I think this strategy was still helpful. It also helped me to become aware of my English words that I did not know in my target language so I could make a mental note to look them up later when I returned home. Arriving back at my host family's house I would immediately go to my room and pick up a dictionary. I usually remembered two or three words that I had made a mental note about, but oftentimes I did not remember even one. I began writing them down throughout my day so that I would stop forgetting them by the time I got home. ~ Erin Leline, Ecuador*

> *When I speak, I try to plan out what I am going to say in advance, and I try to control the conversation so we can talk about things I know about. I also try to anticipate where the conversation is going. ~ Mary Jo Loch, Germany*

Communicate more

Not only does speaking more give you a chance to practice your skills, it forces others to speak directly to you, giving you a chance to have more personal conversations. Remember that initiating the conversation can seem like a very hard task, but once you do it you'll find that people will be willing to talk with you, even if they have to listen to your broken language. The following is an example of how not participating in the conversation can make the locals feel that you really aren't following the conversation:

> *I was in a restaurant with my Venezuelan boyfriend, and we were sitting at a table with many other Venezuelans. They were all speaking Spanish, and I understood everything that they were saying. I didn't jump into their conversation because I didn't know any of the other people sitting at the table. So, naturally, I just sat and listened as I would do in the U.S. Well, they ended up asking my boyfriend if I knew how to speak Spanish! I*

said, 'Sí, hablo español' (Yes, I speak Spanish). And they all looked at me in surprise. I continued to stay quiet and only answer questions directed toward me. And then throughout the conversation they would ask, 'She doesn't understand, does she?' yet I understood every word! I was so frustrated. I had already told them I knew how to speak Spanish and I had been answering their questions, but they continued to believe that I did not understand because I was not speaking! ~ Tammy Yach, Venezuela

Keep the conversations going

Second language learners often get stuck trying to come up with the perfect word or phrase. Here are a few tips to help you continue speaking, although maybe not perfectly.

Borrow words

Use a word from your native language. For example, you can insert the English word "computer," "taxi," or "OK" into the target language with the hope that the word will be understood.

Translate literally

You can perform word-for-word translation. For example, to tell someone that you are 20 years old in Spanish, you say "*Soy veinte años viejo*," when the correct form is "*Tengo veinte años*," literally "I have 20 years." While you may not be right, you can often get the point across.

"Foreignize" words

Use a word from your native language and fit it into the target language structure or pronunciation. A native Korean speaker may not understand you when you say "ice cream" with American pronunciation, but if you pronounce it "ah-ee-se-ke-lim" in Korean pronunciation, they will probably know what you mean.

I do this all the time with German verbs (e.g., 'interpretieren' for 'interpret'). For better or for worse, however, these words often really exist in German! ('Interpretieren' really is one of several words meaning 'interpret.') ~ Molly Zahn, Germany

Co-author Cohen had such an experience in Brazil some years ago. When he kept asking for a "hot dog" at a kiosk in São Paulo, the woman didn't understand at all. When he remembered to say "hachee dogee," the way Brazilians say it, she understood immediately!

Use descriptions

If you do not know how to say something the way you wish to, try saying it with the vocabulary and sentence structure you know. For example, one student wanted to thank her host family for driving her to the bus stop. Not knowing how to say, "to drive," she said, "Thank you for your car." Another example would be that if you do not know the past tense very well, you could describe the consequence instead of describing the action. So, rather than, "Cynthia gave birth to a 6-pound baby boy," you would say, "Cynthia is now the mother of a 6-pound baby boy."

Use a simple word if necessary

Use the word for "animal" instead of "deer," "tool" instead of "hammer," or simple words such as "big" for "huge" or "gigantic." You could also attach an intensifier like "very," "a lot," "many," or other descriptive words to achieve a closer approximation. For example, before co-author Julie Chi knew more than a few words in Spanish, she wanted to ask her Mexican friends about the ocean. She used these simple words: *grande* (big) and *agua* (water), and learned that the ocean was far away from where she stayed in Monterrey.

> *I would always need to ask my host mom for more toilet paper when I ran out. I did not know how to say toilet paper so would just ask, 'Hay papel para el baño?' (Is there paper for the bathroom?) ~ Tammy Yach, Venezuela*

Coin a new word

Make up a new word in the target language to communicate the unknown word (you create "air ball" because you do not know "balloon").

> *Sometimes, I use English words but make them sound German, or I make up a word. My made-up words are usually understood because Germans use so many compound words as it is. ~ Mary Jo Loch, Germany*

Act out or draw the word

When you don't know the word, you may try nonverbal means for getting the idea across. Co-author Andrew Cohen was in a Brazilian supermarket attempting to buy fresh mushrooms without remembering the word. So he drew what he hoped the store clerk would interpret as a mushroom. He was ushered over to the garlic! So he tried to refine his picture. When it looked more mushroom-like, the clerk asked, "*Cogumelo?*" At first, Andrew was slow to understand whether the clerk got the message. First, such a funny-sounding word didn't seem, on the face of it, to mean anything like "mushroom!" And second, the store was out of mushrooms!

> *I had no clue how to say 'alarm clock' in Spanish. The first night I understood my host mom saying, 'Should I wake you up in the morning?' I wanted to say, 'No, I have an alarm clock.' I used the word for watch and added, 'but it is not a watch, it's a....' Then I made a square in the air with my fingers and put my hand to my ear, then put my hands together, and laid my head on my hands as if to sleep. 'Oh, un despertador' (an alarm clock), she said! ~ Tammy Yach, Venezuela*

Fake your understanding

Study abroad students have reported to us that, depending on the speech community you are in, faking that you understand what a speaker has said may be more socially acceptable than continually asking the speakers to repeat themselves. You need to determine what works best in your situation.

Abandon certain words

Give up the search for a particular word if it is not really necessary for the conversation.

Ask for help

Natives may be more than willing to serve as "experts" on their language and to provide you the word or words you need. They may be flattered that you are so interested.

Rather than simply avoiding words or topics you don't know, you may wish to make the situation into an opportunity for language learning.

- If you don't know the word for cherries, you can say, "I would like a kilo, please" (pointing to the desired fruit). To improve your language, you could point and ask, "What is the word for cherries?" and then ask for the kilo of cherries.
- You are writing an e-mail to a native speaker friend and want to tell about your weekend trip to the mountains. You realize you don't have the necessary vocabulary to say very much, but instead of just saying you had a nice weekend in the mountains, it would be more of a learning opportunity to use words you do know and to ask for your friend's help.

When controversial topics come up (e.g., U.S. military operations in other countries, environmental degradation, globalization, social justice, gender roles, sex, and racism), you can use the opportunity to learn language. You may be tempted to avoid the topic altogether—either because you feel you are lacking the vocabulary and grammar structures to express yourself effectively or because you are reluctant to get into a touchy issue.

- First off, be cordial and polite.
- Think through your views on the topic and be ready to discuss them; claiming you don't have views on the topic probably won't sound very believable.
- Try to use the opportunity to gain more information by asking others about their opinions and to get background information on the topic. For example, if the topic is abortion, you could ask questions like, "How does your government view abortion?" or "Has it always been this way?"

Learning from Your Mistakes

Establish a relationship with some native speaker that will permit that person to actually correct your mistakes. In some cultures that's hard because people worry you will be offended. I remember that when I was in the Peace Corps in Venezuela it took months before I finally was able to convince one person—a close colleague at my work—that I really did want her to correct every mistake I made. Once she began to do so, she was an invaluable aid to my language learning. ~ Chip Peterson, Venezuela

Correct yourself

You are bound to make mistakes. But did you know that you are capable of correcting about half of your mistakes by yourself? You simply need time to hear just what it was you actually said. If you are in a situation where a teacher or other speaker of the language corrects your errors as soon as you say them, you could:

- Request that they wait until you have had a chance to self-correct
- Ask that they let you finish speaking before they provide the correction

Accept feedback on your errors

For those errors you can't self-correct, you need to be able to digest the corrections that come your way.

Co-author Andrew Cohen tells of missing a bus and consequently arriving late to a language center where he was studying Arabic. Who should greet him in the corridor but one of his Arabic teachers, who proceeded to correct his Arabic explanation of how he had missed the bus! At that moment, Cohen wanted to be able to hold up a sign saying that he was simply in the "communication-of-message" mode while he was explaining being late, and that he wasn't in the "attentive-learner" mode, when he would presumably be more receptive to the corrections his teacher was offering! However, given that Cohen is an avid language learner and respectful of his instructor's status, he did eventually pay attention to the corrections from his teacher. The point is to be open to being corrected, even when you are focused on another goal.

- To make the most of corrections, write down the correction in a notebook—possibly in a special section for that kind of information (see example under "Feedback on Written Work," p. 238) and verify the correct form with a native speaker of the language (possibly the teacher) at a later time.

> *I found that the best way I learned was when I would speak with my host mother and she would correct my speaking errors. I think she was a little reserved when I first arrived, but after about two weeks she started helping me. ~ Erin Leline, Ecuador*

Creating Opportunities for Speaking the Language In-Country

The truth is that for many reasons, you may find yourself associating primarily with other English speakers rather than with native speakers. In addition, you may actually be taking most of your courses in English. As a result, your exposure to your target language may not be quite what you had expected. What can you do about that?

Gather up your courage and speak to strangers

Let's say you are shy by your very nature and have trouble walking up to strangers and starting a conversation. All the same, you can probably find some strategies that will make it relatively easy for you to strike up conversations with strangers. One study of effective language learners found, for example, that elderly people and young children may provide two good types of conversational partners since they are likely to be more interested in what you have to say rather than in how you say it, and more importantly, they may be happy to talk with you and readily excuse your obvious deficiencies as a target language speaker. So here are some strategies for non-native speakers who are hesitant about starting up conversations with target language speakers:

- Seek out elderly people sitting on park benches or at malls, as it's possible they may have time on their hands and may not be in a hurry to cut off your sentences, finish your remarks, or correct your grammar.
- Young children are another resource for casual conversations since they will be less likely to correct your grammar. They may correct your vocabulary, but that could be helpful. Co-author Barbara Kappler found a note she had written to her host family in Britain edited by her 12-year-old host brother! He seemed to enjoy the opportunity to correct the vocabulary in her U.S. American English, and it became a weekly ritual for them. This turned out to be a fine way for Barbara to learn the local dialect.
- Taxi drivers are usually more than happy to talk with you and typically won't correct your language. They will just be happy that you can speak their language at all. Here is how one study abroad student benefited from this opportunity:

> *Some of the most beneficial conversations I had in Spain were with taxi drivers. When we traveled, we took taxis a lot. In the cars, the drivers would usually start up conversations. These were very helpful because they spoke very fast and they used a lot of slang words. In these situations, I would rely on my global learning style. I would not try and plan out what I was going to say, instead, I just let the conversations happen. Since I usually had other English speakers in the car with me, it was easy for us to communicate with the drivers because if one person missed what was said, another person was able to explain. ~ Amanda Smith, Spain*

Take advantage of program opportunities

Your school or other organizations in your host country probably offer various programs to help you meet native speakers. Don't miss out on these organized opportunities to meet people. One student, after reading the recommendation about talking to strangers, gave this advice:

> *People are chickens, and it is much easier NOT to strike up random conversations with people on park benches—for me, this is VERY difficult. But my language program offered several special opportunities to interact with native speakers—a visit to a clinic to talk with the patients, special arrangements with a permanent resident of the city, etc. Of course this depends on the program, but it seems many offer such opportunities. The point that needs to be made is that if such opportunities exist, take advantage of them! ~ Molly Zahn, Germany*

Become a regular at local establishments

Maybe you don't like to talk to strangers and your program offers few opportunities to meet native speakers. In this case, you need to create a way to get to know people over time. One solution is to go to the same stores, the same coffee shops or delis, or the same discos so that you can slowly get to know people.

> *Instead of eating my lunch in the English-speaking cafeteria, I often went to the nearby taco place and ordered, in Spanish, different types of tacos. I didn't know what some of them were, so I asked questions. ~ Julie Chi, Mexico*

> *When I first arrived in Malaysia, I felt a bit timid about going very far so I ended up eating my meals frequently in the same local restaurant. Because I went often, I soon became a regular and ended up having lots of time to get to know the waiters and other restaurant staff. One of the waiters ended up inviting me to go to his village to see a typical Malay wedding—I was amazed that such a great opportunity grew out of hanging out at a local restaurant. ~ Karin Larson, Malaysia*

Be careful in choosing housing

Some study abroad programs offer a choice among various types of housing. If yours does, take language into account in making your selection. A homestay, an apartment with native-speaking roommates, or some other arrangement that will surround you with the target language daily is preferable to an apartment with U.S. American roommates, a dorm just for foreign students, etc. Think carefully about the goals of your program. While you may lose some freedom in selecting a homestay or give up some familiarity by selecting host nationals for roommates, this decision could have the greatest impact on reaching your language-learning goals.

Be persistent about making new friends

Your stay is temporary. It can be hard for locals to want to befriend you, only to have you leave in a few weeks or months. The burden is on you to make the extra effort to meet new people. You might notice that these connections lead to others, too. And not surprisingly, research has shown that those who date a native speaker show rapid language improvement. (More comments about cross-cultural dating are on p. 80.)

> *I dated a native from Venezuela while studying abroad, and since I did not want to speak to total strangers, I could talk to him. This way my Spanish really skyrocketed! I am so glad that I dated him because if I hadn't I would have been like all the other American students there—talking to each other without really learning much Spanish. ~ Tammy Yach, Venezuela*

Here's co-author Julie Chi's story on her experience in Seoul, South Korea. With only a year of formal Korean instruction under her belt, Julie set off for Korea with her husband, a native Korean, to live with her in-laws, whom she had never met:

> *I knew that in order to make a good impression, I had to be able to make myself understood in Korean. I had my husband, a native Korean, to help me some of the time, but there were many times when I had to make myself communicate in Korean without his help.*

I woke up every morning very early to help my mother-in-law cook breakfast for the family. I learned the vocabulary for all the ingredients, and I also learned how to describe the processes for cooking the new foods. Even though it was hard for me to wake up before everyone else because of my exhaustion from speaking Korean the day before, I made myself get up to speak with my mother-in-law.

In addition to helping out in the mornings, Julie also enrolled in a swimming class with her mother-in-law and used this class as an opportunity to have casual "chatty" conversations with her mother-in-law's friends, expanding the topics for discussion as she became more comfortable in Korean. Julie also reconnected with a Korean woman that she had become friends with in the United States, and she in turn introduced her to other Korean friends Julie could practice her speaking with.

I made every effort to speak that I could. I even talked with my two-year-old nephew! I made sure to use a lot of gestures and ask a lot of questions like, 'How do you say __________ in Korean?' I made up words, talked around the topic until they understood, and most importantly, I knew when to take a break so as not to burn out. I was very lucky for my experiences, and now that I'm back in the U.S., I continue to practice Korean with a new friend when we meet each week for coffee.

Although Julie had opportunities that you may not, if you are living with a host family you can try to do some of the things Julie did. If you're not, make friends and spend some time with their families or attend some of their activities regularly.

Tips for staying in the target language

So far the emphasis in this section has been on getting you comfortable speaking the language of the host community. The assumption was that you may be fearful about speaking the target language at all, or at least anxious about making mistakes. It was also thought you may need some communication strategies to ensure that you keep the conversation going (such as using paraphrases like a circumlocution: "I need something to cover my clothes while I cook" = "I need an apron"). Finally, suggestions were given for how to create speaking opportunities, such as going up to strangers, taking advantage of program opportunities, frequenting local establishments, finding a housing arrangement where the target language is needed, and meeting local people.

But let's assume you have gotten over your inhibitions and are now putting yourself out there. What do you do when you encounter host country natives who want to practice their English with you and are really insistent about it? Or what if they perceive your target language efforts to be so weak that they switch to English so as to "put you out of your misery" or to move the action along more quickly? While you may feel annoyed or put down, they may think they are doing you a service!

Here are some options for you to follow if you really do want to use the target language more, especially if the host country native speaker is a member of your host family, a friend from the community, or a fellow student, rather than a stranger:

- Just persist in the target language and see what happens. The native speakers may recognize your persistence and switch back to the target language.
- Let it be a bilingual conversation. You speak in the target language and the other person speaks in English. Why not? This way you're both getting practice at the other's language. Although it is not a wise long-term strategy, this may help initially in keeping the conversation going.
- Conduct the conversation first in English and then go back over it in the target language.
- Have periods during the day when only English is used and other periods when only the target language is used. It can be soothing to you to know that your language partner will continue on in the target language, despite difficulties you are having finding words and phrases. Switch the times during the week for each language so that the conversations may vary. Thus, you're not always talking about breakfast and the weather if you choose breakfast time for your language practice.

What should be clear from this is that sometimes it may be necessary to "negotiate" when and how your language is used, and when the target language is used. Rather than leaving it to chance, you can actually discuss the issue with your conversation partners and arrive at a solution that works for everyone.

Beyond Knowing the Vocabulary

Have you thought about how you would deal with sensitive situations like apologies or complaints while studying abroad? What about accepting or declining invitations in the target language? Do you know the right kinds of expressions to use? If so, do you know when and how to use them?

Suppose the following things happen to you in the United States:

1. You do not want to go to a party thrown by some high school friends. You feel out of touch with many of them and want to spend time with new college friends. What do you say to get out of going to the party?
2. You are five minutes late for a doctor's appointment. What do you say to the receptionist? Then, you wait 45 minutes to see the doctor. What do you say to the doctor when you finally get in?
3. Your friend meets you for lunch, looking great in a new sweater. What do you say? What if this person is "more than a friend"? What if you don't want the person to think of you as more than a friend?

Knowing how to refuse invitations, apologize, complain, make requests, and give compliments in your own language requires intricate knowledge of cultural rules and norms. Here are a few ways you might respond:

1. While you may value being direct in your communication, you might feel it's a bit rude to tell your high school friends, "I have outgrown our relationship and would rather spend time with my new friends." You may

feel it is more polite to explain, "Thanks for the invite, but I can't make it on Thursday—I have other plans."

2. In the doctor's office many would make a small apology to the receptionist for being late but would not expect to have the appointment canceled. Most would not expect an apology from the doctor. Making a direct complaint to the doctor may also be considered disrespectful, given the status of the doctor and prior knowledge that doctor's appointments often run behind schedule.
3. How do you give a compliment to a friend? Maybe you would say, "Hey, nice sweater." But to impress someone or show that you have a romantic interest, you may emphasize how good your friend looks in the sweater: "Wow, you look really nice today. Great sweater. Is that new?"

Some days, it might be complicated enough to feel competent in your own language. How do you do this in a second? The rules that govern the way we say things to get across our intended meaning are so subtle that they are very difficult to decipher by non-native speakers.

The following example is from Hebrew. You want to take a window seat on a bus and need to get by the woman in the aisle seat. You say *sliha*, which you know means "excuse me" in other situations. But this time the woman reacts as if *she* had just stepped on *your* foot. You were unaware that in Hebrew *sliha* is a bit rude. In this situation, the means of requesting access to the window seat would more likely be either *Efshar lashevet*? (Is it possible to sit there?) or *Eyfshar la'avor*? (May I get by?).

Have patience. The subtlety of language and culture means it can literally take years to feel confident about how to say these things.

Perhaps the safest way to develop your ability to have your language function in a culturally acceptable way is to check out what it is appropriate to say before you say it. The following are two activities you could do in order to gather information before speaking. The first deals with compliments and the second with requests.

ACTIVITY: Gathering culturally appropriate language

Consider the following scenarios and what you might say in the target language.

1. **You are by nature a friendly person and like to compliment people on how they look and on the things they do well. The following are two compliments you are likely to extend:**

    a. *Hey, ____________, I really like what you're wearing today! That's a really cool _________.*
    b. *Hey, ____________, I thought your talk was outstanding. You did a nice job of presenting that material.*

Because you really like to pass on well-deserved compliments, you have been advised that in your host community, it is easy to offend people by doing compliments wrong. You have heard, for example, that depending on your age, your status, or your gender, an intended compliment may at worst be taken as an insult and at best may be considered inappropriate coming from you. In some cultures, the person being complimented, say on their jewelry, may feel obligated to offer it to you.

Find someone who is a native speaker and gather information from that person about how to perform the above two compliments in the target language. Be sure to check out your compliments with regard to their acceptability depending on who the sender is and who the recipient is.

2. **You are living in a host community where you find people making requests of you that you want to refuse. The problem is that you never learned in your language textbook how to refuse tactfully. The following are two typical situations:**

    a. You are invited to a friend's party, but you don't want to attend because there is usually a lot of smoke, noise, and drinking. In addition, such parties usually go on too long for you (since you start working early in the morning), and you know from experience that it is difficult to leave early. How do you decline the invitation?
    b. Your colleague asks you to edit a paper for her in English because she would like to get it published somewhere. Not only is your time very limited but also you know she is a weak writer, both conceptually and in terms of language proficiency. You absolutely need to turn down her request without offending her. How do you do it?

Find someone who is a native speaker and gather information about refusals in the target language. Ask this informant about some acceptable ways to perform each of the two refusals above, depending on who you are (age, status, gender) and who the recipient is.

Now let's assume you already checked with a native speaker and know what to say. The following are a few situations where you can try out conveying your message in culturally appropriate language.

ACTIVITY: An exercise in 'getting what you want'

The most frustrating situation is often when you need to request something specific from another person. Try your skills out for the following situations in the language and cultural context you are dealing with:

Situation 1: Your family has decided to visit. There is no convenient public transportation from the airport. You need to ask your host (friends or family) for a ride.

What would you say in your home country?	What rules/values/differences might be involved in the target culture?	What would you say in the target language?

Situation 2: Your friend is often late to meet you to walk to school. You would like to walk together but have been arriving late to class and don't feel comfortable. You want to ask your friend to arrive on time.

What would you say in your home country?	What rules/values/differences might be involved in the target culture?	What would you say in the target language?

Situation 3: You found a cheap airplane ticket to visit friends in a neighboring city. In order to take the trip, you need to ask your instructor for an extension on a paper due next week.

What would you say in your home country?	What rules/values/differences might be involved in the target culture?	What would you say in the target language?

LANGUAGE: *Speaking*

Should you be expected to say things with the same finesse as a native speaker? In many cases, the words you say will be accepted even if you violate certain rules. If people recognize that you're a non-native speaker from your accent, they'll be less likely to be offended by the way you say things. In other cases, your communication may be accepted but would still be viewed as inappropriate. In still other cases, it may not be acceptable at all. Take advantage of your time in another country to learn these nuances.

What co-author Julie Chi has done is practice with a friend who isn't offended by what she says but teaches her how to say it better. She asks her friend to tell her whether or not it is appropriate to talk about a certain topic, for example, or how to say something with which she previously had a blundering experience. It's OK to make mistakes, and you can learn from them with some assistance of a friend.

"I'm SO sorry": Strategies for apologizing

Nothing is as simple as an apology, right? Don't you just show you feel bad and say, "I'm sorry?" Well, it's not quite that easy. There are a few things you may want to know about apologies.

You may breeze through your entire study abroad program, never offending a soul and never causing a problem. If that's you, skip to the next section. However, if you are like most travelers—including all of us writing this—you will probably need to apologize at some time. And when you do so, given that you've already offended someone or caused a problem, you want to make sure you don't rub salt in the wound by apologizing in a manner that makes things worse.

The following chart is a list of strategies for apologizing that apply universally to apologies in any language. The trick is knowing which one(s) to use in a given situation in a given language. Ask a native speaker to help you fill in the chart with some target language phrases that you can use in various situations.

Strategy	Apologizer	Notes about Use in English
Apology expression	Use a word, expression, or sentence with a verb such as "sorry," "excuse," "forgive," or "apologize"	Can be intensified whenever the apologizer feels the need to do so by adding "really" or "very"
Acknowledge responsibility	Absolute acknowledgment of responsibility ↓ Rejection of responsibility	**High:** It's my fault. **Middle:** I was confused; you are right. **Low:** I didn't mean to. **Lower:** I was sure I gave you the right information. **Reject:** It was not my fault.
Explanation	Describe what caused the offense (e.g., the bus was late); the explanation is intended to set things right	Used by the speaker as an indirect way of apologizing
Offer of repair	Makes a bid to do something or provide payment for damage	Only appropriate when tangible damage has occurred
Promise of nonrecurrence	Commits to not having the offense happen again	

Target Language Phrases	When Appropriate?

(Adapted from Cohen and Olshtain, 1981.)

Note that in some cultures no apology may be effective in rectifying the situation:

> *I was flying out of Athens, and when we landed I accidentally hit the man behind me in the head with the bag I was getting out of the overhead compartment. I apologized immediately, and he didn't say anything. We had to wait to get off the plane and out of the corner of my eye I could see him touching his head and rubbing it. I felt uncomfortable and guilty, so I turned to him and apologized again. At this point he started yelling at me, going on about how this had happened because I was impatient, and now he was hurt and it was just no good to be so impatient. After a few moments I realized that saying anything more was going to aggravate the situation, so I simply turned and faced forward until the line started moving and I was able to get off the plane.*
>
> *If the same thing happened in the U.S., my experience has been that the other person would have accepted my apology, especially the second time. In retrospect I should have realized that getting yelled at was a possibility. I spent a year in Greece, and there were a few instances where I personally got 'scolded' by someone in public or witnessed public arguments between strangers. From what I'd seen and experienced, it seemed to be true that when someone yelled at someone else in Greece, the other person didn't automatically apologize but defended themselves by yelling back. In my airplane incident, I don't think anything would have appeased that particular man. Possible alternatives would have been to say nothing at all and act as if I hadn't hit him with my bag or after he started yelling at me, I might have argued back that he was standing too close to me in the first place, and so on. ~ Suzanne Hay, Greece*

In contrast to the experience above, co-author James Lassegard had the following to say after he and Suzanne Hay compared their respective experiences in Greece and Japan:

> *If this same incident happened in Japan, a very lengthy apology accompanied by much bowing and expressing of concern for the health of the hapless victim would be warranted. Also, in most cases in Japan, an explanation for a wrong caused by someone comes off as simply an excuse and would never be accepted in lieu of an apology.*

The following situation gives an example of how culture impacts the use of language:

> You completely forget a crucial meeting with your instructor. An hour later you call to apologize. The problem is that this is the second time you've forgotten such a meeting. Your instructor gets on the line and asks, "What happened?"

If you were an Israeli Hebrew speaker, your culture may support two types of behavior in your reply. First, you would emphasize your explanation. For example, "Well, I had to take my roommate to the doctor and then there was a problem with the landlord...." Second, you would not try to repair the situation by saying something like, "I am so sorry. I'd like to reschedule the meeting whenever it's convenient for you." In the Israeli culture, it is up to the boss (instructor) to determine the next step. It would be presumptuous for the lower-status person to suggest what happens next.

Take a look at this example of how cross-cultural misunderstandings can occur:

> At the campus coffee shop, Rebecca, an exchange student from Israel, accidentally bumps into her friend Mary, a U.S. American who is holding a cup of hot coffee. The hot coffee spills all over Mary, soaking her clothing. Mary shouts, startled: "Oooh! Ouch!" Rebecca says, "Sorry." Mary glares at her. Rebecca assumes Mary is really mad at her for bumping into her.

What happened? Rebecca, an Israeli Hebrew speaker, directly translated the expression of "sorry" from Hebrew to English. In Israel, it would be understood that she is very sincere in her apology; however, to Mary, a speaker of U.S. English, this does not sound at all like an apology. Mary is expecting an intensifier: "I'm really sorry. Are you OK?" And even possibly an offer of repair: "Oh! Here, let me help get something on that burn and clean up the mess."

Improve your competence

You cannot learn the most appropriate way to say things on your own. It is essential to immerse yourself in the culture and connect with native speakers. However, don't expect to learn these things naturally. You will need to become a language detective and seek answers to specific questions.

Ask native speakers how they would apologize in situations from those involving only a minor offense (e.g., slightly bumping into someone or interrupting their conversation) to those involving a major offense (e.g., hitting their car or hurting them physically). Try to imagine situations you could be in, or those which you have been in, if you have past experience with native speakers.

Ask a native speaker whether there would be any difference in each of these apologies depending on whether the person being apologized to is:

- of higher status (e.g., a boss or a parent), equal status, or lower status
- a friend/acquaintance or a stranger

Sometimes you may find that specific intensifiers are only used for certain speech acts that are different from the English words "very" or "really." For example, the word *domo* in Japanese can be used to heighten the expression of gratitude or regret, but it is not used to enhance words or phrases in a sentence like "very" is.

We use apologizing in this section as a way to introduce the topic of using language appropriately in different cultural situations. You should also learn how to express yourself in a number of other situations such as:

- Giving and receiving compliments
- Making refusals
- Giving directions
- Thanking
- Making requests
- Making complaints
- Giving advice
- Greetings

Post-Study Abroad Speaking Activities

The number one complaint from returnees is that friends and family are not interested in hearing the details of their experience abroad. What is also frustrating is that you will have fewer opportunities to speak in the target language. You may even feel lost among your fellow Americans. To keep up your language skills and to feel connected to your study abroad experience, you need to find people to talk to.

Where do you find these language informants?

- Locate clubs on campus and in the community that promote your country of interest and target language.
- Use the Internet to find native speakers or people interested in conversational exchange. There are many great Web sites that allow you to have live chats with people living on the other side of the world.
- Check newspapers or the Internet for upcoming cultural events or celebrations of holidays such as the Chinese New Year. Attend other activities like foreign films or art exhibits that are specific to your country or region of interest, and actively seek out others with whom you can practice speaking the target language.

LANGUAGE-LEARNING STYLES AND STRATEGIES: READING FOR COMPREHENSION

Being able to understand the text in another language helped me feel self-sufficient. It allows a freedom from dependency on others. ~ Jon DeVries, world traveler

Like an awakening, there's a point when you realize you're relying more on instinct than a dictionary to breeze through your French novel. Even if fleeting, at that moment I've felt like a cultural insider...as if I might have been born in the wrong place. ~ Kristin Mishra, France

If I can read a local newspaper in a place that I travel, it's empowering, exciting. Feels like another window opens on a different world. ~ Steve Theobald, world traveler

Pre-Departure Reading Activities

Like to read poetry? Science fiction? Cookbooks? Whatever you like to read in English is the best thing to read in your target language before study abroad. Why? Because you'll have the motivation to read it! Here are a few tips for finding resources in your target language:

- Ask your language teachers.
- Check your university or local library's collection for subscriptions to international and national newspapers.
- Search the Internet using your host country's name as your keyword.
- Check out online bookstores to find foreign books.
- Talk to local native speakers for their suggestions.
- Ask fellow students, local native speakers, or your language teacher if you can borrow materials.
- Choose a dictionary that's best for you to aid in your reading practice.

  Bilingual dictionaries (English to/from another language) can be misleading because there may not be direct equivalence between the English word and the word in the target language.

  Monolingual dictionaries (single language) can be more helpful in truly understanding the meaning of words, but then you need to be knowledgeable enough in the language to understand the definition!

  Monolingual and bilingual dictionaries. There are some dictionaries that are both monolingual and bilingual in the same book, which solves the problem of either/or.

  Electronic dictionaries make word retrieval quicker. Many electronic dictionaries allow you to store vocabulary you come across when you are out and about. You can review this vocabulary at your leisure, with the dictionary taking on the role of flash cards.

Learner dictionaries. Such dictionaries may be more helpful to low-intermediate learners because they make some effort to use simplified language. Nonetheless, be prepared for them not to be simplified enough at times. A classic case is a learner dictionary of English that defined "to moor" as "to secure or fasten to the dock." The learner didn't know what "secure," "fasten," or "dock" meant, so the definition was useless! In this case, the learner needed to look up the unknown words in the definition before she finally could understand the word "moor."

Get the Most from Your Reading

Reading in a second language can be like taking a ride on a roller coaster. There's frustration—and sometimes fear and self-doubt—when you feel you're getting nowhere and need to look up every word. There's a big thrill of excitement when you can quickly cruise through and know you understand nearly everything. And sometimes it's just hard to keep going as you read the same sentence over and over and over. This section contains strategies for helping you with the ups and downs of reading in another language. These strategies have worked for hundreds of students, and they can work for you too!

Strategies for increasing your comprehension

Decide why you need to read it

You probably feel overwhelmed sometimes because you try to understand every word or idea. Determine if you really need to understand the entire text or just get a grasp of the main topic. In most contexts, you may only need to get the main idea. Then you know whether to read the material thoroughly or just skim it.

Skim the text

Gathering clues about the context is critical in increasing your understanding and retention when reading in another language. Skimming before you read the text from start to finish helps provide this context. You are probably experienced at skim reading, but here are a few reminders:

- Read through all the headings.
- Jump to the end to see if there is a useful summary, discussion, or conclusion.
- Outline the main sections of the text.

Use both top-down and bottom-up tactics

Just as with listening, you may have preferences for whether you are a "top-down" or "bottom-up" reader. Ideally, you will be able to use both. Top-down reading is when you already know something about a topic and apply this to a new reading. For example, you are reading an article about AIDS. Since you already know something about the disease, you expect certain topics to be discussed, such as the number of cases reported and the number of countries affected by the disease. This prior knowledge helps you intuit the meaning of the new article. On the other hand, when you focus exclusively on the words and sentences of the text in front of you and use only those words to assist you in creating meaning, this is referred to as bottom-up reading.

If you are a beginning learner, you may find more success in the top-down approach. Also, if your goal is just to get the main idea, you would use the top-down approach. However, if you intend to get fine details, or if you know nothing about the topic, you may find that the bottom-up approach is better suited to your needs.

Don't overuse your dictionary

A good rule of thumb is to use a dictionary sparingly. Why? Because dictionary use:

- Distracts you from the text and takes twice the time
- May cause errors, especially if you use a bilingual dictionary (e.g., an English/Spanish dictionary) because languages often do not have direct equivalents; and in some cases, different countries have different dialects of the language
- May result in your forgetting the meaning immediately after looking it up anyway!

The following is a comment about bilingual dictionaries from co-author James Lassegard, a longtime resident of Tokyo:

> *Now that I am abroad, I've learned so much language here 'in context' whether written or spoken that I would find it difficult to give English translations unless I really thought about it. I think trying to get a precise English translation (when there isn't one) is one of the biggest obstacles learners have and results in the overuse of dictionaries, which tends to compound the frustration.*

Consequently, it may be most beneficial for you to learn as much vocabulary as possible in context rather than from the dictionary. But if you are going to use the dictionary, you may wish to have some effective system for recording a meaning. It is often the case that learners keep looking up the same words over and over because they forget the entry immediately after finding it. The more effort you use to figure out the word, the more likely you will be to remember it.

Read between the lines

Keep your eyes open to clues in the reading itself. For example, you are reading in a popular magazine about outdated fashion, and the writer tells you not to wear a shirt with a loud pattern. Does this mean that you should not wear a shirt with musical instruments on it or one that plays loud music? No, of course you know from the context that it means that the pattern is wild and disturbing, so you would not want to offend other people by wearing it.

Get some background information first

Before reading a new text:

- Ask someone (a friend, native speaker, or someone with more reading proficiency than yourself) to give you an introduction to the material, such as an explanation of the topic. This discussion will give you background information for understanding the text.
- Ask this person to help you define difficult vocabulary in advance.

I had a difficult reading to do for one of my Spanish classes in Venezuela. It was on folklore, so I had no clue where the text would be taking me with the different mythical characters and the things that they were engaging in. However, my Venezuelan friend helped me by explaining certain parts of the text to me, and from this I was able to grasp the concept and understand what I would be encountering in the reading. This was a lot faster and easier than using the dictionary, and it also helped me use my target language to help understand the reading. ~ Tammy Yach, Venezuela

Strategies for remembering what you read

Write summaries

Ever feel like you understand each sentence as it goes by and then get to the end and don't remember anything? This is common! The mind has to perform mental gymnastics in order to get at the meaning from a target language text. What helps is to make ongoing summaries every few lines. This keeps the meaning of previous material fresh while you continue on to new material. To keep your mind thinking in the target language, try to write the summaries in the target language rather than English. Writing them in English only slows you down by forcing your mind to switch back and forth between languages.

I found that making summaries of each Spanish reading was very helpful. I could always refer back to my notes if I was confused or use them as study material for the test. Other students would always ask me for my notes so they could understand the reading. If they had just made their own notes, they too would have easily remembered what they read in the beginning of the reading. A foreign language is difficult to learn, thus when reading and retaining what a second language text says, taking notes is necessary for ultimate comprehension. ~ Carrie Borle, Spain

Generate questions

When the reading feels slow and plodding—even if the topic seems interesting—it's easy to fall asleep or get bored reading in a target language. One way to stay alert and curious is to predict actively what the writer is likely to write about next. Try turning each heading and subheading into a question, using words such as *who*, *what*, *when*, *where*, *why*, and *how*. Then, predict the answers to each question. While you're reading, notice whether or not your prediction was close to being correct.

For example, you are reading a magazine article with a title that translates to "New Drug Approved." You'll ask yourself, "What is the drug and what is its use? Who created and approved this new drug? Where can one get the drug? How was it created? Should I use this drug?" You might have some possible answers already floating around in your mind, so you read to find out whether or not your predictions were right. You might be surprised that the drug is more (or less) effective than you expected!

Strategies for getting feedback

How do you know you are doing a good job reading? This can be a bit of a challenge since reading is basically unobservable unless you are reading aloud, which isn't very common unless you are practicing to give an oral reading. In that case you could have someone check your reading for how natural it sounds. Consider meeting with a teacher during office hours to practice, or pair up with someone who speaks the target language fluently and read the material aloud.

When you are doing silent reading, you could ask a native-speaking friend to read a text you had difficulty with (or a portion of it) and see if the friend has the same understanding of it as you. If it is a popular novel or essay that your friends have read themselves, you could try to summarize it for them and see whether they agree with your summary. The daily newspaper can be a good source of feedback on reading if you can find a friend who reads it. Check whether your interpretation of a lead story is accurate. You can always ask friends to confirm or correct your understanding of given words as well.

> *You know you are doing a good job reading when you can read through the text and understand the general concept. You do not let hard words bog you down or cause you to keep turning to the dictionary. You continue reading and make notes while you read. You can always go back to your notes if you do not understand. ~ Tammy Yach, Venezuela*

ACTIVITY: Filling in the gaps

As you read texts in a second language, there are going to be numerous words you do not understand. Strategic readers use both general knowledge and clues from the words they do know to fill in the gaps. The following is an exercise involving a story about daily planners in which certain words have been deleted. Your task is to read the text as is and to answer the comprehension questions without attempting to fill in the blanks. When you have finished, you can check the source text, but you may surprise yourself to see just how many words you "filled in" without having to check the original. You will almost certainly notice that it was not necessary to fill in the blanks in order to complete the task.

LANGUAGE: *Reading*

Daily Planners: Now You See Them, Now You Don't

Directions: *Read the text below without filling in the blanks and then answer the comprehension questions that follow.*

It used to be that you would organize your life by means of a printed annual calendar book that also had a place for storing phone numbers. It was with a ________ like this that you would ________ track of the events in your ________. Each year you would dutifully recopy the ________ and addresses of your friends, acquaintances, and others who you ________ to keep in touch with and discard the others. The ________ would be to see how small a ________ you could use and still have ________to make the entries you wanted. If you could fit it in your ________ or purse, that would be ideal. You took it with you almost ________.

Then in the name ________ progress these simple calendar books got ________ by more elegant loose-leaf "daily planners." These ________ often came encased in expensive leather binders, some ________ a zipper on them and sporting a ________ of accessories such as a ruler, a magnifying ________, a map of the world, a ________ album section, and so forth. The use of replaceable ________ meant that parts of the book ________ be preserved into the ________ calendar year. It was no longer ________ to copy over all your names and ________. But it now became a bigger ________ to set up your annual organizer because they ________ special fillers for different categories of ________. There were sections for long-range ________, for commitments, and for ongoing projects. These ________ got to be almost exorbitantly ________ with all these special sections, the clip-on rulers, and other stylish ________ like the photograph pages. These planners were not ________ expensive but also heavy. And you could no longer ________ them in your pocket or your purse. They took on a life of ________ own.

But just as quickly as these organizers ________ on the scene, they were replaced. In ________, the exquisite leather planners became a ________ of the past as the electronic planners made their ________ on the scene. All of sudden people were doing their ________ with handheld devices that stored everything forever. The actual electronic ________ was synced to a computer so that ________ was a backup for everything in your handheld ________ organizer. What a boon, since when you used to ________ your leather organizer on a plane, that was the last you ________ of all your plans and contact information. Now if you ________ or damaged this electronic organizer, you could get another one and ________ it with your stored information from your ________. Also when you wanted to check an ________ from several years back, if you hadn't ________ your old calendar in a closet you were out of ________. Now the ________ just sits there in electronic storage, waiting to be called up. In addition, you used to have to ________ until the new organizer pages came out in order to ________ events in the future beyond the calendar year. Now this was no longer the ________. In addition, you now didn't have to ________ over your address book information and you could easily update it whenever you ________ to. No longer would you have ________ with fading pencil and smudges. That was all a thing of the ________.

But what is state-of-the-art ________ is likely to be outdated and devalued tomorrow. The simple ________ device is itself becoming almost anachronistic as people are increasingly ________ a more sophisticated personal digital assistant (PDA). Not only do they now manage your personal ________, such as contacts, appointments, and to-do lists, but also ________ to the Internet, act as global positioning system (GPS) devices, and run multimedia software. What's more, ________ have combined PDAs with cell phones, multimedia players, and other electronic gadgetry.

The real ________ is whether we are better organized ________ than we were when we used a little calendar book we kept in our pocket or purse. Do we ________ our lives better? Do we show up for ________ more on time than ever before? Do we think in grander terms about the ________ we can do in life? Are we more in ________ with our friends than in the ________? There are clearly more bells and whistles ________ to our personal planning, as well as a more ________ price tag. Whether we are better ________ remains to be seen!

Comprehension questions

- What is the main point of the passage?
- According to the author, what features has technology brought to personal organization?
- What are the advantages and disadvantages of these advances?
- Does the author feel that people are better organized today than in the past?

Complete text

Daily Planners: Now You See Them, Now You Don't

It used to be that you would organize your life by means of a printed annual calendar book that also had a place for storing phone numbers. It was with a book like this that you would keep track of the events in your life. Each year you would dutifully recopy the names and addresses of your friends, acquaintances, and others who you wanted to keep in touch with and discard the others. The challenge would be to see how small a book you could use and still have room to make the entries you wanted. If you could fit it in your pocket or purse, that would be ideal. You took it with you almost everywhere.

Then in the name of progress these simple calendar books got replaced by more elegant loose-leaf "daily planners." These planners often came encased in expensive leather binders, some having a zipper on them and sporting a series of accessories such as a ruler, a magnifying glass, a map of the world, a photo album section, and so forth. The use of replaceable pages meant that parts of the book would be preserved into the next calendar year. It was no longer necessary to copy over all your names and addresses. But it now became a bigger expense to set up your annual organizer because they had special fillers for different categories of planning. There were sections for long-range planning, for commitments, and for ongoing projects. These books got to be almost exorbitantly expensive with all these special sections, the clip-on rulers, and other stylish extras like the photograph pages. These planners were not only expensive but also heavy. And you could no longer stick them in your pocket or your purse. They took on a life of their own.

But just as quickly as these organizers appeared on the scene, they were replaced. In fact, the exquisite leather planners became a thing of the past as the electronic planners made their entrance on the scene. All of a sudden people were doing their planning with handheld devices that stored everything forever. The actual electronic organizer was synced to a computer so that there was a backup for everything in your handheld electronic organizer. What a boon, since when you used to forget your leather organizer on a plane, that was the last you saw of all your plans and contact information. Now if you lost or damaged this electronic organizer, you could get another one and fill it with your stored information from your computer. Also when you wanted to check an event from several years back, if you hadn't stored your old calendar book in a closet you were out of luck. Now the information just sits there in electronic storage, waiting to be called up. In addition, you used to have to wait until the new organizer pages came out in order to enter events in the future beyond the calendar year. Now this was no longer the case. In addition, you now didn't have to copy over your address book information and you could easily update it whenever you wanted to. No longer would you have pages with fading pencil and smudges. That was all a thing of the past.

But what is state-of-the-art today is likely to be outdated and devalued tomorrow. The simple handheld device is itself becoming almost anachronistic as people are increasingly purchasing a more sophisticated personal digital assistant (PDA). Not only do they now manage your personal information, such as contacts, appointments, and to-do lists, but also connect to the Internet, act as global positioning system (GPS) devices, and run multimedia software. What's more, manufacturers have combined PDAs with cell phones, multimedia players, and other electronic gadgetry.

The real question is whether we are better organized now than we were when we used a little calendar book we kept in our pocket or purse. Do we plan our lives better? Do we show up for meetings more on time than ever before? Do we think in grander terms about the projects we can do in life? Are we more in touch with our friends than in the past? There are clearly more bells and whistles attached to our personal planning, as well as a more handsome price tag. Whether we are better organized remains to be seen!

(Text from Cohen and Weaver, 2006.)

OK. So what strategies did you use to read the text with gaps? Which strategies were most successful for you? Did you get a sense of how you don't need to understand every word to get the gist of a reading?

Reading During Your Time Abroad

One benefit of being in your host country is that you'll have mounds of written information in the native language available to you. The trick is to find material at your level of reading ability. For example, one of the first challenges you may have is simply doing a bank transaction at an automated teller machine.

> *One of the problems I have currently in Japan is using the ATMs for anything more than withdrawing cash. There are eight selections in kanji (Chinese characters) that are specific to banking transactions that I never quite learned in language class. I know the characters for 'passbook,' so when I want the machine to record my latest transactions on my passbook I just push that button, even though I can't read the other characters. Incidentally, many ATMs have a bilingual English selection, but I only use it as a last resort. ~ James Lassegard, Japan*

The bottom line is that some reading challenges will be insurmountable, at least at first. The important thing is to persevere. Here are some readily available sources for reading:

- Advertisements
- Packaging instructions
- Newspaper headlines

- Maps (When on walks with a group, don't just rely on a better speaker to lead the way. Take out the map and guide the group yourself. You can work on your reading and speaking skills at the same time!)
- Instructions at the local ATM machine in the target language—if you have someone to help you in case you have trouble

Reading academic texts

As a student—especially if you take courses intended for regular students at your host school—you will be faced with the challenge of not just reading extensively in the target language, but reading material that may tax your abilities at a high level. This is both because these readings involve sophisticated writing and because they may not be as exciting as more "popular" reading materials.

What do you need to do when you read academic texts?

- Read for basic comprehension, which calls for an understanding of vocabulary, grammar, and semantics, in order to understand the information presented in the text
- Recognize the organization and purpose of the text
- Distinguish major from minor ideas and essential from nonessential information
- Conceptualize and organize text information into a mental framework
- Understand rhetorical functions such as cause-effect relationships, compare-contrast relationships, and arguments

Reading strategies can been grouped into three broad categories: (1) planning and identifying strategies that help in constructing the meaning of the text, (2) monitoring strategies that serve to regulate comprehension and learning, and (3) evaluation strategies by which readers reflect or respond in some way to the text.

While the list of possible reading strategies is huge, here are some of the more prominent ones:

- Plan how to read the passage
- Identify key words and sentences carrying the main ideas
- Infer the meaning of words and ideas based on clues to meaning in the text
- Check out any notable discourse features
- Determine how the different parts of the text function in the discourse
- Remember why the text is being read
- Check for prior knowledge of the topic
- Read through the entire text (whether rapidly or slowly and meticulously)
- Read portions selectively
- Look for markers of meaning
- Monitor ongoing understanding of the text
- Identify portions of the text that are unclear
- Reread for clarification
- Predict what will come

(Pressley and Afflerbach, 1995; Carrell and Grabe, 2002.)

Here is what some students had to say about their efforts at academic reading:

> *Reading in Spanish has always been my weakness. I sometimes find it very difficult to read assignments for class. In many of my classes we are talking about the history of Spain and Latin America. I do not enjoy reading historical texts in English, so it makes it even more difficult when I have to read boring books and articles in Spanish. I find it is helpful for me to skim the text once very quickly and pick out the things I understood and then go back through and read it with a dictionary nearby. I use contextual cues to form ideas about what I think is happening based on what has already occurred. ~ Amanda Smith, Spain*

> *Reading is one of the toughest parts of the Spanish language for me. I do all right with small children's books or short excerpts from magazines, newspapers, or novels even, but when I have an assignment due and 30 pages of reading on the history of Spain, my brain goes on overload and I cannot function. I try to summarize the story as I go to relate the ideas and happenings to something I am already familiar with. This strategy works well, but when you add a deadline, it becomes that much more difficult to understand the material because it is presented at a rate beyond my capabilities and sanity. I try to read easier writings to keep up with my reading abilities but to not overwhelm myself so I can gradually work my way up to more difficult tasks. ~ Erin Leline, Ecuador*

Reading materials to seek out

- Articles on the Web: After you watch the TV news, go to the Internet and read about one of the interesting stories you saw on the news (of course in the target language).
- Mystery novels: The vocabulary isn't usually too difficult and often the stories provide a comfortable way to increase your reading in the target language.
- Comic books: The drawings give you clues for understanding the text.
- Children's books: Just remember that nursery rhyme language may not reflect everyday language. (For example, while "patty cake, patty cake, baker's man" may still be a popular rhyme in parts of the U.S., the words don't come in handy every day. But as one language learner said, "It still helps!")
- Target language subtitles on American movies: You can listen to the actors and at the same time read the local-language version.
- Books on tape or in digital files: You hear the language read and possibly read along as well.
- Books on tape for foreigners to learn the language
- Newspapers: Make sure you find one with feature articles or human interest pieces written at a level that you can comprehend; some countries even have newspapers written especially in learner language!
- Billboards, phrases on T-shirts, bumper stickers

When I studied English, what helped me was hearing it on a tape and also reading it, so that you get multiple channels. Get a book and audiotape from a library. You improve your vocabulary and you also hear the pronunciation. ~ Tõnu Mikk, Estonian exchange student to the U.S.

Generally, I find reading various texts in German just for fun to be a very useful strategy, especially in regards to hobbies and subjects that I enjoy the most. This type of pleasure reading often boosts my intrinsic motivation for learning and makes up for the onerous reading assigned in class, especially when many classroom assignments very rarely parallel anything that I deem pleasurable to read. Oftentimes I also read over and get the general gist of what is going on, and by going back into the text I attempt to drill into my brain what I just learned and apply it to the concepts that I have already built a base for. ~ Paul Tilleson, Germany

Returning Home

Before you leave your host country, pick up some books, magazines, newspapers, and other media in your target language that you can read when you return. You may even choose to bring home a computer guide or some instructional book written in the target language.

Once you have returned home it may be hard to speak the language frequently, but you can still keep up on your reading. Here are some suggestions to help you:

- Seek out people who have had similar study abroad experiences and trade reading material so that you aren't limited to what you are able to find on your own. Talk to native speakers of the language and ask them to borrow a novel, a comic book, magazine, or newspaper. They also might have more insight on specific websites for your country of interest.
- Start a book club with returnees or students in your language classes.
- Use the Internet to actively seek out pen pals in the target language, even if they are not native speakers.

Co-author Lassegard finds that when he writes email in Japanese he gets 10 times more responses than when he writes in English. That's a pretty strong motivation to keep reading and writing coherent sentences in the target language. Also, keep in contact with people you met in the host country. E-mail is an easy way to keep in touch. Co-author Chi still emails her friend in Mexico who she met more than six years ago! Finally, a recent returnee had this advice to offer:

You should make sure that you keep in contact with native speakers from the country you visited. They can write you emails...and this is the most effective form of learning. They can help you with your language, and if you have questions, you can ask. They also use language as you would most likely use it in day-to-day conversations. This is the best form of continuing your reading skills and comprehension. I am doing this now that I have come back. ~ Tammy Yach, Venezuela

It is essential to do as much reading as possible in order to become a more fluent reader in the target language. Find different sources, like the ones mentioned above, or others that will supply you with a variety of native writing styles for diverse age and interest groups.

> *Drink nothing without seeing it; sign nothing without reading it. ~ Spanish proverb*

WRITING

Pre-Departure Writing Activities

To get some practice in writing, try writing down some of the things you'll want to say when you first arrive in your host country. Who are the first people that you will meet in the new country? Who will you need to interact with the most when you first arrive? Most often, these people are your host family members, a supervisor, or a landlord. What will you say to them when you first meet them? What do you most want to tell them about yourself?

Since you may be very nervous, and a little tongue-tied, you might find it helpful to write a letter of introduction. This way you have the opportunity to tell them exactly what you want to say without leaving out a detail, and you also will be able to use the language correctly. If you are not sure how formal or informal to be in your letter, it may be best to err on the side of more formal. In general, the U.S. has a relaxed writing style (calling people by their first names, using contractions, following casual rules of grammar). In some languages, writing too informally may send a signal that you are not respectful of the recipient's status, age, etc.

Advice from Second Language Writers

The following strategies are from second language writers, detailing ways that you can improve your writing. Though these suggested strategies apply mainly to the writing of term papers and other academic texts, some may also apply to the writing of letters and other shorter pieces, especially when it is important that they be well written:

- **Go back to go forward:** Writing builds on itself. Go back over what you have written to determine what to write next.
- **Repeat key words and phrases:** Good writing is cohesive—the ideas are clearly connected. Going back over your writing helps you to make sure that ideas are linked clearly. To link your ideas, deliberately repeat key words and phrases and use conjunctions ("and," "but") to guide the reader. So, for example, if in English you wrote "the second language learners" in the first reference, you would write "the language learners" the second time, "the learners" the third, and perhaps "they" the fourth time. The important thing is to ensure that the reader will understand what the reference is to. In some languages cohesion is marked somewhat differently, so it is crucial to check this out in your host language context.
- **Plan out what you are going to write:** Expert writers either have a plan thought out in advance for a text or make workable plans as they go along that draw on their knowledge of effective writing. Inexperienced writers tend to work in small planning units, writing one phrase at a time, and then asking themselves what to say next.
- **Discuss what you want to say with someone else before writing:** Some learners prefer to talk about what they are going to write before writing it to clarify their ideas. Later, they may also read what they wrote out loud to help discover unintended glitches.

- **Leave a blank for words you don't know:** If you don't know a word in the target language, leave a blank, perhaps with a circle around it, or write in the English word temporarily. This way you don't unnecessarily distract yourself from the writing process.
- **Edit grammar and mechanics after your ideas are written:** Postpone editing for grammar and mechanics until an appropriate time because it often distracts you from getting your ideas down. Don't stop the flow; save editing for later.
- **Make major revisions after your ideas are written down:** Major revisions also should be postponed so as not to interrupt the writing process. For example, if you find a problem, make a quick mental or written note but finish working on the current section before dealing with it. This way, you can revise your writing without disrupting the flow of ideas.
- **Distance yourself from the writing:** Step back from your writing for hours, days, or weeks (if possible). When you are caught up in the text, it's hard to see the strengths and weaknesses of your writing.
- **Give yourself extra time to write:** At your home university, you may start your term paper only a few days before it's due. When you're researching and writing in your target language, you may want to allow yourself extra time since the process is bound to take longer.
- **Read in the target language in order to improve your writing in that language:** Reading books and articles in your host community's language can improve your writing because reading not only keeps up your comprehension skills, but also contributes to your writing by providing you with new ideas for vocabulary and sentence structure, among other things.

A technique that I have found to be useful is to take writing in small doses, often trying to get my ideas down and only revising it later. I usually take steps in revising the essay many times. I often consult class notes and sometimes, although it does not necessarily involve a second language speaker, find others to get feedback from and pay close attention to how they would similarly write it. ~ Paul Tilleson, Germany

In reference to writing strategies in a target language, I find that the best strategy for me is to plan out in advance how to write an assignment, and then check how well my writing reflects what I want to say. This seems natural given that I possess a very reflective learning style. Before I consider something to be complete, I always have to go back over it multiple times checking it. Going along with this strategy, I tend to wait to edit my writing until I have everything written that I wanted to get down, and then I will revise the work a couple times before considering it completed. ~ Brian Trolander, Germany

Feedback on Written Work

One of the biggest mistakes novice writers can make is assuming they have to go it alone. Good writing is often best accomplished as a group project. And like any other group project, giving careful attention to the feedback of others in your group can be a great help.

Written feedback works when:

- You are interested in feedback on the topic or are particularly concerned about vocabulary
- You know what to do with the feedback because it is clear and specific.
- You have the knowledge necessary to understand the correction. For example, in a French essay, a female student writes: *J'ai arrivé à Paris il y a trois jours,* or "I arrived in Paris three days ago." The teacher corrects this sentence in her essay as follows: *Je suis arrivée il y a trois jours.* The student is confused because she doesn't really know the rule that certain verbs in French use the "to be" rather than the "to have" verb. The student is also confused that the past participle is inflected for the feminine gender of the writer! In this case, the student still needs to pursue why the initial writing was incorrect.
- You record the feedback to help you make improvements in the long run. For example, if you create your own learner's log in a notebook with meaningful definitions, translation equivalents, and examples, each vocabulary correction or suggested alternative could be added to it. If you have included grammar rules in your learner's log, you can also update these based on the feedback that you receive.

A Special Means of Getting Feedback: Using the Reformulation Technique

Want to sound "more authentic"? Frustrated that your writing, while fairly error free, seems unnatural and stylistically awkward? Curious about how your writing compares to native writers? Try reformulation.

> *Reformulation...shows exactly what the issues are—what you're doing that is not German but rather English translated into German (or Portuguese, or whatever language), and how you might make it sound more 'authentically' written. ~ Molly Zahn, Germany*

Even after spending much time on a piece of writing, you may have the uncomfortable feeling that a native would not have written it that way. Here is one example from a student:

> *I can write in fairly sophisticated German with relatively few grammatical errors. I don't (usually!) do things like mess up subject-verb agreement or make mistakes with number or gender. The biggest thing I noticed when writing was the way sentences were constructed. In English, I tend to create complex and laborious sentences. (Germans are famous for this, so it shouldn't intrinsically be a problem.) The problem is, my complex sentences in German, although grammatically and, even from a technical point of view, stylistically correct, are structured more like English sentences than German ones. For example, I tried to convert directly into German the following very English sentence:*

> Because the first two years at an American university are taken up with general liberal education and because there is no cumulative exam at the end of the degree program, most American students come away from their B.A. programs with merely superficial knowledge of their subject area.

While it is grammatically OK to begin a sentence with 'because' in German, it's not very natural—it doesn't sound so good. Also, the English 'come away with' in the sense of 'gain, receive as a result of an experience' can't really be directly translated. It can, grammatically and everything, but it just isn't something a German would say. The same with 'take up with.' My native speaker restructured the sentence like this:

> In contrast [to the German university system], one studies primarily general topics in the first two years at an American university, and one is not tested on the contents [of his/her degree] upon finishing. Therefore, after the completion of their B.A., most American students have only superficial knowledge in their subject area.

Steps for using the reformulation technique

What then is reformulation? Reformulation entails having a native writer of the target language rewrite one of your compositions so that it sounds more stylistically "native-like." You then compare the original version to the reformulated one, noting differences in specific categories such as vocabulary, syntactic structures, and rhetorical functions. Reformulation is basically a refinement and is intended to complement the feedback that you currently receive regarding your target language writing, rather than to replace the other forms of feedback. You will notice that it is designed to be done outside the language class. If you are currently studying a language, your teacher's role is only to provide grammatical corrections on what you write. The process of reformulation takes your writing to the next level.

Reformulation is generally most useful for intermediate and advanced second language writers. It is a method that can be used to improve your ability to write "like a native."

Getting Started:

1. Write a short paper (200 to 300 words). Make revisions until it reflects your thoughts accurately. Self-check for mistakes in grammar and mechanics.
2. Give the paper to a competent native writer at least once for feedback. This writer should go over the paper for vocabulary and grammatical errors. This person could be your language instructor if you are currently in a language class.
3. When you receive the native writer's comments, revise your paper based on that feedback. This version is referred to as a reconstruction since it has been corrected to reflect what you meant to say.

Reformulation Tasks

4. Next, give the reconstruction to a competent native writer (not your teacher) to rewrite or *reformulate* the entire paper or a portion of it (say, the first 100 words, since the beginning of the paper is often written with extra attention). It is usually advisable to find someone other than the teacher to do the reformulating because the teacher is perhaps too close to the text already, having gone over it already for correction and other comments. Also, you do not want a reformulation that is too polished. The reformulator's purpose is only to shift the message to a form that is more stylistically similar to that of an average native writer, not a professional.

   Once someone has agreed to do the reformulation, he/she should rewrite the paper, preserving as many of your ideas as possible while making the piece sound more appropriate in the target language. Clearly, it is not always possible to preserve every idea—either because the original idea was not that clear to begin with or because the use of a different word or phrase shifts the meaning to some extent. It is important for your helper to stay as close to the original ideas as possible to ensure that the writing still reflects your work and not theirs.

5. With the help of a native writer (possibly your language teacher if this person has the time) or on your own, compare your original corrected version with the reformulated one. You are encouraged to do this in several steps in the order listed below:
   - **Compare the way things are phrased in your version and the reformulated one.** How does the native speaker phrase sentences? Look at the native writer's approach to questioning, defining, hypothesizing, asserting, etc. For example, in your target language, you had written the equivalent of, "I am sorry if I did something wrong." The reformulator wrote with more formality and with a few flourishes: "I wish to apologize sincerely for any inconvenience I may have caused you." These are ritualistic formulas that natives know how to write and that you as a learner may well want to learn! They may come in handy during your stay abroad and beyond.
   - **Compare the means of linking one idea with another and its effect on the clarity of the writing.** Does it flow? Does it hang together? Look at the ways that the native writer linked together ideas—within and across sentences and paragraphs. Such ties or connectors consist of grammar forms such as conjunctions—combining ideas together ("and"), contrasting them ("but"), or showing one causes the other ("so")—and personal pronouns ("he," "it," "they") and demonstrative pronouns ("this," "that," "they"). Check to see if the reformulator organized your writing so that it is understandable. For instance, you could check whether he or she identified the topic (or topics) that you are writing about more clearly. You could also see if the native writer changed the order of ideas. The ideas may flow better in a different order in the second language. In addition, you could also see whether any ideas have been enhanced by the addition or elimination of words or phrases.

- **Compare the selection of vocabulary.** What vocabulary works best? Pay attention to whether the native used more precise words, more concise phrases, or more/less formal words. Also note how the reformulator combined certain words. Pay particular attention to prepositions used with particular verbs, verbs used with particular nouns (e.g., "to perform an operation"), and adjectives with nouns (e.g., "the fruit is ripe"). Frequently, the changes that the native writer has made are slight, representing subtleties of vocabulary use.
- **Compare the choice and ordering of grammatical forms.** How is the reformulated writing structured? Check whether the native writer has changed some of the grammatical structures—clauses, sentences, or clusters of sentences. If so, note what structures were used in place of the ones in your version. Did the native use more or less complex structures to convey the same meaning? What did the native writer do to avoid repeating the same structure over and over? You will see structures that you already know but haven't used, as well as those that you do not know. Write down new grammatical patterns (in your learner's log) and try to use them in your own writing to help you improve your skills.

Example of reformulation

We will now look at an example of reformulation—a four-sentence paragraph from an essay by a university student studying English as a foreign language:

> One of the severe problems of the social life on campus is the problem of the relationship between Arabs and Jews. It is well known that the mixture of the two cultures causes tension between students, and it especially effects students who live in the dormitories of the university. In my opinion this problem would not have been so severe if unreliable sections from the Students Union did not deliberately wake students to act violently. I therefore suggest that an imediate change of the group which dominates the Students Union will be done by free elections on campus.

The teacher's corrections were as follows:

1. "social problems" for "problems of the social life"
2. "better structure than coordination?"—a comment in the margin regarding the second sentence
3. problem with the word "effects"
4. "university dormitories" instead of "dormitories of the university"
5. "why a past idea 'would not have been'?"—a comment in the margin regarding the third sentence
6. another word for "sections"
7. deleted the plurals in "Students Union" in both places it appeared
8. comment about tense and choice of verb in "did not deliberately wake"—suggested "provoke"
9. spelling of "immediate"
10. a comment in the margin, "Structure!" with regard to "will be done" in the last sentence — suggested "to make a change"

The student incorporated the teacher's corrections into a revised version, and the paragraph came out as follows:

> One of the severe social problems on campus is the problem of the relationship between Arabs and Jews. It is well known that because of the mixture of two cultures, tension exists between students, especially those who live in the university dormitories. In my opinion members of the Student Union provoked students and encouraged them to act violently, therefore I suggest that these members must be changed through free elections on campus.

As in the previous example, we see that surface mistakes have been cleaned up. There are now no glaring verb tense errors, for example. But if we look closely, we notice several vocabulary problems—"the mixture of the two cultures" and "these members must be changed." Also, in the first sentence the noun "problem" is repeated, rather than a demonstrative pronoun, producing somewhat awkward cohesion in English.

The following is a reformulated version:

> A serious social problem on the Hebrew University campus is that of relations between Arabs and Jews. It is well known that cultural and political differences between these groups lead to tension and conflict within the student population, especially among those who live in contact with one another in the dormitories. In my opinion, members of the Student Union provoke violence among students. For this reason, I suggest that these members be replaced through new campus-wide elections.

Note that in the last sentence, "For this reason" provides a more specific connective marker than "therefore." Also note that the awkward phrases have been replaced: "cultural and political differences between these groups." for "the mixture of the two cultures," and "I suggest that these members be replaced" for "these members must be changed." The awkward repetition of the noun "problem" in the first sentence is avoided by use of the demonstrative pronoun "that": "A serious social problem…is that of…." With regard to syntax, the second sentence is simplified by eliminating the subordinate clause introduced by "because of" after "It is well known that…."

Practice!

To make this approach to feedback on writing more real for you, we suggest that you write a short essay or select one that you have already written in a target language. If you are required to produce target language writing in a specialized area, such as business correspondence, medicine, law, culture, or whatever the case may be, you may wish to prepare as an exercise a piece of writing reflecting the field, then go through the step-by-step guide to reformulation.

Writing a Term Paper in the Target Language

You already know a great deal about writing a term paper in your native language, including that organization is key. But what about writing an academic paper in your host country's language? You may want to consider some differences in writing style and expectations:

- Organization is still crucial, but you need to check with your local professors about their expectations, since how papers are organized varies across academic cultures.
- In addition, you should familiarize yourself with the conventions for writing academic papers in your target language. You can learn about some of these conventions if you have a native writer reformulate some of your term paper for you. In this way, you can see more graphically how native writers turn phrases in their language—for instance, how to hedge when something isn't known to be definitively true (e.g., the equivalent of "it would appear that," "one might assume," "all things being equal," etc.).
- The third major hurdle is to use the appropriate academic terminology. Sometimes these terms are evident but other times you need to check with other students, with the professor, with textbooks, or elsewhere to find out the terms used to refer to the concepts you wish to express. In fact, it is sometimes nontechnical terms used technically that cause the most problems in academic writing—terms that take on a technical meaning in a given academic field (e.g., "mechanism," "process," "mode," "scheme," etc.).

Other Kinds of Writing in the Target Language

It is possible and even likely that you will do at least some writing in the target language that is not academic in nature. After all, there are many study abroad programs that do not necessarily involve academic writing. You may, for example, be asked to include some creative writing of a non-academic nature in your final course project. You may also be called upon to do some journalistic writing. And outside of class, you may get involved in a community project where you may, for example, need to write material for posters or leaflets. In addition, there are always friendly letters to write, whether on paper or as emails. In many ways, e-mail messages constitute a genre of writing somewhere between a spoken register and a relatively informal written one. Each type of writing has its own features—its characteristic vocabulary and structures. You need to find out what these features are if you want to have your writing be consistent with local norms.

All these types of writing could probably benefit from the reformulation technique discussed previously. Find out how your friends and acquaintances would write the same kind of text that you need to write. Pay attention, for example, to how they write email messages. Here are some questions you may want to ask yourself as you embark on your target language writing project:

- What conventions do host community writers use when writing a particular genre of text (e.g., a literary story, an editorial for a newspaper, or a friendly letter)?

- What vocabulary and language structures tend to be associated with the given genre of text? For example, what types of adjectives would be used to describe a funny incident at the market? Would you use adjectives that are more colloquial than ones you would use in an academic essay?
- How do people write journalistically in the target language? Are there stylistic ways to signal truth versus speculation?
- Are there characteristic ways to use vocabulary and syntax in email messages? For example, what do greetings and closures look like in such messages? Is there a slang used to describe things that are pleasing or displeasing?

Post-Study Abroad Writing Activities

When you return home from your time abroad, it may be difficult to continue practicing your writing skills. Here are a few quick ways to keep up your writing:

- Write a letter to your host family every so often. You may also be able to e-mail them.
- Keep a short journal on aspects of your experience abroad that are particularly memorable by using your newly learned language skills.
- Continue writing about how your life has changed since the experience, and try to explain your feelings regarding these changes.
- If you are rather fluent in the second language, find a local newspaper that is written in that language and send in an article. Before submitting the article, take it through the writing process and find someone to give you honest feedback on your writing. You might discover a talent you never knew you had!

TRANSLATION STRATEGIES

We all translate to some degree while learning and using a second language. For example, you may want to know what something means in your native language before going any further. You may go rushing to a dictionary to get the meaning of *cogumelo* in Portuguese (mushroom) before continuing to read a Portuguese text about poisonous mushrooms. Very possibly, you already use many of the strategies described in this section, even if you are only somewhat aware that you are doing so. The goal is to raise your awareness about translation strategies used because once you are aware of them, you can then decide consciously when to employ a certain strategy and when it might be possible to try a new one.

Choosing between Mental and Written Translation

Choosing between mental and written translation is partly a question of your own learning-style preference.

- You may prefer, for example, to write out or type a translation if you like to take in new language material visually.
- You may also wish to produce a word-for-word translation according to the order that the words appear in the target language.
- On the other hand, you may prefer to keep the material in your head, perhaps focusing on how it sounds, not how it looks.
- Or you may prefer to get the gist of the message, rather than look at each individual word.

Some situations are more appropriate for mental translation, such as in an informal conversation where written translation would be impractical. Other situations would probably call for a written translation no matter what your learning-style preferences are (for example, when you need to produce a written text or give a formal talk). While it may be useful to prepare a written translation of a short target language passage while reading, translating fully anything of length can be so time-consuming and tiring that you don't learn much of the language at all. The choice between written or mental translation will depend both on what kind of learner you are and what the situation is.

> *One translation strategy I try to use is translating in my head while reading in order to understand the text. For me this is the best way to approach a written text, especially since I do not feel fluent in the target language. ~ Brian Trolander, Germany*

Translating when Languages are Either Very Close or Very Far Apart

You may wish to translate a certain type of sentence just because the languages are dramatically different with regard to this pattern. In such cases, translating may help you to accentuate the differences and fix them comfortably in your mind.

For example, there may be cases where a verb in a foreign language has two very different meanings and you feel a need to translate both options to make sure that you do not mistakenly use the wrong one. So, for example, a native speaker of Hebrew uses the same verb, *levaker*, for both "to visit" and "to criticize." It should be clear to the reader how dangerous it might be to use the wrong translation equivalent in an English conversation with a native English-speaking person and find yourself expressing your desire to criticize when that is the farthest thing from your mind!

On the other end of the spectrum are cases where the meaning of a given word is almost the same in two languages, but translation can still help to clarify the range of coverage of a word. So, for example, *sensible* in Spanish means both "sensible" and "sensitive" in English.

Translating Idioms, Sayings, and Expressions

If you are learning a second language, sooner or later you are bound to run across a phrase or a saying whose meaning leaves you baffled. In an attempt to understand it, you may look up each word in the dictionary and double-check your grammar book. It is very possible that, despite these measures, you will find the meaning of the phrase still eludes you—in fact, it might even seem nonsensical or absurd. If that is the case, chances are likely that you have hit upon an idiom.

Each language has its own set of idioms that act as a lively shorthand to express ideas or describe events. Consider the following:

- If Carlos tries to tell you that he's going to repay you soon, I'd *take it with a grain of salt*.
- "*There are always other fish in the sea*," my mother said after Abby and I broke up.
- We tried to throw a surprise party for Leo, but Erica *let the cat out of the bag* when she was talking to him after work on Friday.
- Donald's *name was dragged through the mud* when he was accused of stealing at work.
- The whole experience with Uncle Bill's inheritance *left a bad taste in my mouth*.

If you are a native speaker of U.S. English, it is almost certain that you immediately understood each sentence without getting bogged down by the literal meanings of the idioms because, really, what does a tiny amount of salt have to do with repayment of a loan? Nothing. Why would letting a feline out of a sack ruin impending party plans? Unless it was eating the birthday cake, it wouldn't. As you can see, it is not the literal meaning that is important but instead the culturally understood sense of the expression, the figurative meaning of the idiom.

Translating idioms from U.S. English to the language of the host country or vice versa can be tricky business. There are a few idioms, such as "to kill two birds with one stone," that have near word-for-word equivalents in a number of different languages. However, for the most part, it is wise to avoid the direct translation of idioms, as they will most likely be confusing at best and offensive at worst.

Learning the idioms and colloquial expressions of your host country will allow you to interact with those around you in a more native-like, natural way, and will move your language learning beyond your textbook into a new, colorful realm. When translating from the language of the host country, our suggestion is to ask a host country native to explain the figurative meaning of any idiom that you run across. If you are translating to the language of the host country, you might want to ask if there are similar idioms in the host country language that would match what you are trying to express.

For example:

It's about the same either way.

- English: It's six of one, half a dozen of the other.
- French: It's cabbage green and green cabbage (*C'est chou vert et vert chou*).

To be resentful or angry about something from the past

- English: To have a chip on your shoulder
- Italian: To have a fly on your nose (*Avere las mosca al naso*)

> *Recently my husband, Keon, and I ate at a nice restaurant. Keon did not like his meal at all and he complained about it the next day saying, 'If I go there again, I will change my name.' I was confused. I didn't know what he meant, so I asked him to explain it for me. He said that it was a Korean expression that meant the food was so bad that he never wants to eat there again. I figured out that he meant, 'I'll change my (last) name before I ever eat there again!' So it's very similar to our expressions like 'when pigs fly' or 'when hell freezes over.' ~ Julie Chi*

Translating While Speaking

The use of translation strategies in speaking depends on whether you are speaking informally in everyday conversational contexts or more formally, for example when giving a presentation or speech for which you need to spend time preparing.

- If you are giving a prepared speech, you may wish to jot down translations of specific words or key sentences. These sentences may highlight certain key grammatical features.
- While speaking, you could monitor what you are saying by keeping in mind the translations you've jotted down.
- Both for prepared speeches and for informal speaking, you could work back through what you said mentally, translating several items to see if you used the language correctly.

Translating While Writing

For some of you, your writing will be better organized if you plan first in your native language, simply because you have more tools in the native language. It may be easier for you to see the "big picture" that way and to get a sense of what you want to say. You will likely have vocabulary to find workable equivalents in the target language. In any case, when you actually begin to write in the target language, you should find a proper balance between choosing vocabulary you know, using a dictionary, and consulting with a native speaker.

ACTIVITY: Different approaches to translating while writing

This activity will help you determine which translation method works best for you when writing.

What I like most about my favorite friend. (Write a paragraph in your native language.)

What I like most about my favorite friend. (Translate what you wrote above into the target language.)

What I like about a very special relative. (Write a paragraph directly in the target language.)

Now compare the two processes: writing in your native language first and translating versus writing directly in the target language. Which approach are you likely to prefer? Your choice may in part reflect your learning-style preferences. There are learners who prefer to write out their thoughts in their native language first and then translate them into the target language to be sure they have it right. They may do this to develop their ideas fully before trying to write them in the target language and also to organize them in an integrated fashion. It may also serve as a strategy for enhancing self-expression if they are able to use translation as a way to avoid writing too simplistically in the target language—that is, settling for low-level vocabulary that doesn't really express what they had in mind. Then there are others who prefer to write directly in the target language, even if they end up making mental translations from their native language as they go along.

Especially among beginning and intermediate-level learners, there will be learners who do better in their target language writing if they first write in their native language and then translate to the target language. Others, especially more advanced learners, may be more successful writing directly in the target language. It may also depend on what it is that needs to be written. Use whichever of these approaches works best for you at your level of proficiency.

Translating While Reading

Be aware that your brain can process and store information a lot quicker and more efficiently in your native language. You can use that to your advantage while reading—and maybe you already do.

> *I realized that I [perform mental translation] all the time while I read. I stop at the end of paragraphs and try to form a flash mental image or explanation of the topic of the paragraph. Because this all happens so fast, the main terms are almost always in English. ~ Molly Zahn, Germany*

Translating While Listening

Listening is the skill where the information stream can be the most relentless—as in movies and TV (where you don't have access to a playback mechanism). In such cases, it is not possible for you to rewind the tape a few times until unintelligible gibberish is heard sufficiently well to understand any of it. Fortunately, this type of listening is not a high-stakes situation since no one really cares if you understood everything correctly. In an academic context, however, especially in lectures, the understanding and retention of information may be crucial. You may, in some cases, be able to stop the lecturer for clarification or check with a TA afterwards. Still, you will most likely need a method for writing some things down effectively—which will probably call for using your native language.

In fact, you may translate at the same time you are taking notes on lectures in the target language if it is easier for you to remember the lecture that way and easier to study from the notes. Of course, you may lose more sentences along the way than if you take notes in the target language directly because your mind is busy processing the translation in addition to understanding and organizing the information.

> *For me, it's mostly a question of speed. Because what I write down is usually only a summary of what the professor has just said, I sometimes find myself groping for words in German. So I get the thought down in English and then go back to German. There's also the issue that I have my own personal abbreviations and method of taking notes in English that I haven't yet developed for German. That's another reason that taking notes in German is slower. ~ Molly Zahn, Germany*

CONCLUSION OF THE LANGUAGE STRATEGIES SECTION

Throughout the language strategies part of the guide, you have been advised to keep an open mind about trying new strategies for language learning and use. Hopefully you have learned more about your own learning styles and what you can do to improve your language skills, especially in the study abroad context. You have explored a variety of strategies, and you should feel free to adapt them in any way that helps you learn best.

We realize that this guide provides a lot to absorb in one sitting, so feel free to page through it as often as your language needs require. The activities presented are meant to be used as often as you like, depending on your goals, so don't be afraid to try them again at a later time—for example, when your language skills have improved or when you have gained more insight. Again, adapt these activities according to your particular situation and, most of all, enjoy them.

In this guide, we have made an effort to combine ideas about language and culture. Since the two concepts are so intertwined, we would like you to be able to use some of the strategies offered in the language and culture sections of the guide together. In many cases, you will find that language and culture come together naturally, so you can take these as opportunities to maximize your entire learning experience in your host country.

Recommended Reading on Language-Learning Styles and Strategies

Brown, H. D. (2002). *Strategies for success.* White Plains, NY: Longman/Pearson Education.

This is a book for ESL learners, covering the following in short chapters: learning-style preferences, right and left brain, motivation, self-confidence and lowering anxiety, taking risks, language-learning IQ, first language influence, learning a second culture, learning strategies, group strategies, and test-taking strategies. Every chapter has a questionnaire to help learners delve into the issues. Exercises are included for practicing language skills.

Cohen, A. D. (2011). *Strategies in learning and using a second language* (2nd ed.). New York/London: Routledge/Taylor & Francis Group.

This book examines what it takes to achieve long-term success in languages beyond the first language. The author uses his extensive experience in researching and teaching language use strategies to outline language strategies are and how they can enhance performance. Entirely new material has been developed for this second edition based on examples of specific strategies supplied by actual learners, mostly drawn from a website featuring these strategies in the learning of Spanish grammar.

Griffiths, C. (2013). *The strategy factor in successful language learning.* Bristol, UK: Multilingual Matters.

This book addresses fundamental questions regarding the relationships between successful language learning and strategy use and development according to learner, situational or target variables. It considers strategy effectiveness from an individual point of view and discusses pedagogical issues, especially relating to teacher perceptions and training, classroom and learner factors, methodology and content. Rather than focusing on strategies divorced from the 'real world' of the classroom, this book explores the issues from the teaching/learning point of view.

Mendelsohn, D. J. (1994). *Learning to listen.* San Diego, CA: Dominie Press.

This book starts by discussing theoretical assumptions concerning the learning process, listening process, and listening strategies. The author then makes the case for a strategies-based approach, discusses the essential features and design of a strategies-based course, deals with the linguistic proficiency required to be a competent listener, and gives examples of the strategies-based approach.

Oxford, R. L. (1990). *Language learning strategies: What every teacher should know.* Boston: Heinle & Heinle/Thomson International.

The most famous of the strategy books, Oxford's text contains two versions of the Strategy Inventory for Language Learning (SILL), which has been translated into several foreign languages and provides students with a hands-on method to self-diagnose their language-learning strategies. The book contains extensive examples of how different strategies can be applied across language skills and tasks. This is a very practical resource for language teachers and strategy teacher-trainers.

Oxford, R. L. (2011). *Teaching and researching language learning strategies.* New York/London: Routledge/Taylor & Francis Group.

This book offers an overview of the field of language learning strategies over the past 30 years. It provides practical, innovative suggestions for assessing, teaching, and researching language learning strategies. It also includes examples of strategies and tactics from all levels, from beginners to distinguished-level learners.

Reid, J. (Ed.). (1995). *Learning styles in the ESL/EFL classroom.* Boston: Heinle & Heinle/Thomson International.

This anthology features the work of authors known in the area of learning styles: Bassano and Christison, Carrell and Monroe, Chapelle, Ely, Oxford, Reid, and others. Included are issues surrounding learning-styles research, classroom activities and curriculum development using learning-styles information, and a look at the relationship between learning-styles research and the classroom. This anthology seeks to define learning styles as opposed to learning strategies. It offers detailed explanations and examples of various aspects of learning styles and includes several assessment tools.

Rubin, J., & Thompson, I. (1994). *How to be a more successful language learner* (2nd ed.). Boston: Heinle & Heinle.

This popular and easy-to-read book provides numerous concrete suggestions for how learners can become more independent, effective, and successful in their attempts to learn foreign languages. Divided into two parts, the book introduces learners to the nature of the language-learning process and then provides step-by-step suggestions on how to improve vocabulary, grammar, reading, writing, listening, and speaking skills.

References

Althen, G. (1988). *American ways: A guide to foreigners in the United States.* Yarmouth, ME: Intercultural Press.

Anderson, C. (2002). *Study abroad: The role that culture plays in relating between U.S. American women and host country men in Latin America.* Unpublished thesis, University of Minnesota.

Bennett, J. M., Bennett, M. J., & Allen, W. (1999). Developing intercultural competence in the language classroom. In R. M. Paige & D. Lange (Eds.), *Culture as the core: Integrating culture into the language classroom.* Minneapolis, MN: University of Minnesota, Center for Advanced Research on Language Acquisition.

Bennett, M. J. (1993). Towards ethnorelativism: A developmental model of intercultural sensitivity. In R. M. Paige (Ed.), *Education for intercultural experience* (pp. 21-72). Yarmouth, ME: Intercultural Press.

Bennett, M. J. (1999). Overcoming the golden rule: Sympathy and empathy. In M. J. Bennett (Ed.), *Basic concepts: Intercultural communication* (pp. 191-214). Yarmouth, ME: Intercultural Press.

Bennett, M. J., & Bennett, J. M. (n.d). *The D-I-E model of debriefing.* Unpublished materials from the Summer Institute for Intercultural Communication, Intercultural Communication Institute, Portland, OR.

Bock, P. K. (1974). *Modern cultural anthropology: An introduction* (2nd ed.). New York: Alfred A. Knopf.

Carrell, P. L., & Grabe, W. (2002). Reading. In N. Schmitt (Ed.), *An introduction to applied linguistics* (pp. 233-250). London: Arnold.

Cohen, A. D., & Olshtain, E. (1981). Developing a measure of sociocultural competence: The case of apology. *Language Learning, 31*(1), 113-134.

Cohen, A. D. (1990). *Language learning: Insights for learners, teachers, and researchers.* New York: Newbury House/Harper and Row.

Cohen, A. D. (1998). *Strategies in learning and using a second language.* Harlow, Essex, UK: Longman.

Cohen, A. D., & Weaver, S. J. (2006). *Styles- and strategies-based instruction: A teachers' guide.* CARLA Working Paper Series #7. Minneapolis, MN: University of Minnesota, The Center for Advanced Research on Language Acquisition.

Crawford-Lange, L., & Lange, D. (1984). Doing the unthinkable in the second-language classroom. In. T. Higgs (Ed.), *Teaching for proficiency: The organizing principle* (pp. 139-177). Lincolnwood, IL: National Textbook Company.

Dörnyei, Z. (1994). Motivation and motivating in the foreign language classroom. *Modern Language Journal, 78*(3), 273-284.

Dörnyei, Z. (2001a). *Motivational strategies in the language classroom.* Cambridge, UK: Cambridge University Press.

Dörnyei, Z. (2001b). *Teaching and research motivation.* Harlow, Essex, UK: Longman/ Pearson Education.

Dörnyei, Z. (2002). *The integration of research on L2 motivation and SLA: Past failure and future potential.* Plenary paper presented at the Second Language Research Forum, Toronto, Ontario, Canada. October 3-6, 2002.

Dörnyei, Z. (2003). Attitudes, orientations, and motivations in language learning: Advances in theory, research, and applications. *Language Learning, 53*(S1), 3-32.

Ehrman, M. E., & Leaver, B. L. (2003). Cognitive styles in the service of language learning. *System, 31*, 393-415.

Gardenswartz, L., & Rowe, A. (1994). *The managing diversity survival guide.* Burr Ridge, IL: Irwin Professional Publishing.

Hall, E. T. (1976). *Beyond culture.* New York: Anchor/Doubleday.

Hess, D. (1997). *Studying abroad/learning abroad: An abridged edition of the whole world guide to culture learning.* Yarmouth, ME: Intercultural Press.

Hofstede, G. (2003). *Culture's consequences: Comparing values, behaviors, institutions and organizations across nations* (2nd ed.). Thousand Oaks, CA: Sage.

Howell, W. S. (1982). *The empathetic communicator.* Belmont, CA: Wadsworth.

Inagaki, Y. (1985). *Jiko Hyogen no Gijutsu (skills in self-expression).* Tokyo: PHP Institute.

Kappler, B., & Nokken, K. (1999). *Making the most of your time abroad.* Minneapolis, MN: University of Minnesota, International Student and Scholar Services.

Kolb, D. A. (1984) *Experiential Learning,* Englewood Cliffs, NJ.: Prentice Hall.

Lewis, T. J., & Jungmar, R. E. (Eds.). (1986). *On being foreign: Culture shock in short fiction.* Yarmouth, ME: Intercultural Press.

Lysgaard, S. (1955). Adjustment in a foreign society: Norwegian Fulbright grantees visiting the United States. *International Social Science Bulletin*, 7(1), 45-51.

Mendelsohn, D. J. (1994). *Learning to listen: A strategy-based approach for the second-language learner.* San Diego, CA: Dominie Press.

Morris, D. (1994). *Bodytalk: A world guide to gestures.* London: Jonathan Cape.

Oxford, R. L. (1990). *Language learning strategies: What every teacher should know.* Boston: Heinle & Heinle.

Oxford, R. L. (1995). Style analysis survey. In J. Reid (Ed.), *Learning styles in the ESL/ EFL classroom* (pp. 208-215). Boston: Heinle & Heinle/Thomson International.

Paige, R. M. (1993). On the nature of intercultural experiences and intercultural education. In R. M. Paige (Ed.), *Education for the intercultural experience* (pp. 1-19). Yarmouth, ME: Intercultural Press.

Paige, R. M. (2005). Culture learning dimensions. In J. Bennett & R. M. Paige (Eds.), *Workshop manual: Training design for international and multicultural programs.* Portland, OR: Intercultural Communication Institute.

Paige, R. M., DeJaeghere J., & Yershova, Y. (1999). *Culture learning in the language classroom: A manual for language instructors.* Minneapolis, MN: University of Minnesota, The Center for Advanced Research on Language Acquisition.

Peace Corps. (1997). *Culture Matters: The Peace Corps Cross-Cultural Workbook.* Washington D.C.: The Peace Corps Information Collection and Exchange. Available on the web: http://www.peacecorps.gov/wws/publications/culture/

Pedersen, P. (1997). *Culture-centered counseling interventions: Striving for accuracy.* Thousand Oaks, CA: Sage.

Pressley, M., & Afflerbach, P. (1995). *Verbal protocols of reading: The nature of constructively responsive reading.* Hillsdale, NJ: Lawrence Erlbaum.

Stewart, E. C., & Bennett, M. J. (1991). *American cultural patterns: A cross-cultural perspective* (Rev. ed.). Yarmouth, ME: Intercultural Press.

Storti, C., & Bennhold-Samann, L. (1997). *Culture matters: The Peace Corps cross-cultural workbook.* Washington, DC: Peace Corps Information Collection and Exchange.

Taylor Nicodemus, N. (1991). The travel journal: An assessment tool for overseas study. *Occasional Papers on International Education Exchange,* 27. New York: Council on International Educational Exchange.

Index

D

E

F

G

H

S

T

U

V

W

Made in the USA
Middletown, DE
18 May 2019